338.4791
SIN

NMV

D0192667

The Tourism Industry

An International Analysis

The Tourism Industry

An International Analysis

Edited by

M. Thea Sinclair and M.J. Stabler

C·A·B International

C·A·B International
Wallingford
Oxon OX10 8DE
UK

Tel: Wallingford (0491) 32111
Telex: 847964 (COMAGG G)
Telecom Gold/Dialcom: 84: CAU001
Fax: (0491) 33508

© C·A·B International 1991. All rights reserved. No part of
this publication may be reproduced in any form or by any
means, electronically, mechanically, by photocopying,
recording or otherwise, without the prior permission of the
copyright owners.

A catalogue entry for this book is available from the British Library

ISBN 0 85198 718 4

Printed and bound in the UK by Redwood Press Ltd, Melksham

Contents

Contributors   ix

Acknowledgements   xi

1   New Perspectives on the Tourism Industry   1
     M. Thea Sinclair and M.J. Stabler
     Introduction
     Research on the tourism industry
     New contributions to tourism industry analysis

2   Modelling the Tourism Industry: A New   15
     Approach
     M.J. Stabler
     Introduction
     Tourists – industry – destination analysis
     An appraisal of tourism models
     Tourism opportunity sets
     The contribution of opportunity sets to the analysis
          of tourism
     Consumer and industry interrelationships: a
          behavioural matrix
     Issues underlying the opportunity sets approach
     Towards an operational model of opportunity sets
     Conclusion

3   Information Technology in Tourism: The   45
     Impact on the Industry and Supply of
     Holidays
     M. Bennett and M. Radburn
     Introduction
     Information technology in the tourism industry
     Current trends and issues in the use of IT
     The role of IT in the supply of holidays
     The potential of IT to influence holiday sales processes
     Spatial differences in the supply of holidays

Contents

The wider implications of the survey: filtering of
    holiday choice

The impact of IT on filtering

Staff training, IT and travel agency operation

Some concluding comments on the impact of IT on tour
    operators, travel agents and consumer choice

The future

Conclusion

4   **Integration in the Tourism Industry: A Case**   **67**
    Study Approach
    Venancio Bote Gómez and M. Thea Sinclair

Introduction

Explanations of integration

The structure of firms in the UK and Spanish tourism
    industries

Foreign investment in the tourism industry

Concentration in the tourism industry

Vertical ownership and contractual arrangements in the
    tourism industry

Summary and conclusions

5   **Tour Operators' Strategies: A Cross-Country**   **91**
    Comparison
    Brian Goodall and J.R. Bergsma

Tour operators

Skiing holidays via inclusive tours

Skiing PHs from the United Kingdom via mass-market
    tour operators

Skiing PHs from The Netherlands via mass-market tour
    operators

Comparison of United Kingdom and Dutch mass-market
    tour operator programmes

Conclusion

6   **Changing Styles of Sports Tourism:**   **107**
    Industry/Consumer Interactions in Canada,
    the USA and Europe
    G. Redmond

Introduction

New facilities for the athletic tourist: hotels, resorts
    and spas

Sport vacations

Sports halls of fame and museums

Multi-sport festivals and world championships

National parks

Conclusion

7   **Products, Places and Promotion: Destination**   **121**
       Images in the Analysis of the Tourism
       Industry
       G.J. Ashworth
       Marketing as an analytical framework for tourism
       The elements of place marketing as applied to
           tourism
       The special function of place images in marketing
       Tourism place marketing images in the Mediterranean
       From analysis to strategy

8   **Guest-host Perceptions of Rural Tourism in**   **143**
       England and Portugal
       J. Edwards
       Introduction
       The development of rural tourism in south west
           England and northern Portugal
       Economic diversification and rural tourism
           development
       English and Portuguese hosts' perceptions of rural
           accommodation
       A comparison of guests' and hosts' perceptions of rural
           accommodation in south west England
       Similarities and differences between guests' and hosts'
           perceptions of rural accommodation in northern
       Portugal
       Hosts' and guests' perceptions of accommodation in
           rural areas: an overview
       Hosts' and guests' assessments of rural areas in south
           west England as locations for tourism
       Hosts' and guests' assessments of rural areas in northern
           Portugal as locations for tourism
       Hosts' and guests' perceptions of the attractiveness of
           rural tourism: a comparison
       The implications of the study

9   **Understanding Holiday Choices**   **165**
       P. Kent
       Introduction
       Elements of choice
       The range of products on offer
       Other choice considerations
       The objectives of the analysis
       Results
       Discussion
       Conclusion

Contents

10   The Tourism Industry and Foreign Exchange   185
     Leakages in a Developing Country: The
     Distribution of Earnings from Safari and
     Beach Tourism in Kenya
     M. Thea Sinclair
     Introduction
     The tourism industry in Kenya
     The demand for tourism in Kenya
     Total and per capita foreign currency earnings from
         tourism
     Foreign exchange earnings and leakages from
         safari and beach tourism
     Tourism earnings distribution: the role of air
         transport
     Conclusions and implications

11   Government – Industry – Community   205
     Interaction in Tourism Development in
     Mexico
     Veronica H. Long
     Introduction
     The effects of tourism on local communities
     Tourism in Mexico
     Government participation in tourism development
     Las Bahias de Huatulco
     Developmental impacts
     Socio-cultural impacts
     Socio-economic impacts
     From Santa Cruz to La Crucecita
     Social impact mitigation by FONATUR
     Community response to mitigation
     Exclusion of locals from a changing tourism
         industry
     Discussion
     Conclusions
     Epilogue

12   Challenge and Change in East European   223
     Tourism: A Yugoslav Example
     Douglas G. Pearce
     Introduction
     A tourism development strategy for Yugoslavia
     Tourism in Split
     The regional and national content
     Constraints and challenges
     Conclusions
     Postscript

Index   241

Contributors

G. Ashworth Dr. Gregory Ashworth is Reader in Urban and Regional Planning in the Faculty of Spatial Sciences, Rijksuniversiteit, Groningen, The Netherlands. He is an expert on urban tourism and tourism images. He has numerous publications on tourism marketing and the historic city, as well as in the area of tourism geography and policy-making.

M. M. Bennett Dr. Marion Bennett, formerly a marketing executive with American Express, is currently Lecturer in Tourism at Strathclyde University. Her research interests lie in the area of information technology and the tourism industry.

J. Bergsma Jan Bergsma is Head of Department in the Sektor Toerisme en Rekreatie, Nationale Hogeschool voor Toerisme en Verkeer, Breda, The Netherlands. He is joint originator of one of the main ERASMUS initiatives in the area of tourism education, involving students from three European countries. His research interests and publications include tourism planning and policy.

V. Bote Gómez Dr. Venancio Bote Gómez is Director of the Tourism Programme at the Institute of Economics and Geography, Consejo Superior de Investigaciones Cientificas, Madrid. He is one of the World Tourism Organization's main tourism consultants and has undertaken joint research on integration in the tourism industry (with Thea Sinclair) for Spain's National Research Plan, and has written numerous reports, articles and two books on tourism.

J. Edwards Dr. Jonathon Edwards is Senior Lecturer in Tourism at the Department of Tourism and Heritage Conservation, Bournemouth Polytechnic. He has undertaken original research on rural tourism in European regions and is currently researching on tourism–environment relations.

B. Goodall Brian Goodall is Professor of Geography, Consultant Director of the NERC Unit for Thematic Information Systems and Dean of the Faculty of Urban and Regional Studies at the University of Reading. His wide-ranging research interests and publications cover time-share development, tourism marketing and holiday choice.

Contributors

P. Kent   Dr. Peter Kent is Marketing Manager for British Rail's Network South-East London area. He was previously employed by Air Europe, where he gained inside knowledge of the operation of the tourism industry. His main research interests and publications are in the area of tourism and consumer choice.

V.H. Long   Veronica Long has lived in Mexico, where she obtained first hand experience of tourism development planning. She worked on 'ecotourism' for the World Wildlife Fund, and is currently undertaking research on sustainable tourism development projects in Indonesia.

D. Pearce   Dr. Douglas Pearce is Senior Lecturer in Geography, University of Canterbury, New Zealand. He has numerous publications in the field of tourism, including one of the most popular textbooks on the subject. He is also a tourism consultant for the World Bank.

M. Radburn   Dr. Mark Radburn is Senior Lecturer in Tourism and Leisure Management at Herefordshire College of Technology. His research includes work on the management of water recreation resources and on the structure of the tourism industry in the UK and other European countries. He is currently researching the economic and social effects of tourism in rural areas.

G. Redmond   Professor Gerald Redmond lectures in the Department of Physical Education and Sport Studies at the University of Alberta in Canada. His main research interests are in the field of sports tourism, and include new tourism products and lifestyles.

M.Thea Sinclair   Dr. M. Thea Sinclair is Director of the Tourism Research Centre, Canterbury Business School and Department of Economics, University of Kent. She has published extensively on the economics of tourism and has undertaken tourism research for the United National Centre on Transnational Corporations and World Bank.

M.J. Stabler   Mike Stabler is Lecturer in Economics at the University of Reading, and his main research interests are urban and rural conservation, tourism and leisure, as well as on agriculture, housing and the financial management of non-profit organisations. His wide-ranging publications include theoretical and applied research on the economic and environmental impact of leisure development and the structure of the tourism industry.

Acknowledgements

We would like to give our warmest thanks to Abi Gillett and Yvonne Penford, without whose dedicated processing efforts this book would not have appeared.

Thea Sinclair and Mike Stabler

Chapter 1

New Perspectives on the Tourism Industry

M. Thea Sinclair and M.J. Stabler

Introduction

During the past few decades tourism has emerged as one of the world's major industries, exceeding the importance of many manufacturing industries and other services in terms of sales, employment and foreign currency earnings. The growth of the tourism industry has occurred in both industrialised and developing countries, and has been accompanied by an increasing number of ownership and contractual relationships between firms at the international level. The considerable changes in the structure and operation of the tourism industry have not, however, been the subject of detailed investigation. The lack of analytical research in the past stems, in part, from the heterogeneous nature of the tourism industry, which comprises not only the supply of transportation, accommodation, catering, entertainments, related facilities and natural resources used for tourism purposes, but intermediaries such as tour operators and travel agents, as well as tourism marketing associations. The public sector also has considerable involvement in the industry both directly, for example, via tourism boards and ministries, and indirectly via its regulatory role.

This book provides a variety of new, analytical perspectives on the tourism industry, using the insights of a range of disciplines: economics, geography, psychology, anthropology and sociology. It includes an evaluation of previously formulated models of the tourism industry, and presents a new conceptual framework encompassing the producers, consumers and destinations. Contributors to the book discuss the effects of innovations in information technology on the industry and consumers, as well as the changes in the structure and operation of the industry which result from different types of integration between tourism enterprises at the national and international level. The tourism products supplied are examined in terms of both their actual characteristics and the images which are projected by producers and perceived by consumers. The distributional effects of the tourism industry in developing country destinations are considered, together with the role of the public sector and related policy making. The book also aims to facilitate further analysis of the supply side of tourism by highlighting new methods of analysis. This chapter will first

1

provide a review of research on the tourism industry, evaluating past contributions and identifying the areas requiring further investigation. The subsequent section will outline the ways in which the authors in this book fill key gaps previously identified in the literature, thereby contributing to the body of knowledge of the industry and providing new directions for future research.

Research on the tourism industry

Past research on the tourism industry can be classified into three main categories: first, descriptions of the industry and its operation, management and marketing; second, the spatial development and interactions which characterise the industry on a local, national and international scale; and third, the effects which result from the development of the industry, including economic, social, cultural, political and environmental repercussions. Confining attention largely to books which are representative of the literature, a number have provided descriptions of the tourism industry, for example, Burkart and Medlik (1974), Cleverdon and Edwards (1982), Hodgson (1987), Holloway (1990), Lundberg (1989) and McIntosh and Goeldner (1986). These texts are often written from a practitioner's viewpoint, outlining the structure and operation of particular sectors of the tourism industry, and suggesting trends and their possible consequences.

Texts of a more applied nature on management and marketing reflect the need for handbooks for practitioners. A relatively early example was that by Wahab (1975) and more recent texts include those by Foster (1985) and Witt *et al.* (1991). Discussions of tourism research for managers are provided in Ritchie and Goeldner (eds.) (1987). Several books combine the examination of management with marketing, for instance Hawkins *et al.* (1980a) and Witt and Moutinho (1989), Acerenza (1985) discusses management and planning and Laws (1991) considers tourism marketing in the wider services context. There are well established texts solely on marketing, which provide a general application to the tourism industry, for example, Acerenza (1986), Holloway and Plant (1988), Jefferson and Lickorish (1988), Middleton (1988) and Wahab *et al.* (1976). Other texts have considered specific topics related to tourism marketing; for instance, Buttle (1988) deals with hotels and catering and Shaw (1986) with air transport, whereas Brooke *et al.* (1985) and Buchanan and Hyczynski (1985) examine the topic of forecasting organisational behaviour.

Goodall and Ashworth (1988) and Ashworth and Goodall (1990) are collections of contributions on the structure, operation and management of the tourism industry, including the marketing role of tourism intermediaries, and also include some discussions of the spatial, planning and economic effects of the industry. Additional texts on planning, development and related issues are exemplified by Gearing *et al.* (1976), Gunn (1988) and Hawkins *et al.* (1980b). Useful reviews of research on various aspects of the tourism industry are included in Cooper (ed.) (1989; 1990; 1991).

The literature on spatial factors, which can be found in publications by Lozato (1985), Mill and Morrison (1985), Pearce (1987; 1989), Robinson (1976) and Smith (1983), has largely concentrated on the pattern of development of the tourism industry and the origin–destination linkages. Models of the structural development of tourism destinations over time and space, and typologies of tourism development, are provided by Miossec (1976) and Pearce (1989). Particular interests of contributors to the geographical branch of the literature concern the modelling of the generation, magnitude and patterns of travel. Williams and Shaw (eds.) (1991) surveyed tourism development in Western Europe, Hall (ed.) (1991) considered development in east European countries and Lea (1988) discussed developing countries.

Studies of the effects of the tourism industry, with the notable exception of Mathieson and Wall's (1982) broad review of economic, physical and social issues, have concentrated on particular aspects of tourism development. For example, Edington and Edington (1986) examined the environmental repercussions of tourism development, which are also the subject of reports by the OECD (1981) and World Tourism Organization (1983a; 1983b). The emphasis of past literature on the economic effects of tourism has been on income and employment multiplier effects resulting from tourist expenditure (i.e. demand). These studies are exemplified by Archer (1973; 1977a; 1977b; 1989), Henderson and Cousins (1975), Pye and Lin (eds.) (1983) and Varley (1978). Research reports have also been concerned with particular countries, for example Archer (1982), Fletcher (1985, 1986, 1987) and the World Tourism Organization (WTO) (1980; 1981; 1983c). Diamond (1974; 1977), Erbes (1973), Mitchell (1970) and Wanhill (1982) have examined, in journal articles and/or reports, the implications of tourism development for factor utilisation, and provided estimates of the relevant capital–output ratios. Moreover, a variety of economic effects of rural tourism were considered by Bote (1988). Some attention has also been paid to the tourism industry's contribution to foreign currency earnings, the balance of payments and economic development, particularly in non-industrial countries, for example Ascher (1985), Bryden (1973), Cleverdon (1979), English (1986), Erbes (1973), Sinclair (1990), UNCTAD (1973) and WTO (1988).

There has been little analysis of the political effects of tourism apart from, for example, Richter (1989). Investigations of the social effects of tourism development include Murphy's (1985) discussion of resident/tourist interactions and the effects on communities experiencing tourism development, Smith's (ed.) (1989) study of the social implications of interactions between tourists and hosts, Urry's (1990) analysis of sociological factors and Thurot *et al.*'s (1976) examination of socio-cultural effects. Early discussions of the economic, social, cultural and political effects of tourism development were included in de Kadt (ed.) (1979), and more recent research was provided in Britton and Clarke (eds) (1987). The collection of studies in Harrison (ed.) (forthcoming) constitutes a compilation of analyses of tourism development in non–industrialized countries, based on a variety of disciplinary perspectives.

The content and range of tourism books generally reflect those of the wider journal literature. Inspection of the journal literature reveals not only the areas in which examination of the tourism industry is well covered but also where it is deficient. Useful descriptions of the structure, operation and management of the industry, and of its attempts to influence consumer demand via marketing strategies, can be found in such journals as *International Tourism Quarterly, Tourism Management, Travel and Tourism Analyst*, the *Service Industries Journal* and the trade press. Rather less is known about the characteristics of well established or new tourism products, or about the product images which are promoted by producers and received by consumers.

In general, there is little research on the tourism industry and its operation which is analytical in emphasis, providing explanations of the processes which occur, their causes and effects. The interrelationships between the industry, the consumer and the destination have been neglected, largely because modelling has been insufficiently integrated. The dynamics of tourism supply and decision-making have also received little attention; even in those areas where the pattern of change has been observed, it has frequently not been well documented. For example, innovations in information technology have been reported in the trade press but academic researchers have only recently considered their implications for the organisation and development of the industry.

The considerable volume of journal literature on the spatial development and interrelationships which characterise the tourism industry is well represented in the *Journal of Travel Research, Journal of Leisure Research* and *Tourist Review*, and contributions have also been included in specialist geographical journals, for example *Annales de Géographie, L'Espace Géographique, Geoforum, Geography, GeoJournal* and the *New Zealand Geographer*, and also in *Norois* and *Tijdschrift voor Economische en Sociale Geografie*. However, there is considerable scope for further work on the processes which characterise the formation of the tourism industry, although geographers, for example Pearce (1984; 1985), have provided some interesting contributions in the area of planning. The role of the public sector, with respect to the planning and promotion of tourism, has not been widely investigated. The related issue of the effectiveness of initiatives undertaken by central and local governments and tourism organisations, particularly with respect to social and environmental factors, is another area meriting detailed attention.

Examination of the effects of the tourism industry and tourism development is varied. Articles in journals such as *Annals of Tourism, Estudios Turísticos, Leisure Studies, Tourism Management* and the *Tourist Review* range from the merely descriptive to those providing in-depth analysis. Some topics are attracting increasing attention, for example, the environmental effects of tourism, examined in journals such as *Industry and Environment* and the *Journal of Environmental Management*. However, others have been largely ignored in western journals. A notable example is that of gender and the tourism industry which, though researched in the general leisure field, appears rarely in either western tourism journals or books, apart from a few exceptions, for example Barry *et al.* (1984), Castelberg-Koulma (1991), Guerrier (1986) and Lee (1991). The issue of prostitution and tourism, involving the treatment of women as tourism commodities, has been discussed in *ISIS International Bulletin,* the *Far Eastern Economic Review* and the *Southeast Asia Chronicle*. The distributional consequences of different types of tourism products and development, and of intervention by the public sector, have received little detailed attention in the literature.

Underlying most of the gaps identified in both the book and journal literature are economic aspects, which themselves are not strongly represented. Gray (1970) and Peters (1969), in early texts, examined the economics of international tourism, and Singh (1975) considered the tourism industry at the beginning of the period of its dramatic expansion. A later book by Sessa (1983) on the elements of tourism economics provided only an introduction to its principles. Similarly Baretje and Defert (1972), Figuerola (1985) and Bull (1991) address issues in the travel and tourism industry from an economic standpoint at an introductory level. Even a text such as that by Smith (1989), which is expressly concerned with the analysis of tourism, only touches on specific aspects of the industry, namely market segmentation, business location and its geographic structure. Thus the analysis of the tourism industry is partial and scanty.

New contributions to tourism industry analysis

It is against the background of rapid growth and change in international tourism and the current state of the literature on the industry that this text was compiled. It seeks, by providing an analytical, interdisciplinary emphasis, to fill important gaps in the literature, discussed above, and to provide new perspectives on key issues in the tourism industry and new methodological directions which might be pursued. Underpinning the book is the theme of the internationalization of tourism's industrial structure. Cross-country linkages occur via total and partial ownership, by transnational corporations, of firms in different countries and via a range of contractual relationships whose effects can be of equal or more importance than those of ownership. The different forms of economic integration, discussed in the book, can lead to the exercise of monopoly power by large tour operators, airlines and hotel chains, which can have important effects on both tourists and destination areas. Internationalization also occurs through the development and application of information technology (IT), as will be shown. Although IT systems for buying holidays and other tourism services are not, as yet, standardised, there is pressure for increasing standardization as a means of decreasing the industry's costs and increasing efficiency. Contributors to the book examine the ways in which trends towards internationalization affect the range and characteristics of the tourism products supplied, as well as consumers' opportunities and choice. They also have implications both for individual firms within the industry and for policies at the local, national and international level. However, while acknowledging the power of large firms and their ability to affect consumer choice, the authors recognise the role played by tourists in influencing the nature and growth of the tourism products supplied.

This book includes contributions both by established and new researchers from Europe, the USA, Canada and New Zealand, and examines the tourism industry from a variety of disciplinary standpoints. The authors provide four main perspectives on the theme of tourism industry and its internationalization, embodying research on key areas, previously neglected within the literature: first, in Chapters 2–4, an economic, analytical perspective, focusing upon the actions of the intermediaries in the industry; second, in Chapters 5 and 6, an analysis of the nature and characteristics of existing and new tourism products; third, in Chapters 7–9, examination of the projected and received images of tourism products and destinations; and fourth, in Chapters 10–12, the distributional consequences of tourism development, and the role of the public sector.

Stabler, in Chapter 2, provides a useful context for the book by reviewing current and past models of the tourism industry, formulated within different disciplinary spheres. After demonstrating the partial nature of the contributions made by each set of models, he provides a general analytical framework encompassing the interrelationships between the tourism industry, the consumers and the destinations. The model can be used to examine the process of decision-making both by producers and consumers, taking into account the determinants of the decisions made and the dynamics of the process itself. Stabler also indicates the ways in which the model provides the foundation for future applied research involving the testing of specific hypotheses concerning the operation of the industry.

Chapter 3 by Bennett and Radburn is useful not only in documenting some of the most important changes in information technology (IT), but also in analysing their effects upon competition between producers. Innovations in IT have the potential advantages of increasing consumers' awareness of a wider range of products, and of increasing the speed of information retrieval. However, they can also bias consumers towards products supplied by particular producers. This is especially likely to occur when consumers purchase package holidays from travel agents which are integrated with major tour operators. In discussing the role of IT as a strategy in inter-firm competition, Bennett and Radburn demonstrate the means by which producers influence the process of consumer choice, previously discussed in Chapter 2 and also examined in Chapter 9. They also indicate the advantages of integration between tour operators and travel agencies, examined further in Chapter 4.

Bennett and Radburn's discussion raises questions about the future viability of the travel agency sector of the tourism industry; innovations in IT could have the effect of enhancing the role of travel agents or of rendering them unnecessary. The actual outcome will be affected by legislation at the national and international level, for example, permitting or prohibiting direct sales by tour operators or attempting to eliminate bias in computer reservation systems. Legislation is thus highly influential in determining the framework for competition both at the national level and in such wider groupings as the European Community. It can also affect the relationships between firms from industrialised and developing countries, discussed in Chapter 10.

The nature, causes and effects of different types of integration between firms in the tourism industry are examined by Bote and Sinclair in Chapter 4. Cross-country integration can take place via the obvious form of foreign direct investment, or via less obvious arrangements, for example long–term contracts. Examination of different types of inter-firm integration is important because of the effects of integration on the extent and nature of competition between producers and the prices charged and output supplied to consumers. Bote and Sinclair compare the types of integration which underly changes in the structures of the tourism industries of different European countries, and the increasing market dominance by large firms. The internationalization of the tourism industry in the form of both foreign direct investment by transnational corporations and contractual arrangements is clearly demonstrated, and it is argued that economic integration has important implications for competition policy at the international level.

Chapters 5 and 6 retain the international theme of the book but shift the perspective towards the tourism product and innovations in supply. In Chapter 5, Goodall and Bergsma use the conceptual framework provided by Stabler, in a cross-country comparison of the role of tour operators as producers and the nature of the product they supply. A comparison of the characteristics of the products indicates variations not only between different tour operators within a given country, but between all tour operators in different countries. Intra-country differences may be explained by product differentiation and market segmentation, aided by information technology, as a means of avoiding competition. However, inter-country differences are more difficult to explain as tour operators generally only sell to their domestic market. Further research is necessary to examine the possible effects of differences in consumer tastes between countries, and of producer ties in the form of integration between tour operators, carriers and hoteliers in specific destinations. Considerable differences between the products supplied to consumers of different nationalities may imply the existence of barriers to competition which impede the formation of a single European market for the tourism industry.

Innovations in the tourism product, examined by Redmond in Chapter 6, are important as a form of inter-firm competition, and both cater for and create consumer demand for an increasingly diversified range of products. Redmond's discussion of sports and health tourism in Canada, the USA and Europe not only illustrates changes in the products supplied by the tourism industry, but also indicates competition in the form of the quality of provision and product diversification. The implications for destinations and tourism intermediaries are that competition takes place in the form of both price and non–price characteristics; those destinations and intermediaries which compete most successfully are those which supply an appropriately priced range of high quality, new and established tourism products. Changes in consumer tastes, for example, for tourism in 'natural areas', can be satisfied and/or stimulated by the provision of new products.

It is important to examine not only the actual tourism products and destinations which are supplied, but also the product and destination images projected by the industry and the public sector, and the images received by the tourists themselves. The third new perspective on the tourism industry focuses on behavioural approaches which consider projected and received tourism images in both tourist generating and destination areas. In Chapter 7, Ashworth examines tourism images in destination areas as diverse as Turkey, Egypt, Tunisia, Malta, Cyprus and Languedoc in France. Ashworth demonstrates the frequent contradictions between the images promoted by the industry or public sector and those received by tourists. Conflicts in images can occur in terms of the projected and actual behaviour of tourists, the facilities supplied and character of the destination, the means of image transmission and the spatial scale of the image promoted. Such contradictions can result in disillusionment with the product on the part of tourists, and future decreases in demand. Disillusionment is often an intractable problem over the short run because, once established, an image is often difficult to alter, and future demand is also dependent upon recommendations (positive or negative) by past consumers. Ashworth argues that a successful approach to marketing should be holistic. This type of approach would take account of the factors underlying the production, promotion and reception of images, thereby avoiding potential mismatch with its detrimental consequences for both tourists and suppliers. He also points out the possible strategy of projecting different images to different markets. By providing a more comprehensive framework, Ashworth's analysis constitutes a departure from conventional approaches, and offers new insights into marketing processes.

Chapter 8 by Edwards provides further evidence about images and the perceptions of producers and consumers, in this case at the micro level of accommodation supply in areas of rural tourism in south west England and northern Portugal. There is often little knowledge of the extent to which the characteristics of tourism products supplied coincide with those demanded by consumers, or of the degree to which the perceptions of suppliers match those of their clients. Mismatch between supply and demand could result in decreased satisfaction of both hosts and guests. Edwards' study facilitates greater understanding, both of producers' supply decisions and consumers' holiday choice process. The finding that, in general, producers' and consumers' perceptions of rural accommodation and destinations coincide is perhaps more probable at the local level. However, significant differences in perceptions can still occur, for example, in terms of the importance of recommendations resulting from past experience and of value for money. Such disparities indicate the need for tourism producers and promoters to acquire detailed knowledge of their potential clients' perceptions and priorities.

Further insights into consumers' choice processes are provided by Kent in Chapter 9, and are important for holiday provision and planning, also discussed in Chapters 11 and 12. Kent shows, through the use of a realist method combined with a more conventional survey technique, that knowledge of the characteristics of target groups of consumers, including the consumers' position in the family life cycle, social position and special needs, is necessary if the industry is to fulfil consumers' requirements. Consumers engage in a process of search for desired attributes, as indicated by hedonic pricing models, although the latter have not taken account of the dynamics of holiday demand or supply. Destination is found to be of prime importance in the search process. Kent points out that further research on the scale of the destination which is relevant to the tourist's search process would facilitate appropriate promotion by the industry and public sector. Improvements in the destination's environmental quality, accommodation and access, as well as value for money, appear to be significant determinants of consumer choice. However, such improvements could be undertaken in a manner allowing for specialisation rather than competition between tourist destinations.

In the final part of the book, the perspective shifts towards the distributional effects of tourism development and the related policy measures and planning which can be undertaken by the public sector. In Chapter 10, Sinclair considers the effects upon a developing country, Kenya, of involvement in the tourism industry by foreign intermediaries, in particular tour operators, travel agents and airlines. Foreign intermediaries participate in the tourism industry in the destination country not only via ownership but by other forms of integration, previously discussed in Chapter 4, as well as by negotiating short term contractual arrangements. Such participation often increases total demand but may decrease the destination's earnings per tourist. The supply of and demand for tourism can also be concentrated both spatially and in terms of the tourism products supplied and consumed.

Sinclair's study shows that Kenya's share of expenditure by tourists on package holidays supplied by foreign intermediaries is higher for package holidays involving a wildlife component. This indicates that developing countries can benefit from supplying 'new' forms of tourism, as discussed by Redmond in Chapter 6. The destination's share also increases considerably if the destination supplies the tourist transportation, raising the issues of the quality of service and protection by governments of their national carriers. There are no uniform or easy means by which a highly diverse range of developing countries can obtain increased earnings from their tourism industries. However, consideration of the appropriate balance, for each country, between local and foreign participation in the tourism industry, private and public involvement, and relevant pricing, taxation and related regulatory measures, is necessary. Relevant policy formulation could be undertaken at the level of the individual country, or by groups of countries, as has occurred in the area of information technology.

In contrast to the study of Kenya, which examined the distributional effects of tourism development at the inter-country level, Long's study of tourism development in Mexico focuses upon the effects on members of the local community. Whereas Kenya relied on the private sector to stimulate tourism development, resort development in Mexico occurred in an area selected by the public sector, which also supplied local infrastructure and facilities. The advantages of tourism development for the local community included increases in employment and income, but there were also considerable disadvantages, including soaring inflation and an unequal distribution of the benefits not only between foreign and Mexican developers and the local community, but within the local community itself.

Long's study poses the question of appropriate development – for whom? In the Mexican case it was the members of the local community who were expected to adapt to a change in their environment, imposed by outside developers. Long shows that an inequitable distribution of the social costs and benefits of the tourism development not only raises issues of social justice, but also threatens the long–term sustainability of the tourism industry. Sustainability is not only dependent upon the supply of physical assets and the natural environment but, crucially, on the attitude of the local population. The degree of support or hostility on the part of the local community depends, in turn, upon their participation in, effects on and returns from the process of tourism development. The study thus raises the issue not solely of whether the public sector should participate in tourism development, but of the nature of its involvement and its relevance to the needs of the local community.

The final chapter uses a case study to illustrate the constraints and challenges facing eastern European countries which contemplate the development of tourism as a contribution to their economies. In Chapter 12, Pearce examines the question of appropriate planning for tourism, demonstrating the need for a comprehensive tourism development strategy, embracing the local, regional and national contexts. Many of the issues requiring consideration by tourism planners in eastern Europe were also identified as important in previous chapters. They include the development of new tourism products, the maintenance of environmental quality and a positive destination image, effective promotion and marketing, access and transportation, and the appropriate balance between private and public sector participation and local and foreign involvement. Pearce, like Long in Chapter 11, recognises the need for local debate and participation in planning the objectives and form of development of the tourism industry. Pearce and Long thus show that the entire process of planning for tourism development may require a radical re-think if the tourism industry is to benefit those directly involved in destination areas.

References

Acerenza, M.A. (1985) *Administración del turismo. Planificación y dirección.* Editorial Trillas, Mexico, D.F.

Acerenza, M.A. (1986) *Promoción turística. Un enfoque metodólogico.* 4th edn. Editorial Trillas, Mexico, D.F.

Archer, B.H. (1973) *The Impact of Domestic Tourism.* Occasional Papers in Economics No.2, University of Wales Press, Bangor.

Archer, B.H. (1977a) *Tourism Multipliers: The State of the Art.* Occasional Papers in Economics No 11, University of Wales Press, Bangor.

Archer, B.H. (1977b) *Tourism in the Bahamas and Bermuda: Two Case Studies.* Occasional Papers in Economics No.10, University of Wales Press, Bangor.

Archer, B.H. (1982) *The Economic Impact of Tourism in Seychelles.* Commonwealth Secretariat CFTC/SEY/51.

Archer, B.H. (1989) Tourism and island economies. In: Cooper, C.P. (ed) *Progress in Tourism, Recreation and Hospitality Management*, Volume One. Belhaven, London, pp. 125-34.

Ascher, F. (1985) *Tourism Transnational Corporations and Cultural Identities.* UNESCO, Paris.

Ashworth, G.J. and Goodall, B. (eds) (1990) *Marketing Tourism Places.* Routledge, London.

Baretje, R. and Defert, P. (1972) Aspects économiques du tourisme. Berger, Levrault, Paris.

Barry, K., Bunch, C. and Castley, S. (1984) *International Feminism: Networking Against Female Sexual Slavery.* IWTC, New York.

Bote Gómez, V. (1988) *Turismo en espacio rural.* Editorial Popular, Madrid.

Britton, S. and Clarke, W.C. (eds) (1987) *Ambiguous Alternative: Tourism in Small Developing Countries.* University of the South Pacific, Suva.

Brooke, M.Z., Buckley, P.J. and Witt, S.F. (1985) *The International Travel and Tourism Forecast.* Industry Forecasts, London.

Bryden, J.M. (1973) *Tourism and Development: A Case Study of the Commonwealth Caribbean.* Cambridge University Press, Cambridge.

Buchanan, D.A. and Hyczynski, A.A. (1985) *Organisational Behaviour.* Prentice Hall, Englewood Cliffs, New Jersey.

Bull, A. (1991) *The Economics of Travel and Tourism.* Pitman, Longman Cheshire.

Burkart, A.J. and Medlik, S. (1974) *Tourism: Past, Present, Future*. Heinemann, London.

Buttle, F. (1988) *Hotel and Food Science Marketing: A Managerial Approach*. Cassell, London.

Castelberg-Koulma, M. (1991) Greek women and tourism: women's co-operatives as an alternative form of organization. In: Redclift, N. and Sinclair, M.T. (eds), *Working Women: International Perspectives on Labour and Gender Ideology*. Routledge, London, pp. 197–212.

Cleverdon, R. (1979) *The Economic and Social Impact of International Tourism on Developing Countries*. Economic Intelligence Unit, London.

Cleverdon, R. and Edwards, E. (1982) *International Tourism to 1990*. Abt Books, Cambridge.

Cooper, C.P. (ed) (1989) *Progress in Tourism, Recreation and Hospitality Management*, Volume One. Belhaven, London.

Cooper, C.P. (ed) (1990) *Progress in Tourism, Recreation and Hospitality Management*, Volume Two. Belhaven, London.

Cooper, C.P. (ed) (1991) *Progress in Tourism, Recreation and Hospitality Management*, Volume Three. Belhaven, London.

de Kadt, E. (1979) *Tourism – Passport to Development*. Oxford University Press, Oxford.

Diamond, J. (1974) International tourism and the developing countries: a case study in failure. *Economia Internazionale*, 27 (3-4), 601–615.

Diamond, J. (1977) Tourism's role in economic development: the case reexamined. *Economic Development and Cultural Change*, 25 (3), 539–553.

Edington, J.M. and Edington, M.A. (1986) *Ecology, Recreation and Tourism*. Cambridge University Press, Cambridge.

English, E.P. (1986) *The Great Escape? An Examination of North–South Tourism*. North–South Institute, Ottawa.

Erbes, R. (1973) *International Tourism and the Economy of Developing Countries*. OECD Development Centre, Paris.

Figuerola Palomo, M. (1985) *Teoriá económica del turismo*. Alianza Editorial, Madrid.

Fletcher, J.E. (1985) *The Economic Impact of Tourism on Jamaica*. WTO/UNDP.

Fletcher, J.E. (1986) *The Economic Impact of Tourism on Western Samoa*. WTO/UNDP.

Fletcher, J.E. (1987) *The Economic Impact of International Tourism on the National Economy of the Solomon Islands*. WTO/UNDP.

Foster, D. (1985) *Travel and Tourism Management*. Macmillan, Basingstoke.

Gearing, C.E., Swart, W.W. and Var, T. (eds) (1976) *Planning for Tourism Development*. Praeger, New York.

Goodall, B. and Ashworth, G. J. (eds) (1988) *Marketing in the Tourism Industry*. Croom Helm, Beckenham.

Gray, H.P. (1970) *International Travel – International Trade*. DC Heath, Lexington.

Guerrier, Y. (1986) Hotel Manager: an unsuitable job for a woman? *The Service Industries Journal*, 6 (2), 227–240.

Gunn, C.A. (1988) *Tourism Planning*, 2nd edn. Taylor and Francis, New York.

Hall, D.H. (ed) (1991) *Tourism, Eastern Europe and the Soviet Union*. Belhaven, London.

Harrison, D. (ed) (forthcoming) *International Tourism and the Less Developed Countries*. Belhaven, London.

Hawkins, D.E., Shafer, E.L. and Rovelstad, J.M. (eds) (1980a) *Tourism Marketing and Management Issues*. George Washington University, Washington.

Hawkins, D.E., Shafer, E.L. and Rovelstad, J.M. (eds) (1980b) *Tourism Planning and Development Issues*. George Washington University, Washington.

Henderson, D.M. and Cousins, R.L. (1975) *The Economic Impact of Tourism: A Case Study of Greater Tayside*. University of Edinburgh, Tourism and Recreation Research Unit, Research Report No 13, Edinburgh.

Hodgson, A. (ed) (1987) *The Travel and Tourism Industry*. Pergamon, Oxford.

Holloway, J.C. (1990) *The Business of Tourism*. MacDonald and Evans, Plymouth.

Holloway, J.C. and Plant, R.V. (1988) *Marketing for Tourism*. Pitman, London.

Jefferson, A. and Lickorish, L. (1988) *Marketing Tourism: A Practical Guide*. Longman, Harlow.

Laws, E. (1991) *Tourism Marketing – Service and Quality Management Perspectives*. Stanley Thornes, Cheltenham.

Lea, J. (1988) *Tourism and Development in the Third World*. Routledge, London.

Lee, W. (1991) Prostitution and tourism in South-East Asia. In: Redclift, N. and Sinclair, M.T. (eds), *Working Women: International Perspectives on Labour and Gender Ideology*. Routledge, London, pp. 79–103.

Lozato, J.P. (1985) *Géographie du tourisme*. Masson, Paris.

Lundberg, D.E. (1989) *The Tourism Business*, 6th edn. Van Nostrand Reinhold, New York.

MacIntosh, R.W. and Goeldner, C.R. (1986) *Tourism Practices, Principles, Philosophy*. Wiley, New York.

Mathieson, A. and Wall, G. (1982) *Tourism: Economic, Physical and Social Impacts*. Longman, London.

Middleton, V.T.C. (1988) *Marketing in Travel and Tourism*. Heinemann, London.

Mill, R.C. and Morrison, A.M. (1985) *The Tourism System: An Introductory Text*. Prentice-Hall, Englewood Cliffs, New Jersey.

Miossec, J. M. (1976) *Eléments pour une théorie de l'espace touristique*. Les Cahiers du Tourisme C-36, C.H.E.T., Aix-en-Provence.

Mitchell, F. (1970) The value of tourism in East Africa. *East African Economic Review*, 2 (1), 1-21.

Murphy, P.E. (1985) *Tourism: A Community Approach*. Methuen, London.

Organization for Economic Cooperation and Development (OECD) (1981) *The Impact of Tourism on the Environment*, OECD, Paris.

Pearce, D.G. (1984) Planning for tourism in Belize. *Geographical Review*, 74(3), 291–303.

Pearce, D.G. (1985) Tourism and planning in the Southern Alps of New Zealand. In: Singh, T.V. and Kaur, J. (eds), *Integrated Mountain Development.* Himalayan Books, New Delhi, pp. 293-308.

Pearce, D.G. (1987) *Tourism Today: A Geographical Analysis.* Longman, Harlow.

Pearce, D.G. (1989) *Tourism Development.* Longman, Harlow.

Peters, M. (1969) *International Tourism: The Economics and Development of the International Tourist Trade.* Hutchinson, London.

Pye, E.A. and Lin, T.B. (eds) (1983) *Tourism in Asia: The Economic Impact.* Singapore University Press, Singapore.

Richter, L. K. (1989) *The Politics of Tourism in Asia.* University of Hawaii Press, Honolulu.

Ritchie, J.R. Brent and Goeldner, C.R. (eds) (1987) *Travel, Tourism and Hospitality Research: A Handbook for Managers and Researchers.* John Wiley, New York.

Robinson, H. (1976) *A Geography of Tourism.* MacDonald and Evans, London.

Sessa, A. (1983) *Elements of Tourism Economics.* Catal, Rome.

Shaw, S. (1986) *The Marketing of Air Transport.* Pitman, London.

Sinclair, M.T. (1990) *Tourism Development in Kenya.* World Bank, Washington D.C.

Singh, T.V. (1975) *Tourism and Tourist Industry.* New Heights, Delhi.

Smith, S.L.J. (1983) *Recreation Geography.* Longman, London.

Smith, S.L.J. (1989) *Tourism Analysis: A Handbook.* Longman, Harlow.

Smith, V.L. (ed) (1989) *Hosts and Guests: The Anthropology of Tourism,* 2nd edn. Pennsylvania Press, Philadelphia.

Thurot, J.M. *et al.* (1976) *Les effets du tourisme sur les valeurs socio-culturelles.* Centres des Hautes Etudies Touristiques, Aix-en-Provence.

United Nations Conference on Trade and Development (1973) *Elements of Tourism Policy in Developing Countries.* Report by the Secretariat of UNCTAD, TD/B/C3/89 Rev.1, United Nations, New York.

Urry, J. (1990) *The Tourist Gaze.* Sage, London.

Varley, R.C.G. (1978) *Tourism in Fiji: Some Economic and Social Problems.* Occasional Papers in Economics No.12, University of Wales, Bangor.

Wahab, S.E.A. (1975) *Tourism Management.* Tourism International Press, London.

Wahab, S.E.A., Crampon, L.J. and Rothfield, L.M. (1976) *Tourism Marketing.* Tourism International Press, London.

Wanhill, S.R.C. (1982) Evaluating the resource costs of tourism. *Tourism Management,* 3(4), 208–211.

Williams, A.M. and Shaw, G. (eds) (1991) *Tourism and Economic Development. Western European Experiences,* 2nd edn. Belhaven, London.

Witt, S.F. and Moutinho, L. (eds) (1989) *Tourism Marketing and Management Handbook.* Prentice Hall, Hemel Hempstead.

Witt, S.F., Brooke, M.Z., Buckley, P.J. (1991) *The Management of International Tourism.* Unwin Hyman, London.

World Tourism Organization (WTO) (1980) *Economic Effects of Tourism.* World Tourism Organization, Madrid.

World Tourism Organization (WTO)/Horwarth and Horwarth (1981) *Tourism Multipliers Explained*. Horwarth and Horwarth International, London.

World Tourism Organization (WTO) (1983a) *Study of Tourism's Contribution to Protecting the Environment*. World Tourism Organization, Madrid.

World Tourism Organization (WTO)/United Nation's Environmental Programme (1983b) *Workshop on Environmental Aspects of Tourism*. World Tourism Organization – United Nations Environmental Programme.

World Tourism Organization (WTO) (1983c) *Domestic and International Tourism's Contribution to State Revenue*. World Tourism Organization, Madrid.

World Tourism Organization (WTO) (1988) *Economic Review of World Tourism: Tourism in the Context of Economic Crisis and the Dominance of the Service Economy*. Report for the WTO by V. Bote Gómez, World Tourism Organization, Madrid.

Chapter 2

Modelling the Tourism Industry: A New Approach

M.J. Stabler

Introduction

The analytical frameworks in which tourism has been studied have largely been constructed by geographers. This is partly because they made an early entry into the field, but it is also because tourism constitutes their natural milieu, being spatial in character. Indeed, an inspection of the literature on domestic and international tourism reveals that spatial models, being concerned with the origin – destination linkage, with the emphasis on destinations and spatial scale, tend to predominate, notwithstanding the substantial amount of research on demand and income generation. This chapter reconsiders this linkage, having two main aims. First, by widening the scope of existing models it is possible to examine the role the tourism industry plays between the consumer in the origin or generating area and the product in the destination area. Second, stemming from the first, to explain the nature and development of the concept of opportunity sets, an analytical framework referred to by several contributors to this book, embracing economic, marketing, planning and social psychological approaches as well as geographical ones. It is argued that the concept can assist in understanding the structure and operation of the tourism industry, both extending and unifying spatial tourism models.

The concept of opportunity sets is not wholly original for it was employed by Marble and Bowlby (1968) in the examination of retailing. In addition to behaviour by shoppers they analysed the location, number and type of shop, in terms of the goods on offer, which indicated the shopping opportunities open to consumers. In the case of tourism, it has largely been restricted to the analysis of tourists' holiday choice and travel marketing (Woodside *et al.*, 1977; Woodside and Sherrell, 1977) and Um and Crompton (1987) who made reference to it in modelling tourists' destination selection process.

As the term implies, the concept is based on set theory where on the one hand consumers perceive or consider attainable sets of holiday opportunities and, on the other, suppliers offer sets of different kinds of holidays. These opportunity sets are examined in detail in the model developed below, illustrated by an example of summer sun package holidays. However, initially, since the concept contains analytical elements from a number of disciplines, it is of value to review the current state of tourism analysis, in so far as it relates to opportunity set analysis, with the emphasis being on its international aspects.

Tourists – industry – destination analysis

The serious study of tourism, as an aspect of leisure, has been undertaken for little more than 25 years and has not yet established a firm theoretical foundation. This reflects, to an extent, a research effort which has been somewhat piecemeal because those engaged in it have tended to work independently, not only within their own disciplines but also paying little attention to the studies of those outside it. As a consequence there has been virtually no consensus on the direction research should take towards developing a unified and general theoretical structure.

Geographical models
Geographers, such as Miossec (1976), appear to have to have set out the spatial conceptual framework by identifying and analysing spatial demand and supply aspects; the morphology and functions of tourism areas; the use of natural, manufactured and human resources, particularly their organisation within national, regional and local boundaries; travel levels and patterns between generating and destination areas. They have also, more recently, ventured into the field of the analysis of human behaviour and experience, being involved in the construction of models to understand how holiday decisions are related to consumers' psychological and social state and their acquisition and processing of information, especially in relation to images of destination areas. Included in such models is often the classification of tourists with respect to their choice of destination, travel, accommodation and holiday behavioural patterns, thus maintaining the spatial dimension. Finally, geographers have been involved in a continuing debate about methodology.

Geographical models having a bearing on opportunity sets, which emphasises the consumer–industry–product relationship, are those concerned with the origin–destination link, the structure of tourism and the influence of demand and supply. In part following a succinct appraisal given by Pearce (1987), four categories of models can be identified:

- Travel and tourism space;
- Origin – destination;
- Tourism industry core–periphery models;
- Dynamic.

Each of these is briefly outlined in so far as they underpin the opportunity cost model considered later.

Travel and tourism space models

These models emphasise the notion that knowledge of destinations is related to their distance from generating areas. Effectively the analysis of the relationship is through what amounts to tourism travel distance decay functions (Campbell, 1967). Other work of this nature has analysed the volume and pattern of international travel as well as deriving more sophisticated spatial models in terms of natural, built and infrastructural resources, for example, Yokeno (1968) and Miossec (1976).

Origin–destination models

Although origin–destination models are considered here as a distinct category they have really developed out of the travel–space analytical framework. Tourism places are viewed as both origins and destinations and likewise transport structures and routes are two-way, performing both a generating and a receiving function. Places can be ranked according to their role and function in domestic and foreign travel according to their capacity to attract or generate tourists. Metropolitan areas have the greatest ability to do this, followed by peripheral urban and rural areas.

In an international context, industrialised countries are predominant in both generating and attracting tourists whereas as non-industrialised countries, particularly those which possess outstanding environmental attributes, tend only to attract tourists. Locations can be classified either as those where there is a net inflow or a net outflow of tourism, analogous to the inputs and leakages in economic multiplier models. Thurot (1980) and Lundgren (1982) have made a significant contribution to modelling this aspect of tourism, as has Pearce (1981) who incorporated inflows and outflows into an origin–destination model therefore making it more generally applicable.

Tourism industry core–periphery models

These are essentially concerned with international travel and third world countries in core–periphery models which acknowledge the control of multinational companies based in industrial countries over the tourism industry, as exemplified in the work of Britton (1980) and Hills and Lundgren (1977). Development of core–periphery models in tourism has included the idea of concentration both of the market and of the tourism industry at a national level in both generating and destination countries and its dispersal down through regional and local markets. This approach thus embodies tourism industry structural elements into what is basically an origin–destination framework.

Dynamic models

These kinds of models encompass change over time in both the destinations patronised by tourists and their tastes and preferences and therefore holiday patterns and behaviour. Whereas Thurot (1973) considers tourists, socio-economic circumstances and the role they play in the discovery, development and eventual decline of destinations, Plog (1973) stresses their psychological characteristics in establishing tourist personalities. He identifies two main types, namely psychocentrics and allocentrics. Psychocentrics tend to be somewhat conservative and cautious in their choice of holidays, wishing to maintain familiarity in their experiences, while allocentrics are more adventurous looking for new experiences, perhaps even accepting a degree of risk. These two types are therefore likely to choose different destinations. The former, largely constituting mass tourists, favour established tourism areas while the latter prefer more remote or undiscovered destinations. Consequently such models not only investigate motivational, psychological and social factors determining holiday choice and behaviour, but they also consider economic and perhaps physical consequences for destination areas. As such they again reinforce the spatial dimension of what are ostensibly temporal and human geography models.

Economic models

Economists have devoted virtually all their research effort to three aspects of tourism, notwithstanding that it is possible to apply quite a number of the discipline's concepts to other areas of the subject. Dominating research is what might be generically termed 'tourism impact economics' under which can be subsumed: tourism multipliers, concerning the generation of employment and income; the role of tourism in economic development; tourism as a form of international trade, especially the generation of foreign currency earnings and its contribution to balance of payments; the social costs and benefits of tourism, particularly environmental impacts.

In part arising from the first, the second area of economists' research interest has been the study of the structure of the tourism industry, with most attention being focused on its competitive position; only recently has there been serious study of concentration and integration. Economics has made some contribution also to demand studies in which it tends to emphasise the importance of income, price and socio-economic characteristics, such as occupation, class, education, car ownership, period of paid holiday, as key determinants in establishing elasticities of demand. More recent work has considered the attributes of the tourism product in hedonic pricing models (Sinclair *et al.*, 1990; Clewer *et al.*, forthcoming).

Management and marketing models

These are not so much theoretical frameworks as the application to tourism of commercial methods which are often based on and/or open to interpretation from accounting, economic, geographic or sociological standpoints. For example, marketing strategies involving differentiation of the product and market segmentation, have been widely studied by economists as part of the theory of the firm, industrial and market structure. Likewise management studies, drawing on concepts from sociology, social psychology and accounting, as well as economics, have mostly been applied in manufacturing, therefore relating to goods rather than services. Accordingly, it is not necessarily informative or instructive to consider management and marketing concepts in detail, separately from economic ones.

Psychological and sociological models

These largely underlie tourism demand, whatever the emphasis, for the ultimate question which has to be addressed is what motivates people to take holidays. One explanation (Gray, 1970) is that certain needs and desires cannot be met in their home location; seeking the sun would be one example for residents of northern temperate climate areas, such as northern America and Europe. Another suggested by Crompton (1979), is that individuals and or households need a break from routine. Indeed he argues that there are a number of motives related to both the requirement for a change from the home and personal environment and the achievement of specific goals such as social interaction or exploration. However, most writers perceive the taking of a holiday as meeting the need for rest, relaxation and amusement. Accordingly there are factors both pushing tourists away from generating areas and pulling them towards destination areas.

Motivation naturally has to be translated into action in terms of the type of holidays and destinations chosen which are a reflection of the psychological make-up of tourists, the images they hold and the constraints acting on them. The role of images and constraints are examined in some detail by Kent (Chapter 9) who considers the holiday decision process; therefore these factors are not pursued here.

An appraisal of tourism models

The brief review of tourism models above, though not exhaustive in that it considered only those containing elements concerned with the consumer–industry–product link, nevertheless covered those of major importance proposed to date. It is clear, however, that none is sufficiently general to explain consumers' decision-making process in relation to the array of holidays on offer, the structure and the role of the tourism industry (particularly the intermediaries in generating countries pursuing self-determined objectives) and the relationship between origin and destination areas. It has been shown that the common factor underpinning geographical models is the spatial linkage of tourism places but with the emphasis on the outcome of decisions rather than what determines them, i.e. in economic terms they are ex-post models. For example, travel–space and origin–destination approaches record past levels and patterns of tourism flows so that as descriptive models their predictive power rests on the projection of trends. Tourism industry core–periphery models, while similarly explaining observed relationships between origins and destinations, do incorporate and acknowledge the role played by the tourism industry, both official bodies and commercial entities. However, these models have been developed expressly to consider industrial – third world relationships but it can be shown, as Bote and Sinclair do (Chapter 4), that large multinational firms exercise control over industrialised destinations as well as third world countries, for instance the influence of large tour operators in the UK over Spanish resorts, or increasingly in eastern Mediterranean countries, such as Turkey, as Ashworth (Chapter 7) demonstrates. Consequently, the models should include tourists as consumers whose choices and behaviour also have a significant impact on destination areas.

Geographical dynamic models, in concentrating on the characteristics of consumers, largely make good the deficiencies of core–periphery models because they recognise the impact on destination evolution and the decay of changing tastes, preferences and behaviour. However, they virtually omit reference to the tourism industry, particularly the intermediaries, who themselves develop holidays to new destinations, or affect the fortunes of existing ones through changes in their policies, reflecting the economic climate and market conditions, internationally as well as in the generating areas in which they are located. Thus geographic models lack two major elements. First they are insufficiently integrated because they fail to incorporate the tourist and tourism industry adequately into the spatial context. Second they lack an economic and management–marketing base as a means of explaining the actions of the tourism industry in both origin and destination areas.

Given the discipline's tradition, it is not surprising that it is the spatial dimension which is overlooked in economic tourism research, except indirectly in impact studies which focus on destinations. The relevance of economic analyses, and to an extent, management–marketing approaches, to the consumer–industry–product link lies in their satisfactory explanation of business behaviour. A key feature of such approaches is that in addition to the analysis of the market competitive structure, business objectives and marketing strategies are included in relation to both consumers and rival organisations. Such aspects are central to the opportunity sets framework and therefore further discussion is deferred until that concept is considered. Economic analysis of tourists' behaviour is less satisfactory. It tends to make somewhat questionable assumptions about consumer rationality, and also, in relying on observed behaviour, almost completely ignores psychological and sociological explanations, to which attention is now turned.

Psychological and sociological analyses, as has been indicated, have made a valuable contribution to explaining consumer motivation, choice and holiday behaviour. Moreover, in attempting to establish how tourism images are formed and influence choice, together with the constraints to which consumers are subject, they have wider significance than a cursory inspection would suggest. However, this significance for the industry and product (destination areas) is implied rather than explicit. Therefore the spatial dimension is somewhat tenuous. Psychological and sociological models need to be placed in the wider context of the consumer–industry–product link.

The overall picture of tourism analysis which emerges from this exposition and appraisal of the principal models, confirms the assertion made at the outset that their development has been piecemeal and that no general model exists. The problem has occurred because researchers have derived analytical frameworks to meet specific objectives, for example to ascertain travel flow and volume or the impact of tourists from industrialised origins on third world economies, cultures and environments. In constructing a more general analytical framework, though not necessarily an all-embracing model, a number of the approaches examined can be drawn on. However, it must be acknowledged that in doing this there is still a specific objective, namely to consider the central role played by the tourism industry, the focus of this book.

Tourism opportunity sets

Initially, in extending the scope of opportunity sets as a tourism analytical tool, consumer and industry sets were considered separately by Goodall *et al.* (1988). Kent (1990) further refined and developed consumer sets, in line with the approach by Um and Crompton (1990). Goodall (1990) has focused on destination sets and Stabler (1990) has reconsidered industry sets, attempting to link them to the research both of Kent and Goodall and that on destinations by de Haan *et al.* (1990). Here, therefore, the integration of these separate investigations is proposed in what amounts to a review and outline for further development of the opportunity sets concept and its application.

Opportunity sets are the holiday opportunities which exist at any given point in time, and a total opportunity set comprises all possible holidays, both commercial and non-commercial, which are available. How the opportunities are categorised can vary according to how and by whom the holiday is assembled, for example inclusive tour by charter; the type of activity, including skiing, location, season, type of accommodation or combinations of these.

Within the 'total' opportunity set can be embodied the 'consumer' or 'tourist', 'industry' and 'destination' sets. In a comprehensive model a distinction would be drawn not only between aggregative and disaggregative sets, but also between 'inside' or 'subjective' and 'outside' or 'objective' sets. 'Inside' sets reflect the perspective of the particular sector, i.e. consumer, industry and destination, whereas 'outside' sets for each of these sectors are compiled by an independent entity. Inside and outside sets are referred to below in the discussion on destination area opportunity sets. The diagrammatic representation of these sets, given in Figure 2.1, is a simplification and adaptation of that presented by the author elsewhere (Stabler, 1989). It shows that the three sectoral sets overlap, demonstrating the origin–industry–destination link. The analysis of these sets at an aggregated or disaggregated level can best be illustrated by reference to the work of contributors to this book. For example, in examining the general pattern of skiing holidays available through the industry, as Goodall and Bergsma do in Chapter 5 for the UK and Netherlands, an aggregate approach is required. Conversely, the analysis of the marketing of summer sun holidays in a local area and by specific tour operators, Bennett and Radburn (Chapter 3), necessitates a disaggregated approach. Likewise, where the emphasis is on consumers, the analysis may be at a number of different levels of aggregation. For instance, it will be at an aggregate level in comparing holiday choices between one country and another, a more disaggregated level when comparing several socio-economic, say income, groups within a specific country, whereas in identifying the choice process of a holiday by a single consuming unit (Kent, Chapter 9), it will be at a very specific level.

Figure 2.1 indicates that though the three main sectors overlap, none is fully nested within any other. This acknowledges that each sector has portions of its set not subject to linkage with either of the other two. For example, consumers may arrange a holiday without doing so through the tourism intermediaries, i.e. the industry in the generating or destination areas. Clearly also, the industry set is not exactly coincidental with the destination set, even though the latter is part of the product supplied by the industry. As Goodall (1990) shows, there are different destination sets for consumers and the industry in different origin countries. The figure is fully explained by considering the opportunity sets for each sector in turn.

Industry opportunity sets

The industry comprises public and business organisations in both generating and destination areas who supply or promote holidays or their components – travel, accommodation, facilities, services. Within the context of opportunity sets examined here, however, attention is concentrated on the role of the intermediaries in generating areas, particularly the influence they exercise over consumer choice, arising from their competitive structure.

The 'industry' set is shown in the bottom half of Figure 2.1. It is nested fully within the 'total' opportunity set to allow for the fact that not all holidays are arranged through the tourism industry. For example, those with family and/or friends would constitute a 'non-commercial' opportunity set. Various industry subsets can be envisaged, of which an important one in the UK at least, is the 'inclusive tour or package holiday' set which will be considered below in discussing the role of tour operators. At a more specific level it is possible to conceive of 'company' opportunity sets as subsets of industry sets. The industry set overlaps both the consumer and destination sets, for the reasons already given.

Consumer opportunity sets

Starting from the most aggregative level it is possible to derive the nature of the set from which the consumer ultimately chooses a holiday. No consuming unit, whether defined as an individual, household or group, has complete knowledge of holidays available, which is the reason why the 'perceived' opportunity set, consisting of the range of holidays known to it, lies fully within the total opportunity set. In effect those holidays of which there is no knowledge, lying outside the perceived sets, constitute what can be called the 'unawareness' set. The opportunity set from which the consumer makes a final selection is narrower than the perceived set. The consumer possesses an 'attainable' opportunity set comprised of holidays which it is possible to take, for example, they can be afforded. The overlap of the 'perceived' set with the 'attainable' set constitutes a 'realisable' set, i.e. one containing holidays which the consumer is aware of and so is in a position to take (Figure 2.2).

Although other kinds of consumers' sets have been suggested as conceptualising their behaviour (Goodall, *et al.* 1988), the two of most interest are the 'attainable' and 'consideration' sets, the latter containing holidays currently being contemplated. However, the number of choices needs to be reduced to a manageable level so that the consumer can make an informed final selection; a 'choice' set, within which a 'decision' set is nested, can be conceived as lying within the consideration set.

The disaggregation from the 'perceived' opportunity set down to the 'decision' set can be viewed as a sequential process, perhaps with feedbacks to a set at a higher level in the event of the need to reappraise a choice. This choice process by consumers is examined in more detail later in this chapter in analysing opportunity sets behavioural matrices (Figure 2.2). The linkage between the consumer and the industry occurs in the overlap between the former's decision set and the latter's set. This has elsewhere (Stabler, 1989) been called the 'realised' set (not to be confused with 'realisable') but might be better redesignated as the 'operational' set. Obviously it is in the industry's interest that

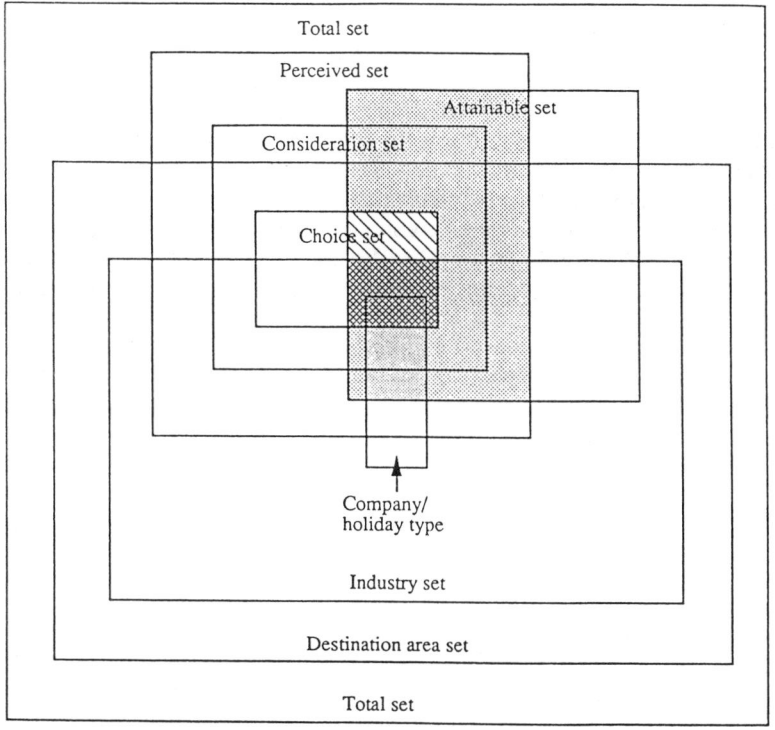

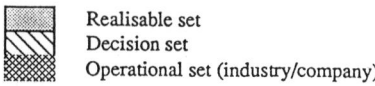

Realisable set
Decision set
Operational set (industry/company)

Figure 2.1 A diagrammatic representation of tourism opportunity sets: consumer–industry–destination links

the overlap of its set with consumers' decision sets should be as large as possible, as it will sell more holidays as a result.

Destination area opportunity sets

It can be argued that 'destination area' opportunity sets, being supply-side in character, are essentially variants or subsets of industry sets. However, one reason why they should be considered as a distinct category is that, as they are concerned with the attributes and resources of destinations, they relate to the tourism product rather than the organisation of holidays and their sale, which occurs in origin areas (for the purposes of analysis, the term 'industry' sets will largely be confined to the tourism intermediaries). Another reason for treating destination area opportunity sets as a separate category is that they are location-orientated. Goodall (1990) suggests that they have a number of dimensions. He argues that destinations should not be viewed as single locations but as resort

23

sets. Considered in this way, destination area opportunity sets may be conceived of as 'environments', i.e. classified according to physical characteristics such as sun–sand–sea, mountains, lakes, sporting centres. Alternatively such opportunity sets may be 'place specific' whether that place is a country, region or sub-region. Goodall's interpretation of destination area sets has both advantages and disadvantages; his assertion that they should be multi-dimensional reflecting different perspectives, is particularly important.

The industry perspective is likely to vary by sector and location. Intermediaries in generating regions will have a view of destinations which reflects their objectives of selling holidays in them. Conversely, the tourism industries located in those destinations will hold a different view as they are more concerned with projecting and promoting them in generating areas. Goodall (1990) refers to these perspectives as the 'outside' and 'inside' viewpoint respectively. They constitute what amounts to industry 'perceived' sets, which is of consequence in that such perceptions govern their actions. Further destination opportunity sets can be derived from different industry perspectives. There are numerous origin tourism industries, each of which will be different in nature. For example, tour operators in the UK project an image of Greece as a destination which certainly differs from that of tour operators in Germany, perhaps reflecting national tastes. Furthermore, destination area sets projected domestically by the industry are likely to be different from those promoted to foreign countries.

Another perspective is that held by tourists, which will be determined by their knowledge of particular destinations, and whether or not they have taken holidays in them. Moreover, there will be a temporal influence on their perspective. Prior to taking the holiday their view will be an outside one, irrespective of their experience of a destination. However, while on holiday in the destination they will hold an inside perspective, if only, as de Haan *et al.*, (1990) suggest, they are literally 'holiday-makers' whose actions and behaviour form part of the product. Finally, tourists who book holidays outside the industry will undoubtedly have a perspective different from those who book through the industry. Thus 'non-commercial' destination area opportunity sets may be distinguished from 'commercial' sets.

Other refinements to destination area opportunity sets can be made. Goodall (1990) stresses the complementarity and interdependency of places and/or environments with a given resort area, region or country, particularly where they are incorporated into two or three centre package holidays offered by tour operators. He also conceives of destination area sets which reflect segmentation by the tourism industry, for example, by accessibility, accommodation, visitor characteristics, degree of commercialism and location.

The contribution of opportunity sets to the analysis of tourism

Modelling the industry

It is possible to give a different perspective on, and to widen the scope of, tourism analysis using the three categories of opportunity sets which have been outlined above, and some indication of this has already been given by reference to research by contributors to this book. However, the value of the concept, which currently is essentially an heuristic device, ultimately lies in its relevance to actual market circumstances. In short, it should have practical applications. In the examination of the contribution of opportunity sets to tourism analysis which follows, most attention is paid to those concerned with the industry.

It has been suggested by Kent (1990) that the investigation of consumer choice within opportunity sets provides a wider analytical framework than economic approaches. Basic economic consumer theory assumes optimality of choice in every dimension through perfect knowledge and rationality subject to a resources limit. It also tends to concentrate on deriving price and income elasticities to ascertain the response of demand to changes in such explanatory variables. In reality consumer decisions are sub-optimal because of lack of information, uncertainty and financial and temporal constraints. Economic analysis, largely through game theory, has only recently addressed this problem, but not to any extent in relation to leisure activity. Similarly, many studies of a more psychological and sociological nature, which concentrate on specific personal characteristics and holiday attributes, overlook the economic constraints and the overall decision process context which condition consumer choice. It is the interaction between these characteristics, attributes, constraints and the choice process which an opportunity sets approach can accommodate. Kent has developed a model of consumer holiday choice behaviour within the opportunity sets framework, which is considered below in suggesting the integration of consumer and industry sets.

Stabler (1989), following the initial exposition by Goodall *et al.* (1988), has considered the opportunity set concept from the standpoint of the tourism industry, concentrating on the intermediaries, especially tour operators in origin areas, in determining the nature and range of tourism products. In doing this he moved away from traditional economic analysis, endeavouring to consider the discipline's concepts within the opportunity sets framework. The economic study of the determinants of tourism supply is not well developed and has not been related to the more extensive research on demand. It has generally been assumed that supply is perfectly elastic, implying that producers have little influence on demand merely responding to changes in its level and pattern. Most attention has been focused on the structure of the tourism industry but with some exceptions, Fitch (1987), Sheldon (1986), Bote *et al.* (1989), the studies have been descriptive rather than analytical. This analytical neglect arises partly from the complex and diverse nature of the tourism industry, covering transport, accommodation, catering and leisure facilities, and partly because of the heterogeneous nature of the product. However, it will be argued here that tourism supply is not reactive but is indeed positively proactive, as demonstrated by the entry of large enterprises into the industry and the increasing concentration which has occurred in some sectors, notably accommodation and intermediaries, both travel agencies and tour operators. These aspects are discussed in Chapter 4 by Bote and Sinclair, who investigated supply linkages between sectors and countries.

The opportunity sets approach has a number of merits as a means of analysing the relationship between supply and demand, given the relatively under-researched state of the tourism industry. These are identified by examining its application in work done by Goodall (1990), Radburn and Goodall (1990) and Bennett and Radburn (Chapter 3) as well as the theoretical development of the concept undertaken by Stabler (1990). An attempt is made to bring out the consumer–industry–destination linkage, illustrating it by considering the role of tour operators in providing package holidays. The study of the provision of package holidays has shown that for some consumers, place is of minor importance, except for the requirement that it contains the essential holiday components. For example, mass summer sun packages are largely sold on the basis of virtually guaranteeing sun in conjunction with sand and sea. Similarly, skiing package holidays, particularly for first-timers, only need to ensure that suitable pistes and apres-ski facilities are available. Thus, provided the requisite components are supplied, the holiday may be taken in any of a number of countries or locations within them. This gives rise to particular supply characteristics because of the possibility of exploiting economies of scale of the transport, accommodation and facilities elements. Consequently the intermediaries in the industry (the tour operators), can exercise considerable control over the providers of these elements. Given the competition between tour operators, there are price advantages to the consumer, but also disadvantages in terms of a standardised, homogeneous product, so that choice is reduced. Commercial considerations determine the destinations which tour operators select and promote (Goodall *et al.*, 1988). Thus it can be asserted that the marketing of holidays starts with the intermediaries, so that consumers tend to be at one end of the industry decision chain and the providers of accommodation and facilities in destinations at the other. This being so, holiday opportunities tend to reflect the intermediaries' objectives rather than those of the industry in destination areas, or consumers.

Although the economic analysis of the competitive structure of the tourism industry can show the domination of the market by large organisations, it does not indicate the interrelationship between them and consumers and the businesses and economies of destination areas. It does not suggest how consumer behaviour is influenced nor, conversely, does it accommodate the power consumers may exercise over the industry through changing tastes and preferences, as they travel more widely, gaining greater knowledge and experience and therefore confidence in selecting and arranging holidays. The characteristics of destinations also condition the industry's activities. In providing mass market holidays, destinations must possess a suitable infrastructure and accommodation to cater for large numbers of visitors, i.e. they must have sufficient capacity to allow for the exploitation of economies of scale by the intermediaries. If this capacity is not forthcoming, the industry in generating areas may need to undertake investment in the destination areas in order to maintain its own growth, thus giving rise to a 'lock-in' effect.

The industry is therefore subject to constraints by both consumers and circumstances in destination areas, notwithstanding its market power. This means that it needs to strike an acceptable balance between its objectives and these constraints. Three principal variables are of concern – the costs of providing holidays, the price which can be charged and the number of holidays which can be sold. Which of the three, either singly or in combination, is given more weight will depend on current circumstances as well as the organisation's longer term strategy in relation to that of its competitors. For example, uncertainties such as the seasonality of holidays, which may be influenced by the weather, and the economic situation make the picture more confused. Modelling the industry is thus very complex. It can be done within a traditional economic or statistical framework in which different expected payoffs, say, low, medium and high, may be posited based on differing assumptions concerning the weights to be attached to specific variables. However, this still necessitates delineating the external environment, i.e. the context in which consumers are making decisions, the market structure and the situation in destination areas. Concerning the second aspect of the external environment, namely market structure, it has been argued that the tourism industry is oligopolistic (Sheldon, 1986; Goodall *et al.*, 1988). However, it is acknowledged within the discipline of economics that there is no clear theory of oligopoly. The current state of analysis is such that the outcome of actions by participants in the market can be indicated in illustrative cases given *a priori* assumptions, but the general predictive power of the theory is weak. Indeed in situations of uncertainty resort has to be made to game theory, in which various scenarios are posited.

In addition to the external environment, the internal one within enterprises comprising the industry is also of consequence, for it is this which determines the entity's objectives and therefore decision–making by management. Economics is somewhat muted on these organisational and human aspects of the operation of firms, notwithstanding some management research by economists and the development of behavioural models as exemplified in the work of Cyert (1988). Moreover, to model the industry, it is essential to incorporate the product (holidays) in some structured way. By this is meant that holidays need to be categorised, for example as commercial/non-commercial, business/pleasure, by accommodation – serviced/self-catering – by season, location, type of activity, organisation or structure, such as inclusive tour by charter or by excursion, or by company. The numbers within each category must be ascertained and their price ranges identified. Finally the spatial dimension of tourism should be replicated in any model. While, as shown earlier, geographical models maintain this spatial dimension, it is absent from economic frameworks, except in relation to location theory, which is not relevant within the context of the analysis of the tourism industry intermediaries.

The opportunity sets framework as conceived takes cognizance of both the external and internal environments of the firm and incorporates the analysis of the product in a predetermined and structured manner. Furthermore, it can incorporate the sequential or temporal process of decision-making by producers, and, in so far as it affects the market, decision-making by consumers. By embodying the industry, consumer and destination sets in a single framework, the spatial dimension is considered.

An issue which economics raises with regard to the opportunity set concept as illustrated in Figure 2.1, is whether it accommodates market clearing with the demand for holidays equalling their supply. From an economic viewpoint Figure 2.1 may be interpreted in two ways. It can indicate the individual consuming unit's holiday choice process and the sale of a specific holiday to that unit by the industry. Such an interpretation does not require the analysis to show market clearing. Alternatively, at an aggregate level, the presentations in Figure 2.1, and in Figures 2.2 and 2.3 below, show opportunity sets at a particular point in time. There is no necessity to assume that the market is in equilibrium. Indeed, given the intangible and perishable characteristics of tourism as a product, and the market structure and its complexities already discussed, both in this chapter and by Bote and Sinclair in Chapter 4, economic analysis would point to market clearance as a special case rather than the general outcome in the short run. In past years, in the UK, there has been a tendency for over-supply to occur in the short run at an aggregate level, as evidenced by late-availability booking and heavy discounting of unsold holidays.

Tour operators' attempts to make supply more elastic in the medium term by incorporating cancellation clauses into contracts with carriers and hoteliers, can sometimes be frustrated by the latter making seats and accommodation available through other channels. Furthermore, as entry costs into the industry are comparatively low, there is an inherent supply instability. In the long term this tendency may lessen if concentration occurs, thus resulting in greater control of the market. Currently, however, in the light of the previous discussion concerning the complexities of supply, the market may be in a state of disequilibrium in the short run but in equilibrium in the medium run. This can be incorporated into the opportunity sets approach through, for example, periodic changes in the supply of holidays. A two-period analysis allows for the adjustment in supply which can often be brought about in the medium run by such means as the cancellation of previously reserved accommodation at little or no cost to tour operators, and for increases in demand which result from measures such as price-discounting. A three-period analysis could take account of the long-run changes in supply which take place in line with changes in the structure of the industry. In a multi-period analysis the opportunity sets for the short, medium and long run would differ.

Consumer and industry interrelationships: a behavioural matrix

The new approach to tourism analysis which the opportunity sets approach provides, where the tourism industry intermediaries play a pivotal role, can be illustrated, albeit in a somewhat simplified way, by use of a behavioural matrix construction devised by Pred (1967) and adapted by Kent (1990) to analyse consumers' holiday choice process. The application of the matrix method to industry opportunity sets was attempted by Stabler (1990), in order to complement Kent's work. The main objective of the application was to conceptualise business behaviour in the more holistic way outlined above, but without fundamentally violating economic principles.

While it is possible to analyse the supply of holidays assuming profit maximisation as the ultimate goal of the industry, this is not necessarily a realistic reflection of the current market situation in which survival is likely to be a short term objective. Moreover, given the structure and characteristics of the industry in the UK, even in a favourable trading climate, the maximisation of sales as a means of increasing market share has been the principal aim of the largest tour operators during the 1980s. An exposition of industry opportunity sets, taking sales maximisation as an aim, serves the purpose of widening the

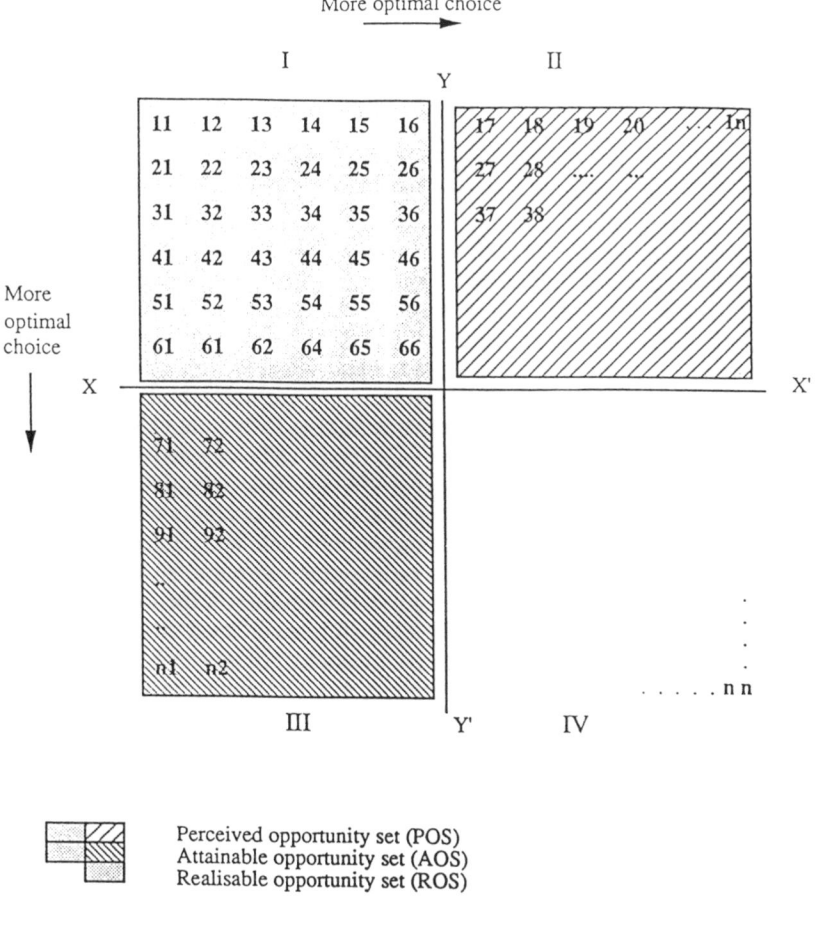

Perceived opportunity set (POS)
Attainable opportunity set (AOS)
Realisable opportunity set (ROS)

Based on Kent (1990); Stabler (1990a)

Figure 2.2 Holiday choice and supply opportunity set matrices

scope of the analysis because destination areas can be included on the assumption that their aims are the same as those of the intermediaries in origin areas.

Kent (1990), following Pred (1967), argued that for consumers there are two basic dimensions to what is essentially a multi-dimensional holiday evaluation matrix. These are the quantity of information or awareness of holiday opportunities (perceived opportunity set) and the quality of information or attainment ability (attainable opportunity set), it being posited that the information can be graded with respect to the types of holidays. This notion is illustrated in Figure 2.2, in which it is assumed that a consumer possesses an attainment level, as indicated by the movement down the columns, and an awareness level shown by the rows. Each of the pairs of numbers represents a holiday choice and the consumer will hold a position in the matrix which reflects

29

his or her awareness of and ability to use information on holidays. The arrangement of the holiday in the matrix is such that by moving to the right along the rows and down the columns, i.e. south east, the consumer will obtain a more preferred holiday. However, the size of the consumer's matrix depends on the boundaries of the perceived (POS) and attainable (AOS) opportunity sets. In Figure 2.2, quadrants I and II constitute the POS while quadrants I and III comprise the AOS. This means that the consumer is aware of holidays in quadrant II but they are not attainable, perhaps because they are too expensive. Conversely holidays in quadrant III are attainable but the consumer is not aware of them. The consumer is neither aware of nor can attain holidays in quadrant IV, i.e. they are not in either the POS or AOS. Quadrant I constitutes the 'realisable' set (ROS) in that it contains holidays which are in both the POS and AOS. The best location for a consumer, i.e. the optimal choice, is holiday 66 in the bottom right-hand corner of the ROS.

The consumer will almost certainly not be able to evaluate all the holidays in a realisable set simply because there are likely to be too many, particularly given imperfect information and the inability to make meaningful use of it. Therefore the size of the set actually evaluated will undoubtedly be smaller. This has been designated the 'consideration' opportunity set. The choice process, i.e. the progression by which the consumer moves down through the 'consideration' set to the 'choice' and 'decision' sets to make a final holiday selection, reflects not only the evaluation of the holidays on offer, expressed preferences and constraints, such as time, income and household composition, but also the attributes of holidays. In theory the process can be viewed as sequential, the 'consideration' set consisting of holidays with appropriate attributes from which those with the most preferred ones are selected ('choice' set) and finally the 'decision' set contains the probable holidays from which one is chosen. Clearly it is conceivable that if a specific holiday cannot be found, or the one chosen is fully booked, the consumer may need to go back to an earlier stage and begin the process again.

In practice different consumers will go through the process in a variety of ways. Many will combine the stages, while others will only reach a decision after redefining goals and preferences a number of times. Nevertheless the whole concept of opportunity sets rests on the foundation that there is a hierarchy of holiday attributes which necessitates the satisfaction of a set of requirements before the consumer can move on to the next decision stage. For one consumer 'place' may be very important, whereas for another the 'accommodation' will be a key attribute.

However, the holidays comprising the matrix in Figure 2.2 merely represent a collection of opportunities with different attributes. Until the preferences of consumers are included, which should be ranked in order of priorities, it is not possible to make the model predictive in the sense of identifying possible choices of holidays. This extension of the model is presented in Figure 2.3, in which the choice process is also shown. In the figure, the two dimensional matrix given in Figure 2.2 becomes a horizontal plane so that preferences are indicated by the vertical plane. Figure 2.3 also shows the opportunity sets referred to above in the order suggested so that the number of holidays in each succeeding set is reduced until only those included in the decision set remain.

It is possible to consider industry sets in much the same way as consumer sets have been analysed. Starting from an almost limitless number of types of holiday in destination area sets, the most specific of industry sets, such as a company set directed at a particular market segment, can be derived by a sequential process. The interrelationship of consumer and industry sets, where in the context of this discussion it is assumed that the industry sets embody destination area sets, occurs when tourists arrange their holidays through the industry.

The overlap of industry and consumer sets is shown in Figure 2.1, but this does not bring out the dynamic nature of the interrelationship. Figure 2.3 attempts to do this in a matrix which is compatible with the approach adopted by Kent (1990) and reflects the three dimensions – sales maximisation, costs and numbers of types of holidays – referred to earlier in this section. As suggested with respect to the sequence of choice by consumers, the process by which the industry assembles, markets and sells holidays is not necessarily in a strict order. It is conceivable that intermediaries first decide on which part of the market to target and then look for locations and types of holidays which fulfil their requirements, rather than the reverse. This does not negate the opportunity sets approach because the industry still needs to identify its goals and rank its priorities, subject to the constraints of meeting the needs of consumers. In short, certain conditions need to be satisfied at each stage of supplying the product before it is possible to move to the next stage.

The process can be traced in Figure 2.3, using package holidays as an example, by starting at the bottom of the figure and working upwards to the point of contact with the consumer. Tour operators in generating areas assemble the components of package tours by selecting accommodation and facilities in destination areas. The range of locations and holidays available is determined ultimately by the number of suitable destination areas. However, it is possible to categorise these into destination opportunity sets as Goodall (1990) has shown. The total opportunity set or universe of holidays from which tour operators make their choice is very large but can expand or contract. For example, the Pyrenees as a location for British skiing tourists is a relatively recent addition to UK destination area sets while some Spanish summer sun resorts have been removed. The selection of holidays by tour operators will be determined by three factors: their own objectives, the degree to which they are influenced by tourism promotion by the industry in destination areas and consumer preferences.

The universe of holidays comprising the initial three-dimensional total opportunity set matrix (embodying destination sets) at the bottom of Figure 2.3 shows, on the horizontal plane, the supply or procurement cost to the industry on the XX' axis and the selling price on the YY' axis. The highest-priced, and highest-cost holiday would be located at X'Y'. However, whether the industry would select and offer such holidays would depend on its cost structure and the market it is serving. As with the consumers' two-dimensional matrix, this plane is purely a collection of holiday types ranked by cost and price. It is only when the third dimension (in the case of the common economic assumption of industrial modelling, profit maximisation) is added that is it possible to determine the optimal collection of holidays the industry would select and

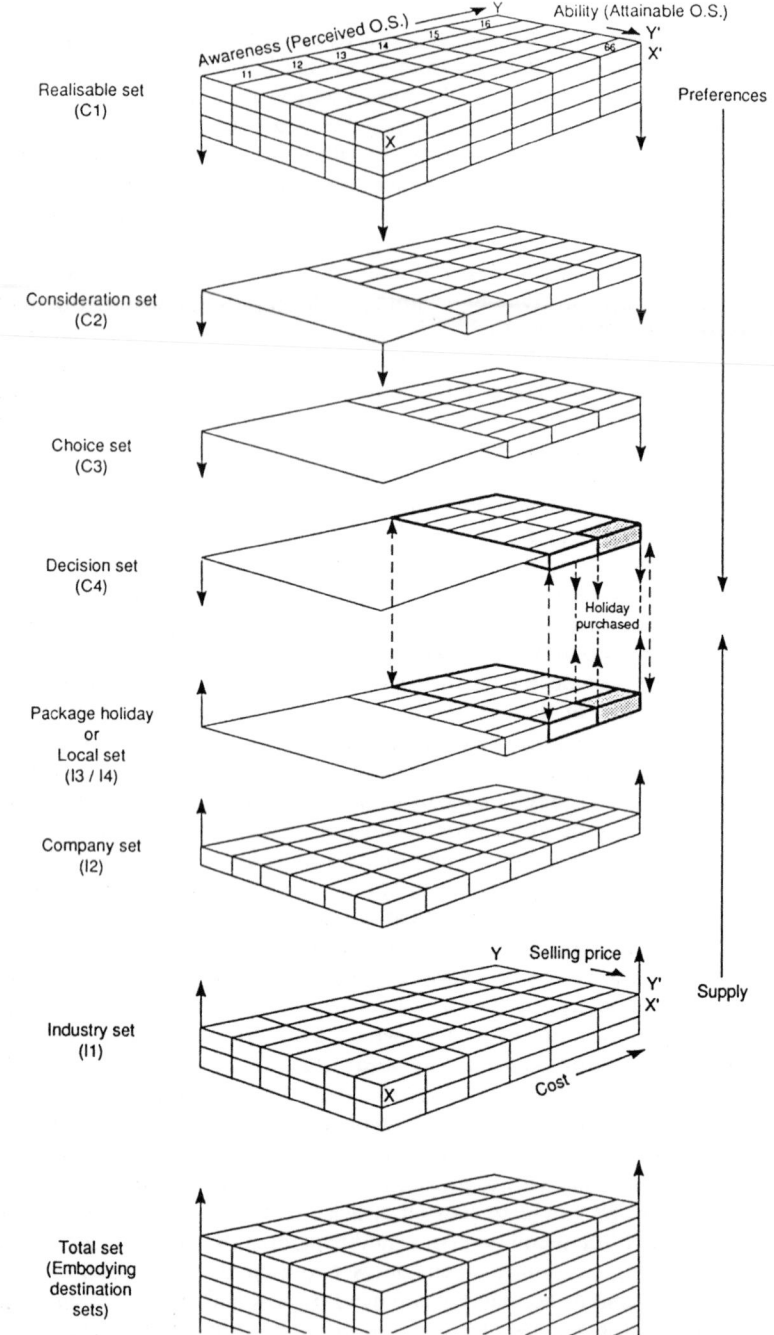

Figure 2.3 The choice and supply of holidays: a three-dimensional sequential matrix for an individual consumer and tour operator

market. For a profit–maximising firm or industry these lie in the south east corner of the matrix at X'Y'.

Stabler (1990a) has examined this matrix for a number of different objectives. He argues that the matrix location at which the industry will select holidays will be a function not only of its objectives but also its cost structure, pricing policies and the market competitive conditions. Since traditional economic theory can explain these notions, it is possible to use the opportunity sets approach, adopting assumptions which reflect current market situations, to indicate the strategy of the industry or individual firms within it. For example, if firms in the industry are pursuing a strategy of endeavouring to increase market share, the policy will be to sell as many types as well as numbers of holidays as possible. Since each 'block' in the matrix represents a type of holiday, the maximum number of different types of holiday would be at X'Y', i.e. all the holidays in the matrix. (To locate also the position in the matrix where the maximum number of holidays is sold would require a fourth dimension, unless the matrix is redefined to contain numbers of holidays rather than types.)

If an individual tour operator's process of selection is now considered, the narrowing down of the range of types of holiday can be accommodated by defining a 'company' opportunity set. The holidays contained in it will depend on the size, nature and objectives of the business. Thus Thomson has a large company set whereas France Direct, as its name implies, markets holidays only to France, concentrating on pension-style accommodation, and has a small set. As with the initial matrix the dimensions of the company set are the same.

Narrowing the focus even more, particular types of holidays can form subsets of either the industry or the company set. For example, all summer sun package holidays offered can be considered in a set designated as such, or the same kind of package holidays for a specific firm can be collected into a set. This kind of set is shown in the fourth matrix from the bottom of Figure 2.3, as I3. Alternatively, industry sets can be made even more specific by composing regional or local sets, i.e. by introducing a spatial perspective. Such a set is shown in Figure 2.3 as I4, for illustrative purposes rather than suggesting that it always features in the sequential process of marketing holidays.

Industry sets which can include destination area sets (designated as I1 to I4 in Figure 2.3) can intermesh with consumer choice and decision sets at any stage between I1 and I4. For instance, a consumer making direct contact in a destination area to book a holiday suggests an interrelationship between C4 and the total opportunity set containing destination sets at the bottom of Figure 2.3, whereas for a consumer buying a package summer sun holiday, the contact will be with C4 and I3 or I4. From the industry's viewpoint the strategy should be to maximise the size of the set which intermeshes with consumer sets, to the extent of entering perceived and attainable sets when choice is in its initial stages. This is true for both domestic and foreign tourism. In the UK, use of the intermediaries (travel agents and tour operators) is not very significant for domestic holiday choice, suggesting that there is potential for such intermediaries to develop their businesses in this direction.

The dashed lines in Figure 2.3 indicate the extent of the intermeshing of the consumer set C4 (decision set) with the industry set I3/I4 (package holiday or local subset). In Figure 2.1 this was designated the 'operational' set, in the sense that industry opportunity sets have penetrated the consumer's decision set, with the probability that a holiday will be purchased.

The review of previous work and the integration of the consumer–industry–destination opportunity sets framework attempted in this section is as far as the concept has currently been developed. It is now necessary for more research to be conducted to refine the approach and to apply it. An evaluation and indication of what needs to be done is given in the next section.

Issues underlying the opportunity sets approach

The theoretical development of opportunity sets has offered insights into the holiday choice and supply process. It has also suggested the importance for the industry, in both origin and destination areas, of consumer behaviour and the characteristics of the product, as well as the structure and operation of the industry itself. It is now necessary to address questions of how to make the concept operational and to test it in an empirical context.

There are essentially two basic requirements. The first is how information on holidays can best be structured into a meaningful data base. The second, interrelated with the first, is more concerned with methodology where there are issues such as how the various sets designated in the foregoing analysis can be demarcated in practice, the empirical evidence required in order to verify the multi-stage process and the means of accommodating the dynamic nature of tourism and the construction of an appropriate predictive model. This last issue is crucial in that the whole credibility of the opportunity sets approach rests on deriving testing prepositions concerning consumers, the industry and the actions and policies of the public sector.

The creation of a data base is a formidable problem but not necessarily insoluble. Similar difficulties are faced by researchers in other fields where information is in the form of promotional material or recorded transactions; for example, the housing market and the retailing of consumer durables. The first stage in the exercise must be to establish definitions and categories of holidays covering the key components of travel mode, accommodation and facilities. Some reference has already been made to possible categorisations of holidays reflecting different dimensions, for example, facilities; package holidays – summer sun and skiing; type of accommodation – serviced or self-catering; location – sea, mountain, forest. The main objective of forming such a data base is to identify the principal attributes of holidays, because this not only influences consumers' choice process but also delineates the industry opportunity sets of which they are aware and can attain. In this connection it is also necessary to ascertain in broad terms the categorisation of consumers concerning their perceived and attainment sets, which reflects their socio-economic characteristics. This suggests that more research along the lines of that conducted by Kent (1990) needs to be undertaken. In effect, consumers' holiday choice profiles need to be built up. Only when this has been done will it be possible to be more confident about identifying the parameters for demarcating different kinds of consumer sets.

The sequential nature of both choice and supply is an important feature of the opportunity sets approach. By emphasising the attributes of holidays which can take *n* dimensions in a more complex matrix, the method resembles a hedonic pricing model. However the sequential derivation of the 'decision' set for consumers and the 'operational' sets for producers, giving rise to the common 'realised' set (Figure 2.1), differentiates the approach. Hedonic models have not yet significantly developed the idea of a multi-stage process. It is implicit in some housing models, for example, Cheshire and Sheppard (1991) and also in a general discussion of the hierarchy of recreational demand by Gratton and Taylor (1985). More empirical work is required to test the hypothesis that the decision process is indeed multi-staged or sequential. Investigation of the process by consumers could be conducted concurrently with work on the construction of holiday choice profiles.

The identification of the industry's decision process may necessitate the simultaneous study of its structure, organisation and operation in destination areas. The shift of the focus from the intermediaries in origin areas to the destination reflects work done by de Haan *et al.* (1990) which suggests that the transaction between consumer and the industry, which forms the central core of an opportunity sets approach, is different if it arises in the destination area as opposed to the origin area. Their study of Languedoc–Roussillon showed that the image projected and marketed in generating areas, such as the Netherlands, UK, and indeed France itself, needs to be assessed in order to ascertain the effectiveness of that promotion by the tourism industry and official agencies in Languedoc and Roussillon. This would require a comparative analysis of the 'inside' and 'outside' destination area opportunity sets, i.e. that projected by the destination as opposed to that received in the generating or origin area, usually filtered through the intermediaries. Where there is a mismatch of the projected and received images embodied in those opportunity sets, then ultimately the objectives of both the origin and destination-based tourism industry are frustrated. Ashworth (Chapter 7) gives further evidence of this mismatch and its marketing implications.

Goodall's (1990) argument for considering the industry in origin and destination areas together in an opportunity sets framework, though it touches on inside and outside sets, is more concerned with the impact of the intermediaries' policies, the tour operators in particular, in destination areas. Tour operators continually seek ways to improve and extend their portfolios of holidays, either to secure repeat business or to maintain or enlarge market share. They may also delete unsuccessful destinations from their programmes. The degree of penetration of destination areas, i.e. the proportion of total holidays available in a specific area being marketed by intermediaries, and the entry or exit ratios of locations in that area in promotional literature, has a large impact on a destination. Clearly the consumer is influenced, in the first instance, not only by whether a destination appears in tour operators' brochures but also by the manner in which it is promoted.

In a study of the marketing of skiing holidays, Goodall shows highly variable descriptions and even omission or distortion of the presentation of resort characteristics. Moreover, inclusion of a destination in a brochure does not guarantee its continued promotion. If it proves unpopular it will be dropped by tour operators. The evidence of entry and exit ratios is scanty but Goodall indicates that for skiing resorts entry ratios are between 20 per cent and 30 per cent. This suggests that in the future, if the growth rate of skiing holidays slows down, exit ratios will be equally high. Goodall's research demonstrates not only the interrelationship between the industry in origin and destination areas, but also their different objectives and roles and the dynamic nature of tourism. It is this last aspect which creates the most acute problems in developing and applying the opportunity sets method, because in addition to the problems of embodying this dynamism, it will tend to destroy the stability of the data base.

These issues concerning the demarcation of opportunity sets, the sequential nature of the decision-making process by consumers and the industry, including the need to take account of differences in the market structure and situation in origins and destination areas, are of importance in the construction of an operational opportunity sets model, to which attention is now turned.

Towards an operational model of opportunity sets

The two previous sections have attempted to indicate the contribution of the opportunity sets concept to synthesising tourism analysis, and to identify the factors which need to be taken into account in constructing a model. This section considers the next steps to be taken in developing a complete opportunity sets model, which needs to be built up by drawing on the consumer and producer elements discussed earlier in this chapter. The foundations of the model lie in deriving testable propositions on the role of the two key participant sectors, namely the behaviour and actions of consumers in choosing and taking a holiday, and the structure, organisation and operation of the industry. In a more general model, the role and the impact of the public sector should be included. However, a two-sector composition of the model, with some reference to public sector influences, may be too aggregative.

To reflect more closely current market circumstances, it might be desirable to disaggregate further the individual sectors by, for example, drawing a distinction between behaviour with respect to domestic tourism as opposed to international tourism. The industry also is certainly not a homogeneous entity. In the origin area suppliers of transport, accommodation and related facilities are very different from the intermediaries who assemble holidays. A similar distinction can be made in destination areas where the product is actually supplied. It is necessary to consider the function of official tourism bodies and central and local government, which interact with both consumers/tourists and producers. The official bodies, often set up and funded by government, become almost a public sector arm of the industry since one of their purposes is to promote the growth of tourism and support producers in achieving this. On the other hand, in their regulatory role they do act to safeguard consumer interests.

For several reasons, attention in this section concentrates on demand to illustrate a step-by-step model-building approach. Given past research, its theoretical foundations are firmer than those of the other two sectors and much more is known about it. Knowledge of demand holds marketing implications for the tourism industry, not only because of the effect of changes in its level and pattern on supply, but also, in turn, because the industry wishes to establish the impact on demand of changes in supply. However, a specific reason for focusing on demand is that consumers' holiday-choice process is a key feature of the opportunity sets framework, as has been demonstrated, and understanding it is essential in constructing an industry-centred model. Nevertheless, a brief examination is undertaken of the supply sector, including public sector aspects, to suggest the lines along which research should proceed.

The model-building approach may involve the amalgamation of theories or analytical frameworks hitherto perceived as separate. For example, psychological and social psychological theories might need to be combined with economic explanations of consumer behaviour. A fundamental requirement is to identify the key variables. In some cases these will be quantifiable but others, of a qualitative nature, may also need to be included because of their explanatory or predictive value. A second requirement is that the sequential process by consumers/tourists should be included in the model, together with the delineation of the constituent opportunity sets.

The methodological issues and the building up of the model, using opportunity sets as a basis, has been initiated by Kent (1990), Chapter 9, who has taken the development of a theory of consumer holiday choice part of the way towards deriving a predictive model. He identified a number of key variables and started to combine psychological and social explanations with economic factors, in a sequential or serial process for selecting a holiday, in an analytical framework which illustrates the hierarchy of goals and preferences. However, in general the state of the art has not progressed much beyond ex-post descriptions of motivations and consumer preferences governed by their choice of determinants, such as the image of a destination, the travel, accommodation and facilities, subject to the consumers' economic and social constraints. Equally, economic theory, though it is well developed in terms of its predictive power if confined to such economic variables as wealth, income, price and occupation, often fails to explain behaviour fully because of its restrictive assumptions. Notwithstanding consumer behaviour theories, for example by Lancaster (1966) and hedonic pricing models, it also has difficulties in encompassing the diverse characteristics of the product which determine demand. Consequently it is only of value in special cases, for example where within a homogeneous holiday opportunity set, such as summer sun packages, price is a decisive demand determinant. What is needed, therefore, is a hypothesis of how and by what process consumers make a choice based on the insights provided by a variety of disciplines.

It has been argued that the holiday search process is initiated when an individual experiences psychological disequilibrium because the current circumstances and/or environment are not satisfactory (Crompton, 1979). A crude hypothesis could be that this sense of disequilibrium will be generated as the period since a holiday was last taken lengthens, or conversely as the date set for annual leave approaches. In effect the hypothesis must suggest the trigger which takes the process to the succeeding phase (or, equally important, why the process does not proceed, as in the case of non-holiday takers). It is in these first two phases, i.e. the disequilibrium and the initial action, that propositions, in order to explain movement to subsequent phases, must suggest the variables or combination of variables which lead to further action. It is possible to adopt well established statistical methods, such as Likert and Thurstone scaling techniques, which are designed to reveal the strength with which individuals hold certain beliefs or attitudes. These could be used to ascertain the importance of

37

identified motivational variables, and to facilitate their measurement. If one or more variables take on a particular value it might be predicted that movement to the next stage would occur. For example it is known that people who have taken holidays before come from backgrounds where holiday-making is a social norm, are members of a particular kind of household composition, experience specific forms of lifestyle, seek certain kinds of experience, are exposed to or have access to particular information sources, will be motivated in identifiable ways.

Motivations, therefore, shape behaviour in the next phase, which is the setting of goals and expression of preferences. One individual's disequilibrium may be restored by an active, sporting holiday while for another imbalance can be overcome by relaxation. Identification of goals and preferences and setting them into hierarchies takes the consumer to the phase of delineating a perceived opportunity set, and into the process of making a holiday choice. The variables underlying the choice of particular holidays and destinations are the most critical from the industry viewpoint. Two sets of variables exert an influence: the goals and preferences which reflect the psychological make-up of the consumer, and the attributes of the holiday. With respect to the latter, i.e. the holiday attributes, knowledge and image of products and destinations are key determinants in holiday choice, so that in order to make predictions about that choice it is necessary to develop propositions regarding them. Moreover, economic, social and time constraints and the supply of holidays available exert an influence and need to be taken into account.

This, however, is as far as tourism research in general has been taken, not just that concerning opportunity sets. The variables to be included in tourism models fall into two groups, those relating to the consumer and those concerning the product. Drawing on the knowledge of consumer profiles which tourism research has built up, it is conceivable that a number of hypotheses of consumer behaviour could be tested which give varying emphasis to particular variables. For example, one kind of profile may identify an 'instant' buyer, very likely the young unattached, in a manual occupation group, who would respond to late availability and package-style holidays. Conversely, an older, higher-income household, with outdoor interests, may be profiled as 'preplanners' to which holidays involving careful and long-term assembly would appeal, such as a tour around Europe.

In considering the product, including the destination, rather than the tourist, image and attributes go hand in hand. For example, what might be described as the 'imageability' of a holiday can be established, by tourists' own experiences and by those of others, as well as promotion by the industry, so that a specific type of holiday engenders predictable responses in certain categories of consumers and a determinable level of demand. Safari treks in Africa, walking expeditions in the Himalayas and green tourism, for instance, not only have a specific image, and are likely to be expensive, but appeal to particular segments of the market. On the other hand summer sun package holidays, particularly those which may constitute a second holiday, are likely to be sold on the basis of convenience where their cheapness, guaranteed sunshine and absence of involvement in prolonged preparations, are the key attributes.

Thus within the opportunity sets analytical framework it is possible, drawing on a data base of categories of consumers and classifications of holidays, to delineate the boundaries of different types of sets containing specific kinds of holidays on the supply side, and classes of consumers on the demand side. The question then arises as to whether it is possible to predict how the consumer will make a choice and what kind of holiday will be selected. It has already been suggested, in explaining the opportunity sets concept, that economic constraints will constrain consumers to certain holidays in an attainable set (see Figure 2.3). Therefore, with knowledge of the distribution of income and level of expenditure on holidays, it can be hypothesised that consumers falling into a particular income group would possess a specific attainable set. In effect the set would contain holidays which they could afford, involving a level of expenditure they would normally incur. Likewise the consideration set could be predicted to contain holidays reflecting the tastes and preferences of specified social profile categories, again based on empirical evidence.

Predicting which holidays will comprise the choice and decision sets is more difficult as these tend to be determined by individual consuming unit characteristics. Moreover, in an empirical context it is possible that much of the choice process, from the holidays contained in the perceived set to the final choice from the decision set, is implicit. There is some evidence (Kent, 1990; Goodall *et al.*, 1988), that the maximum number of choices a consumer can evaluate is around seven. Moreover, Kent (Chapter 9) has shown that the final choice is likely to depend on personal circumstances, preferences and attitudes (which may change at short notice) and even the supply situation (a first choice may not be available) at the time when the decision has to be made. Nevertheless, given the discussion earlier on the hypotheses concerning the most likely holiday to be chosen by consumers with specific socio-economic profiles, reasonable predictions can be made.

This illustration as to how consumers' behaviour may be modelled and related to the opportunity sets concept, reveals in some detail the strengths and weakness of this approach to research in this area of tourism. Much is known about the psychology and socioeconomic characteristics of consumers, there is a well developed economic theory of demand and there is a great deal of ex-post information on the level and pattern of the consumption of holidays. However, the demand models of the various disciplines are compartmentalised, and in some cases, descriptive rather than analytical. What is now required is for the separate analytical frameworks to be aggregated into a cohesive whole and developed so that a predictive model, embodying testable propositions on demand, can be devised. This then needs to be related to the supply side where a similar exercise is required to construct a model containing hypotheses on the behaviour of the tourism industry sector.

The analysis of consumer choice using opportunity sets holds implications for the industry, both in generating and destination areas, in that the promotion of the product (types of holidays and locations) will impinge on consumers in different ways via their perceived and attainable sets, depending on their goals and priorities, and will therefore influence their evaluation and ultimate choice. In effect, the recognition of major holiday attributes conditions information gathering by consumers, and this in turn is a function of how holidays are marketed. Accordingly the industry needs to be aware of the attributes, and their importance, of the holidays which they offer in the different market segments they target. Conversely the intermediaries should be cognisant of consumer goals and preferences, and the hierarchy of attributes which structures their holiday choice decision independently of information received from the industry. This, in a sense, acknowledges the traditional economic tenet of consumer sovereignty.

As shown with respect to the demand sector, the problem of separate and incomplete models or theories must be tackled as a prerequisite for incorporating the supply sector into an aggregate model. For example, economics has sophisticated and predictive theories of individual firms and industries in manufacturing, but its theories of supply in the service industries, particularly where oligopolistic circumstances prevail, the very features tourism exhibits, are much less well founded. For example, the discipline has not fully developed a theory of maximising growth rather than profits, nor has it progressed far in accommodating behavioural aspects. Furthermore, the conceptualisation and construction of models which embody various stages in the supply process, as outlined in the exposition of opportunity sets, is a neglected area of economic analysis. Yet another factor is the need to consider the construction of separate models for the different sub-sectors of an industry which few economists have investigated.

The modelling of the public sector, a possible third main component of a complete tourism theoretical structure, is also in its infancy. As suggested earlier in this section, public sector organisations have already had a marked impact on the tourism industry and tourist behaviour, particularly in countries where tourism is treated as a prime industry and the official tourism bodies play a prominent role, as Ashworth shows in Chapter 7. In common with the consumer and producer sectors, it will be necessary to derive prepositions on the behaviour of public sector bodies in relation to the tourism industry, including the process by which decisions are made and implemented.

Thus the first requirement is to develop fully the fundamental two-sector model of the consumer choice and supply process within the opportunity sets framework. Initially, the public sector role can be incorporated into these two components. However, in a model built up from more disaggregated consumer and supply sectors it might be conceivable to consider the public sector in its own right.

Conclusion

By virtue of its very diversity on both the demand and supply side, the construction of a general theory of tourism is very difficult. The opportunity set concept has been shown to possess the potential to make both a theoretical and practical contribution to tourism modelling by maintaining that essential diversity rather than the oversimplification and truncation which is inherent in the existing methods. However, at a practical level it is still in its infancy. The objective in this chapter has been to establish the terms of the debate and to generate critical communication as a means of sharpening the theoretical focus of the concept. In doing so, the emphasis has been placed on indicating the underlying determinants of observed effects in tourism origin and destination areas of tourist and tourism industry behaviour. Moreover, an attempt has been made to demonstrate the practical necessity of such a conceptual framework, implying that the distinction between theory and practice, like that between pure and applied research, is false. As a concomitant it can be posited that uncritical practice is also dangerous. It is necessary, in such a dynamic field as tourism, constantly to review and revise current business, management and marketing techniques. The performance of the intermediaries in recent years in the UK suggests that such reviews and consequent action have not occurred.

Even at this early stage of its development, the implications for the tourism industry of utilising the opportunity sets concept and its associated analytical framework, as an heuristic device, have been shown. The agenda for developing the approach is a long one. However, the immediate priorities which need to be addressed are to make the concept operational, to examine empirically the nature of the multi-phase decision-making process by consumers and the industry, and to delineate clearly the boundaries of the various opportunity sets which have been proposed.

References

Bote Gómez, V., Sinclair, M.T., Sutcliffe, C.S.M. and Valenzuela Rubio, M. (1989) Vertical integration in the British/Spanish tourism industry. In: Stabler, M.J. (ed.), *Leisure, Labour and Lifestyles: International Comparisons. Tourism and Leisure; Models and Theories*, Leisure Studies Association Second International Conference Proceedings, No. 39, Vol. 8 Leisure Studies Association, Eastbourne, pp. 80-96.

Britton, S.G. (1980) A conceptual model of tourism in a peripheral economy. In: Pearce, D.G. (ed.), *Tourism in the South Pacific: the Contribution of Research to Development and Planning*, NZMAB Report No. 6, NZ National Commission for UNESCO. Department of Geography, University of Canterbury, Christchurch, pp. 1–12.

Campbell, C.K. (1967) An approach to research in recreational geography, *B.C. Occasional Paper No. 7*, Department of Geography, University of British Columbia: Vancouver, pp. 85–90.

Cheshire, P.C. and Sheppard, S. (1991) *Evaluating the Impact of Neighbourhood Effects on House Prices and Land Rents: An Hedonic Approach.* Discussion Papers in Urban and Regional Economics, Series C, Vol. IV, Department of Economics, University of Reading.

Clewer, A., Pack, A. and Sinclair, M.T. (forthcoming) Price competitiveness and inclusive tour holidays in European cities. In: Johnson, P. and Thomas, B. (eds), *Choice and Demand in Tourism*. Mansell, London.

Crompton, J.L. (1979) Motivations for pleasure vacation. *Annals of Tourism Research*, 6(4), 408–424.

Cyert, R.M. (1988) *The Economic Theory of Organisation and the Firm.* Harvester-Wheatsheaf, Hemel Hempstead.

de Haan, T., Ashworth, G.J., Stabler, M.J. (1990) The tourist destination as product: the case of Languedoc. In: Ashworth, G.J. and Goodall, B. (eds), *Marketing Tourism Places*. Routledge, London, pp. 156–169.

Fitch, A. (1987) Tour operators in the UK. *Travel and Tourism Analyst*, March, The Economist Publications Ltd., London.

Goodall, B. (1990) Opportunity sets as analytical marketing instruments: a destination area view. In: Ashworth, G.J. and Goodall, B. (eds) *Marketing Tourism Places*. Routledge, London, pp. 63–84.

Goodall, B., Radburn, M.W. and Stabler, M.J. (1988) Market opportunity sets for tourism. *Geographical Papers No 100: Tourism Series*, 1, Department of Geography, University of Reading, Reading.

Gratton, C. and Taylor, P. (1985) *Sport and Recreation: An Economic Analysis*. Spon, London.

Gray, H.P. (1970) *International Travel–International Trade*. Heath, Lexington.

Hills, T.L. and Lundgren, J. (1977) The impact of tourism in the Caribbean: a methodological study. *Annals of Tourism Research*, 4(5), 248–267.

Kent, P. (1990) People, places and priorities: opportunity sets and consumer holiday choices. In: Ashworth, G.J. and Goodall, B. (eds), *Marketing Tourism Places*. Routledge, London, pp. 42–62.

Lancaster, K.J. (1966) A new approach to consumer theory. *Journal of Political Economy*, 84, 132–157.

Lundgren, J.O.J. (1982) The tourist frontier of Nouveau Quebec: functions and regional linkages. *Tourist Review*, 37(2), 10–16.

Marble, B. and Bowlby, S. (1968) Shopping alternatives and recurrent travel patterns. *Studies in Geography* No 16, Department of Geography, Northwestern University, Evanston.

Miossec, J.M. (1976) *Éléments pour une théorie de l'espace touristique*. Les Cahiers du Tourisme, C-36 C.H.E.T., Aix-en-Provence.

Pearce, D.G. (1981) L'espace touristique de la grande ville: éléments de synthèse et application à Christchurch (Nouvelle-Zélande). *L'Espace Géographique* 10(3), 207–213.

Pearce, D.G. (1987) *Tourism Today: A Geographical Analysis*. Longman, Harlow.

Plog, S.C. (1973) Why destination areas rise and fall in popularity. *Cornell HRA Quarterly*, Nov, 13–16.

Pred, A. (1967) *Behaviour and Location: Foundations for a Geographic and Dynamic Location Theory*. Vol. 1, C.W.K. Gleerup, Lund.

Radburn, M.W. and Goodall, B. (1990) Marketing through travel agents. In: Ashworth, G.J. and Goodall, B. (eds), *Marketing Tourism Places*. Routledge, London, pp. 237–259.

Sheldon, P.J. (1986) The tour operator industry: an analysis. *Annals of Tourism Research*, 13, 349–363.

Sinclair, M.T., Clewer, A. and Pack, A. (1990) Hedonic prices and the marketing of package holidays. In: Ashworth, G. and Goodall, B. (eds), *Marketing Tourism Places*, Routledge, London, pp. 85–103.

Stabler, M.J. (1989) Modelling the tourism industry: the concept of opportunity sets. In: Stabler, M.J. (ed.), *Leisure, Labour and Lifestyles: International Comparisons. Tourism and Leisure; Models and Theories*. Leisure Studies Association Second International Conference Proceedings, No. 39, Vol 8, Leisure Studies Association, Eastbourne, pp. 60-79.

Stabler, M.J. (1990) The concept of opportunity sets as a methodological framework for the analysis of selling tourism places. In: Ashworth, G.J.

and Goodall, B. (eds), *Marketing Tourism Places*. Routledge, London, pp. 23–41.

Thurot, J.M. (1973) *Le tourisme tropical balnéaire: le modèle Caraibe et ses extensions*. Centre d'Etudes du Tourisme, Aix-en-Provence, Thesis.

Thurot, J.M. (1980) *Capacité de charge et production touristique*. Etudes et Mémoires No. 43, Centre des Hautes Etudes Touristiques, Aix-en-Provence.

Um, S. and Crompton, J.L. (1990) Attitude determinants in tourism destination choice. *Annals of Tourism Research*, 17(3), 432–448.

Woodside, A.G., Ronkainen, I.A. and Reid, D.M. (1977) Measurement and utilisation of the evoked sets as a travel marketing variable. In: *Proceedings of Eighth Annual Conference, Travel Research Association*, pp. 123–130.

Woodside, A.G. and Sherrell, D. (1977) Traveller evoked set, inept set and inert sets of vacation destinations. *Journal of Travel Research*, 16, 14–18.

Yokeno, N. (1968) La localisation de l'industrie touristique: application de l'analyse de Thunen-Weber. *Cahiers du Tourisme*, C-9 C.H.E.T., Aix-en-Provence.

Chapter 3

Information Technology in Tourism : The Impact on the Industry and Supply of Holidays

M. Bennett and M. Radburn

Introduction

Information technology, hereafter referred to as IT, is permeating the entire tourism industry. It is being used for a variety of functions, ranging from an internal organisational role to external communication between the different parts of the industry. The implications are equally far-reaching for both the consumer and the industry. This chapter will document the new technology, in particular concentrating on travel agencies, and in turn, will discuss the impact of such technologies in terms of their likely benefits, effects on competition in the industry and the competitive advantage of individual firms within it, as well as assessing IT's impact on consumer choice. Using the example of the marketing of summer sun package holidays in the UK, the chapter shows the effects of IT on the principal providers of such holiday opportunities, namely the tour operators, as well as the travel agencies which retail those opportunities. Particular attention is paid to the role of travel agents who act as intermediaries between the needs and desires of consumers and the tour operators who package products. Finally, speculation on the future provides an insight into how further advances in IT will engender more change in the industry, also highlighting the dynamism characterising the tourism industry.

Information technology in the tourism industry

One of the most comprehensive definitions of the term 'information technology' is given by Poon:

> Information Technology (IT) is the collective term given to the most recent
> developments in the mode (electronic) and the mechanisms (computers and
> communications technologies as well as the software which drive them) used

for the acquisition, processing, analysis, storage, retrieval, dissemination and application of information (Poon, 1988, p. 533).

The tourism industry has proved particularly suitable for the adoption of IT because of its dependence upon the supply and exchange of information throughout the production and distribution chain. Indeed, information can largely be conceived as constituting the tourism product since it is characteristically intangible, perishable, volatile and heterogeneous. Consequently, information assumes a vitally important role which, in turn, generates a need for IT:

> The tourism industry in general is ideally suited for computer technology. It requires a system of registering availability of transport and accommodation at short notice; of making immediate reservations, amendments and cancellations on such facilities; of quoting complex fares and conditions of travel; of rapidly processing documents such as tickets, invoices, vouchers and itineraries, and of providing accounting and management information (Holloway, 1985).

Poon (1988) goes further by suggesting that there is not just one type of IT but a whole system of information technologies. Airlines, for example, use IT not just for schedule displays but for flight planning, departure control, catering, crew management and cargo control. In hotels, reservations management, guest accounting, room management, purchasing, payroll, inventory and food and beverage control have all been pervaded by IT. Internal functions are increasingly performed by accountancy and administration systems, internal networks and extensive databases, while communication within the industry is now principally conducted through the medium of computerised reservations systems (CRS) and viewdata, which together have largely replaced the use of telephones and the post.

A study of the systems in use within travel agencies in the United Kingdom underlines the importance of information technology within the tourism industry in general.

Viewdata

Viewdata, or videotex as it is also known, represents the marrying together of a screen to display information and the telephone network to transmit information from a central computer. Viewdata offers a two-way interactive service, giving access to a variety of databases using 'gateway' software (Forester, 1987). A gateway is a facility allowing a company to connect its reservations computer directly into the network. By dialling into local access nodes, agents are offered local call rates, in theory reducing communication costs. Within five years of its introduction into agencies in 1979, 90 per cent of all UK agencies were using videotex, and by 1987 85 per cent of all bookings were being made through viewdata (Bruce, 1987).

Essentially, there are three network bureaux (Midland Network Services, Istel and Prestel) providing a similar set of services to travel agents. Services vary according to each network but generally they include a hotel and airline booking facility, late availability services, a facility enabling agents to set up their own private data base within the system as well as access to individual tour operators' reservation systems. The three networks are in competition with each other, but combined they provide access to all the main tour operators.

A significant development was that of the Thomson Open-line Program (TOP) which, being the Thomson Travel Group's own private viewdata system, was until recently not available on any other network. In 1986 Thomson Holidays went a stage further by becoming the first tour operator to make bookings available only by interactive videotex. In other words, any intermediary without videotex would not be able to make a booking with Thomson Holidays, currently the largest tour operator in the business.

The latest extension to these network bureaux is that of direct connect or 'hardwiring' as it is also known, i.e. cabling to the individual agent's premises where the access port eliminates the need for a dial-up facility. This is essentially a direct connect link which reduces the time spent trying to access the principal's or supplier's system.

Computerised reservation systems (CRS)

There can be little doubt that CRS have become one of the most technologically advanced sectors of the tourism industry as well as one of the most controversial. These systems enable travel agents to interface with a variety of principals' computers to book airline seats, car hire, rail, ferry services, hotels, theatre tickets and ski equipment rental, as well as numerous other information services. In fact, CRS have been described as a 'total information system' (Poon, 1988) and have had an impact on virtually every sector of the travel trade.

Today CRS have become an essential tool for the business agent and they are almost all airline-owned. This is significant in that CRS were born out of internal airline systems and only later was it realised that they could be used by the retail travel agent. The most prominent systems are American, although two new global distribution systems have been developed, Amadeus and Galileo, which aim to block the penetration of the sophisticated American systems into other markets. This has arisen from the issue of bias and the lucrative nature of these systems, a point which is raised again later.

'Back office' systems

Back office systems basically perform the administration, accounting and ticketing functions. Combined, these systems enable travel agents to store private information, create client profiles and itineraries and undertake invoicing, ticketing and word processing. Perhaps, more importantly, as a by-product they become a useful source of marketing information on which holidays are selling well, where, when and to whom. Information on clients can help agents understand their target market better and assist training and development by indicating which staff are doing the most business. All of this is essential management information, helping to boost the profits of an agency or ensuring the agent's survival.

Who provides these systems? Certainly CRS offer a variety: American Airline's Sabre, for example, has Agency Data Systems (ADS), an accounting and management information package. Other systems such as Delta Airline's DATAS II and TWA's and Northwest Airline's PARS (now combined to form Worldspan) incorporate similar facilities. These systems are particularly important for large business agents. For CRS vendors, of course, it becomes another source of revenue and another method of increasing agent loyalty to the

47

CRS vendor (Wardell, 1987). Numerous other independent and dedicated systems exist, catering for a different mixture of agents. In addition, it is common for the large multiple travel agencies to have their own tailor-made systems, with most administration and accountancy being undertaken centrally.

Current trends and issues in the use of IT

The effects of competition

A significant feature of the new technology is the lack of standardisation. This is a reflection of competition within the industry, leading to fragmented systems resulting in the 'islands of computers' syndrome. Thomson's TOP is a prime example. Until recently, TOP was not available on any other network. Consequently, agents had to link directly into TOP to make reservations. Similarly, tour operators available on one network bureau are not necessarily available on any other, thus creating a problem for the agents in terms of the cost of registering with more than one network bureau.

A lack of standardisation, coupled with competition in the marketplace, is further revealed in the number of 'back office' products available. A plethora of systems on the market creates difficulties for agents in deciding which will best suit the individual agent's needs and at the right cost. This has been exacerbated by the introduction of integrated agency systems which combine front and back office functions, thus allowing reservations to be processed instantly. Paradoxically though, this does represent a step towards standardisation. However, CRS wanting to supply their own hardware, thus preventing agents from being able to use one terminal to access everything, is evidence of the obstacles standing in the way of that goal. It can be observed from this that it is not so much a technical problem as a business political one.

A second point relating to competition is that IT influences the products offered to consumers. The market initiators in IT, and those companies producing the most successful systems, set tomorrow's industry standard. The result is that agents resort to using certain systems because of their ease of use. In research conducted by Bennett (1990), one travel agent stated:

> It's no longer the difference between these companies and their products, it's how easy they are to get at ... The system is taking over the product, the product doesn't matter, it doesn't matter who's offering it – it's the same product anyway and the technology is dictating the choice.

This tendency is reinforced by hardwiring. Since the costs for agents are too great to justify hardwiring into each network, connection into a specific one will ensure that the products available on that network are more likely to be chosen. Consequently, it can be posited, *a priori*, that the service and products offered by the travel agent will, at least in part, restrict the choice available to the consumer using that agent.

The issue of bias on the part of the travel agent can be taken a stage further to include bias by principals. The notable example here is that of CRS which have become infamous for their in-built bias. Of particular significance is the 'halo' effect stemming from screen information giving certain airlines (namely the host airlines owning the systems) a more prominent position in the displays, which in turn leads to that product being chosen more frequently, thus giving such principals more business and larger revenues. Significantly, Robert Crandall, President of American Airlines, is reported to have said that, if forced to sell assets, he would sell the airline rather than Sabre, the American Airlines system, indicating the highly lucrative nature of such systems.

The impact of competition on IT raises two important points. First, IT is being used by the principals to enhance market advantage and power while for the agents, ease of access is the prominent concern. Therefore, it can be argued that the products being offered are not always in the consumer's best interests. Second, this raises the question of for whom the travel agent is an agent – the consumer or the principal, an issue which is examined by means of a case study later in the chapter.

What are the benefits and who gains them?

A major benefit allegedly associated with IT is that it has the potential to lower costs and increase efficiency (Benton, 1986; Blois, 1987; Cullen, 1986; Galliers, 1986; King et al., 1989; McFarlan, 1984; Ward, 1986). For example, Blois (1987), considers that IT offers the following advantages:

- reduced costs of information handling;
- increased speed of information transfer and retrieval;
- increased customer involvement in and control of transactions;
- greater flexibility of product specifications and greater reliability of information transferred.

These, however, are open to dispute.

Reduced costs of information handling

A major benefit of viewdata was that it introduced local call access which *prima facie* should have lowered telephone charges. Thomson, for example, claimed that TOP saved agents £1.5 million in telephone charges during the period 1983–1986 (Rumble, 1986). However, there are counteracting factors, such as the time-related nature of on-line charges (Cullen, 1986). Indeed, it has been found (Bennett, 1990) that communication costs in travel agencies had increased because:

- there is an increase in connection time while clients debate the information shown on the screen;
- connection time is increased as clients increase the number of alternative holidays they wish to consider before coming to any decision;
- clients' use several agents for holiday searches in the belief that one agent has a larger stock of product on-screen than another.

Thus the potential cost savings which agents should have gained through viewdata do not appear to have materialised. However, further research revealed that such cost savings rested with the principals who were responsible for the introduction of viewdata into travel agencies. The rationale behind viewdata was that tour operators could reduce their selling costs by closing their telephone reservation departments. The reservation costs are then passed down to the retailer. If the tour operator dictates that no agent can make telephone reservations, as Thomson did in 1986, then travel agents are forced to conform. Consequently, the greatest benefits rest with the IT initiators. Hence, in the three-year period of 1983–1986 Thomson's own staff productivity improved by 100 per cent (Rumble, 1986).

Increased speed of information transfer and retrieval
Travel agents have certainly gained through the increased speed of information transfer:

> The use of IT has dramatically reduced the time which a customer may have to wait for enquiries to be answered, confirmation of an order to be received or for a service to be delivered. All three results of the increased speed of transaction are visible in many travel agents (Blois, 1987).

Increased customer involvement in and control of transactions
There is greater customer involvement because they can see the information provided by the principal on-screen and consequently are in a position to exercise more control over the booking process. On the other hand, the amount of information clients receive may be more than they can comprehend and ultimately they may have to rely on the agent's advice.

Greater flexibility of product specifications and greater reliability of information transferred
Related to the last two points is the ability to handle bookings more quickly and flexibly, therefore providing scope for an increase in productivity. One example is that of late availability services, the development of which has been facilitated both by the speed of information transfer and its reliability, making it possible to take bookings at short notice. However, some of the benefits of increased productivity have been offset by a number of operational problems faced by agents, including difficulty in accessing tour operators and congestion of lines at peak booking periods. Therefore, IT is not problem-free, but it should be noted that difficulties were prevalent prior to the introduction of the new technology.

The impact on product depth and width

As shown by Goodall and Bergsma in Chapter 5, product depth is the enhancement of and/or extension of the options available for a specific holiday, such as the inclusion of car hire, excursion and insurance services, while product width is the extension of the range of different types of holiday. A benefit of debatable value to travel agents, which is partly the outcome of IT and an example of product depth, is that of late availability services. Holidayfax, BP's Flight and Seatfinder, Holiday Designers and Hogg Robinson's Quick Getaway service are just some of the late availability services on viewdata.

The development of such services has undoubtedly been fostered by IT, but their growth in terms of numbers of bookings is a reflection of a number of other factors too. In particular, it is the result of intense price wars in the UK over the last five years which, during the course of the holiday season, has led some potential tourists to wait and see how far the tour operators will cut prices. Thus, the travel agent, principal and consumer are all players in this field, which serves to reduce the importance of IT.

Furthermore, the growth in demand for such services is partly the result of companies such as Holidayfax entering the market to enable travel agents to profit from this new form of sale. Here, supply has really created the demand. This has added a new dimension to the travel agent's role but it has also meant less commission and less time to benefit from interest on the consumer's money. The point is that late bookings are substituted for earlier bookings. If the availability of late bookings facilities generates new demand, then there would clearly be tremendous benefits to travel agents arising from a larger aggregate market.

Holiday Designers is an especially interesting case in that it enables agents to package empty seats and beds from different tour operator packages, tailor-made to clients' requirements, thus giving extra flexibility to the conventionally rigid Inclusive Tour by Charter (ITC). First Call, too, has extended the scope of travel agency service by providing access to booking facilities for theatres and concerts, constituting an example of product width. As well as enhancing services, IT has thus also spawned new businesses (Griffiths, 1986; Porter and Millar, 1985). For example, Holidayfax, already referred to, emerged as a direct consequence of IT, with the result that a new sub-level has been created in the chain of production which previously did not exist.

From the point of view of domestic holidays, the introduction of domestic products on viewdata has given travel agents a greater impetus to market these types of products. A representative of Haven Leisure stated:

> Many domestic operators criticise agents for their lack of enthusiasm in selling UK holidays. At Haven, we can only praise the retailers for their excellent support. I firmly believe that the provision of a videotex system has had a large part to play in the ever growing volume of Haven bookings coming from agents (English Tourist Board, 1989).

Thus IT has enhanced product depth by extending the range of services offered by travel agents. While this has generally been to their advantage, the economic drawbacks of late availability services highlight the problems of a dependence upon this market.

The increasing application of IT in the tourism industry has also made it possible to differentiate holidays more, thus creating a large portfolio and a finer segmentation of the market. A disadvantage, however, is that it can lead to wasteful competition between intermediaries, where there is apparent duplication of products and where consumers are bewildered by the sheer volume of holidays on offer.

The impact on competitive advantage

Discussion of the impact of IT on the tourism industry would not be complete without inclusion of the issue of competitive advantage. Defined as the 'ability of a firm to create and exploit monopoly or monopsony power' (Bakos and Treacy, 1986), the aim here is to view it in the context of the principal/travel agency relationship. The arguments in favour of increased principal power are strong. Since the principals tend to be the IT initiators and assemblers of the products, it is they who are in the position of greater strength. In research undertaken by Bennett (1990), one travel agent stated:

> ....you get into the position where the man at the end of the line is effectively blackmailed into having to accept the terms and conditions imposed on him. ...The only people that it does any good to, the new technology, is the tour operators, because they are the promoters of it and it was designed with their needs in mind, nobody else's. All of the selling points are based on how best we can get other people to do what we want them to do...There is nothing that we can do to utilise this sort of technology to the benefit of the retail outlet.

Essentially, the power of the principals over travel agents prior to the introduction of IT has been strengthened by technology.

Principal power can be illustrated further by focusing on TAB, the Thomson Automatic Banking scheme, introduced to improve payment methods between travel agents and Thomson. The system operates by automatically deducting money from the travel agent's account on an agreed date after the booking has been confirmed. Although reducing the paperwork for both agents and Thomson, the disadvantage for agents is that if a client defaults on a booking the onus is on the agent to notify Thomson, otherwise the balance will be automatically deducted, which could create a cash flow problem for the travel agent. Related to the last point is the issue of data quality. In the payment reconciliation process between principal and travel agent, it is the businesses with the better systems (at present the principals) which possess better quality information and therefore command a more powerful position.

Finally, extensive databases are increasing the information principals have on their market; for instance British Airways and its Air Miles scheme. One such advantage would be to utilise that information for direct marketing and ultimately direct selling, such as British Airways' Club World. This kind of branding attempts to achieve, through advertising, what is known as 'end-user outreach', i.e. the principal (in this case a carrier) bypassing the intermediary to make direct contact with the consumer.

Clearly, the case for principals endeavouring to increase their power is a strong one. However, there are also arguments for an increase in travel agency power. The key factor is the use of IT as a sales aid which not only improves the speed and efficiency of the booking but also provides the opportunity to offer a better service. This, as already mentioned, increases the consumer's dependence upon the travel agent for advice and guidance on choosing the 'right' product.

A second factor concerns the increased knowledge the travel agent has about the public by capturing booking information and compiling databases. Control of market information could lead to an increase in bargaining power with the principals (Rumble, 1986; McFarlan, 1984). Large multiple travel agents, in particular, would have this advantage. As it is, the multiples' size gives them valuable negotiating muscle with the suppliers.

A shift in power from principal to travel agent is unlikely. The travel agent's greatest assets are in knowing the market, and in forging direct links with the consumer through improved service. However, it is the principals which have gained the competitive edge over the travel agents. To a large extent, this has stemmed from their inherent advantage in being the product supplier and often the larger organisation. Undoubtedly it has also arisen from being the IT initiator and from competition between principals. This has led to fragmentation of systems, where companies have attempted to secure their market by developing their own system. Those larger firms which tended to be early into the field gained a stronger position in the marketplace which has consequently given them increased bargaining power over travel agents and consumers. Generally this competitive advantage continues to rest with the large principals. Only in the case of the smaller principals would the multiple travel agents be in a stronger position. A number of these factors concerning the balance of power and the interrelationship between agents and principals, specifically tour operators, are illustrated by the following case study.

The role of IT in the supply of holidays

The significance of package holidays in the UK tourism industry

Ostensibly travel agents, as the 'retailers' of the travel industry (Foster, 1985), market the products of tour operators, providing a locally accessible point for consumers. Indeed travel agency is the one activity most clearly recognised by the general public as representing the tourism industry. Lavery (1987) goes so far as to state that most consumers are unaware that the travel agent is acting on behalf of a third party.

The 'package' holiday or inclusive tour reflects a significant shift in the holiday habits of UK consumers over a 20 year period. While the last 15 years or so have seen an overall growth in main season holidays of only 3 per cent, the growth in the inclusive tour market has been from about five million holidays in 1974 to around 19 million in 1986 (Price, 1988). This growth has been at the expense of UK based holidays, and also at the expense of other forms of overseas holidays. For example, from 44 per cent in 1976, package holidays accounted for 56 per cent of all UK overseas holiday purchases only two years later in 1978 (Plant, 1988).

The providers of package holidays dominate the UK holiday market, in terms both of their share of overseas holidays sold and of their effect on consumers' perceptions of overseas holiday opportunities. In addition, the five largest tour operators who provide relatively cheap, mass market holidays accounted for 65.5 per cent of total sales of inclusive tours in 1987. The largest company, Thomson, sold 31.5 per cent of the total market (Plant, 1988).

The tour operator's reliance on mass market package holidays during the 1970s and 1980s has, in part, been a response to consumer demand for holidays which conform to a simple sun, sea and sand formula. As the UK tourism industry approaches maturity, this simple formula has become outmoded and consumers appear to be more discerning and sophisticated. In the summer of 1990 the market for package holidays and charter airline seat sales had declined from about 12 million to around 10 million (East, 1990). This decline can be partly explained by increasing consumer dissatisfaction with such products, notwithstanding the economic recession at that time. However, sun–sea–sand holidays remain at the heart both of the industry and of UK consumers' perceptions of it, dictating not only how the majority of packages have been sold but also the actions of travel agents.

The interrelationship of tour operators and travel agents in providing package holidays

In most travel agencies, business is likely to revolve around two main areas of activity: the sale of inclusive tour packages and the sale of airline tickets. It is here that volume sales and therefore most revenue can be most readily obtained. The travel agencies' role in selling package holidays comprises 80 per cent of their business (Keynote Report, 1988) and some 90 per cent of package holidays are sold via travel agencies (Holloway, 1985; Goodall, 1988).

As the UK overseas holiday market develops, largely as a result of more discerning consumers, the interaction between them and travel agents and tour operators must become more flexible and able to satisfy increasingly diverse consumer demands. Information technology will play an important role in developing products and sales strategies which will meet these new circumstances. The package tour may be seen as an important but nevertheless declining feature in the range of holiday opportunities likely to be demanded by consumers in the 1990s.

The potential of IT to influence holiday sales processes

The tourism industry's growth over the last 40 years has seen very little real change in the way holidays are retailed to the consumer. The nature of the product has changed, as have the socio-economic circumstances of consumers, but the distribution or transmission system, that is travel retailing, has changed its relationship with the consumer only marginally. Packaging of holiday opportunities for sale by a retailer is so fundamental to the structure of the UK industry that it remains largely unchallenged, and the opportunities of alternative systems of distribution are not seriously considered. Direct sell, where a one-to-one relationship is established between consumer and supplier, is one alternative strategy which exists in the tourism industry in the UK. It is only in the domestic tourism industry that a large proportion of holiday opportunities are distributed without reference to travel agents or tour operators.

There are many reasons why direct sell for foreign holidays is not more widespread in the UK and why the travel agent remains central to the distribution of holiday opportunities. However, the principal reason for the dominance of the present system of travel retailing is its success. Notwithstanding this, it does seem that an opportunity has been presented to the tour operator as a result of the development of IT systems. They have the ability, as referred to above, to form a more direct relationship with consumers through disintermediation. It is possible that IT might allow tour operators to control the process of consumer information gathering, decision-making and choice to a much greater degree than is presently the case. It is likely, for the foreseeable future, that the dominant role of the travel agent in the exchange of information between producer and consumer is assured. At present it would appear that IT has been designed and implemented to rationalise and reinforce the relationship between travel principals and agents. The possibility of gaining greater influence over consumers' decision-making has been side-stepped by the principals in favour of exercising more control over the travel agents' sales methods and operational procedures. As indicated earlier, the revolution in the holiday sales process and the relationship between consumer and the industry which can be brought about by IT has yet to occur, though the opportunity is apparent.

Spatial differences in the supply of holidays

In a given area, travel agents control the supply of holidays by restricting consumers' access to knowledge of holiday opportunities. It is possible to define, for package holidays, a national industry opportunity set, which includes all package holidays of all tour operations based in the UK (Goodall and Radburn, 1990; Stabler, Chapter 2). This national industry inclusive tour opportunity set can be subdivided into opportunity sets available either regionally, locally or at the level of the travel agent. In theory, the maximum extent of the local package holiday opportunity set is determined by the range of package holidays that tour operators are prepared to offer in a given regional market. There is, in fact, no universal national package holiday opportunity set for the UK because some tour operators may not be represented and products may not be offered in a given region. It is therefore possible to conceive of and identify a local industry package holiday opportunity set which would include all holidays available through travel agencies in a given locality at a given point in time. Further subdivision may produce a travel agency outlet opportunity set. It is clear that it is the local and travel agency outlet opportunity sets which are of principal interest to the consumer, and these are examined in more detail below.

A survey of travel agencies in Reading, Bracknell and Wokingham (Goodall and Radburn, 1990) established a local package holiday opportunity set by recording the range of tour operators' brochures on display in each agency. A total of 857 tour operators' brochures were represented in the survey, but the variation in the extent of each travel agency outlet opportunity set was considerable. Table 3.1 summarises the extent of the survey which demonstrated variation in the number of brochures displayed in national, regional and local multiples and independent agencies, the widest choice being in independent and local chain outlets (see Table 3.2). Differences in the number of brochures displayed between outlets in the same travel agency chain were also apparent (37 per cent variation on the number of brochures displayed in Hogg Robinson's two Reading outlets, and 80 per cent variation between the same company's largest Reading branch and their Bracknell branch).

Table 3.1   The Reading area local opportunity set for 'Summer Sun' package holidays

Travel agency	Type	No. of brochures displayed
<u>Reading</u>		
AA	N	41
Brooking Travel	I	101
Carters Travel	L	38
Thomas Cook	N	51
Co-op Travelcare	N	62
Exchange Travel	L	35
Harvey Thomas	N	108
Hogg Robinson	N	68
Hogg Robinson	N	75
Lunn Poly	N	74
Pickfords	N	60
Pickfords	N	38
British Airways	I	56
Horsemans	L	59
Keith Bailey	I	99
Meadway Travel	N	59
British Rail	N	4
RUSU Travel	I	15
<u>Wokingham</u>		
Eton Travel	L	224
Hogg Robinson	N	72
Pickfords	N	82
<u>Bracknell</u>		
A.T. Mays	N	175
Thomas Cook	N	50
Exchange	N	63
Hogg Robinson	N	21
Ian Allan	R	68
Pickfords	N	66
W.H. Smith	N	95

Number of tour operators' brochures represented in:	
Reading	659
Wokingham	162
Bracknell	131
Local opportunity set	857

Note: key to travel agency type, N = National multiple, R = Regional multiple, L = Local multiple, I = Independent.

Table 3.2 Differences between travel agency types in brochures displayed

Travel agency type	No. of outlets in opportunity set	No. of brochures displayed	
		Average	Median
National multiple	20	65.5	62.5
Regional multiple	1	68	68
Local multiple	5	79	41
Independent	4	68	77.5

Each travel agency outlet opportunity set contained a different range of tour operators. Table 3.3 shows the top 230 tour operators in each of the towns surveyed, together with the top 20 for the area as a whole, based on the frequency of occurrence of the tour operators' brochures in the travel agencies surveyed. Not surprisingly, given the structure of the UK tourism industry, the local industry package holiday opportunity set is dominated by a relatively small number of 'brand names' owned by a few mass tour operators. There is, however, considerable variation. Only one tour operator, Thomson, appears in the top 10 and a further two tour operators in the top 20 for all three towns in the survey.

Most tour operators in the top 20 for each town appear in that town only. Only one-quarter of Reading's top 20 tour operators are not represented in the other two towns in the survey, while half of Bracknell's top 20 and nearly three quarters of Wokingham's are unique to these towns.

The wider implications of the survey: filtering of holiday choice

In this survey, considerable spatial filtering of the regional package holidays opportunity set was taking place. It is possible to explain this variation in a number of ways, including:

- the trading relationship between travel agents and tour operators;
- the structure of the travel agency;
- marketing activity of travel agencies and tour operators.

A number of conclusions can be drawn which have a bearing on all three (Goodall and Radburn, 1990), while Chapter 5 by Goodall and Bergsma deals with the power and strategies of UK tour operators in more detail. Discussion here will concentrate on the effects of filtering of opportunity sets on consumer behaviour.

An emphasis on the importance of the local industry opportunity set is a useful starting point for the understanding of consumers' knowledge of the range of holiday opportunities provided by the industry. As Middleton (1988) suggests,

Table 3.3 The Reading area opportunity set as defined by its top 20 tour operators

Reading	Bracknell	Wokingham
1 Thomson	1 Club 18-30	1 Thomson
2 Intasun	2 Skytours	2 P & O Car Ferries
3 Global Air	= Wings OSL	= Best of Greece
4 Horizon	4 Brittany Ferries	4 Horizon
5 Cosmos	= Sunmed	= Wings (Horizon)
6 Enterprise	= Falcon	= Club 18-30
7 Sunmed	7 Enterprise	= Club Cantabrica
8 Lancaster	8 Wallace Arnold	= Club Med.
9 Sovereign	= Iberian	= Pan World Holidays
10 Wings OSL	10 Thomson	= Scan tours
12 Speedbird	= Crystal Holidays	= Sol Holidays
13 HCI	= Flair	13 Intasun
14 Kuoni	= Global Air	14 Tradewinds
15 Club	15 Rainbow Holidays	15 Cosmos
16 Yugotours	= Sally Tours	16 Kuoni
17 Skytours	= Silk Cut Travel	= Best Travel
= Swiss Travel	= Travel Smith	= Australasia
= Manos	= Wardair	19 Pan Am Holidays
= Flair	20 Lancaster	20 Pegasus

Overall

1	Thomson	=	Kuoni
2	Intasun	12	Club 18-30
3	Horizon	13	Yugotours
=	Cosmos	14	Wings (Horizon)
5	Sovereign	15	Skytours
6	Global Air	16	Global Tours
7	Enterprise	=	Wallace Arnold
8	Wings OSL	18	Poundstretcher
=	Lancaster	19	Select Holidays
10	Falcon	20	Flair

the notion of 'place' in the marketing of inclusive products incorporates not just the location of attractions or destinations, but all the points of sale which give consumers access to the range of package holiday products on offer. No consumer is likely to visit every travel agency in their locality as part of their search for a holiday. Their choice will be made from only part of the local opportunity set and may be restricted to choice from a single outlet opportunity set. The significance of the Reading area survey as an indication of the implications for the consumer is simply that consumer choice is restricted, in a particular area, to access to only a proportion of the total industry package holiday opportunity set. Furthermore, consumers' access to information in that portion of the total industry package holiday opportunity set is dependent on which travel agent(s) the consumer visits.

Perhaps this filtering of consumers' access to information is not very important. Tour operators offer product ranges containing mass-market packages with a high degree of substitutability and produce marketing images for those packages which they hope will encourage volume sales. There is substitutability within the product ranges of individual producers, and there is a high degree of substitutability between the mass market ranges of different producers. Variations in travel agency outlet opportunity sets do not necessarily affect consumers' access to types of package holidays. Indeed it could be asserted that variation in the product ranges available locally is a necessary stimulant to buying behaviour because variation encourages comparative shopping.

The impact of IT on filtering

Filtering of opportunity sets through the use of IT affects not only the range of opportunities available to consumers but also the way in which those opportunities are accessed by consumers. In theory, IT might allow a consumer anywhere in the UK access to the national industry package holiday opportunity set and a wide range of additional services. It is possible that the sheer size and complexity of this extended range of choice is the factor which limits its availability, i.e. the opportunity set available nationally via IT systems is too broad for consumers to handle the information and make holiday choices. A filtering of opportunities allows the industry to structure consumer choice, both as an aid to the consumer's decision-making process and for the competitive advantage principals gain, as discussed earlier in this chapter.

Part of this structuring comes about as a consequence of the use of IT as a competitive tool. It has already been demonstrated, but is worth emphasising, how Thomson, the UK inclusive tour holiday market leader, had, until recently, dominated travel agency IT systems through TOP. This reinforced the potential creation of a filter between consumers and their access to holiday opportunities not on TOP. Again, as suggested, if travel agency outlets 'hardwire' into systems which are incompatible with rival systems, more barriers to consumer access are created. It is the ease of access by travel agency counter staff to systems which will dictate the products offered first to the consumer.

As a sales aid, because of screen-time costs, IT is expensive in comparison with brochure time costs. To minimise this cost, travel agents may limit access by consumers to screened information as well as further limiting access by the number and range of brochures displayed and the number of IT systems they adopt. The only advantage of IT lies with the speed of booking and the efficiency of the booking system. This might tend to increase consumers' dependence on travel agents for guidance through the booking system, where there is also considerable temptation for the travel agent to point consumers towards familiar and easily accessible products.

Staff training, IT and travel agency operation

At the level of an individual outlet package holiday (PH) opportunity set, access to information by consumers is limited by the range of products on display in the agency and by the agency staff's knowledge of those opportunities. Using IT, the agency employee is provided with the means to handle bookings of various kinds with ease and efficiency. However, in itself IT is not a sales aid. Indeed, as already suggested, it is conceivable that once computer systems learn to sell, the tour operator may have little need of the travel agent. One important question for consumers and for the future of travel agencies, wider aspects of which are referred to again in the conclusions to this chapter, is whether or not IT will be used by travel agents as a support mechanism for counter staff, or whether staff will be used simply as an interface between consumers and IT systems. This has serious implications for the way in which travel agencies will operate in the 1990s, whom they will employ and how those employees are trained. The issue at this juncture is how employees react to the introduction and increasing computerisation of travel agency work in the back office as well as the front office environment, and how it will affect their relationship with consumers.

Equipment is becoming technically easier to use and more familiar. In a survey of travel agents in the north west of the UK (Bruce and Kahn, 1989), the introduction of IT systems was seen to demoralise counter staff, who thought that it eroded their traditional skills base, brought monotony to the job and that it was often introduced without negotiation or consultation about its design or operational use. Some illustrative examples are presented here to indicate the influence of IT on travel agents and their staff.

There is certainly an inadequate definition both of the role of travel agency counter staff and the role of IT systems in the training of new and existing staff. Traditional training for travel agency counter staff in the UK is limited in the amount of time and study spent on IT systems. Most travel agency trainees and junior staff have, or are in the process of studying for, a City and Guilds of London Institute qualification known as the Certificate of Travel Agency Competence (COTAC). This certificate forms the basis for a range of further professional examinations and career training routes.

The City and Guilds of London Institute offers schemes in some 400 different subjects and is by no means a tourism industry specialist. Travel industry training is now overseen by the Association of British Travel Agents (ABTA) through its government nominated training arm, known as the ABTA National Training Board. The ABTA National Training Board has approved the schemes offered by City and Guilds (and those offered by other training providers such as the Business and Technician Education Council) and will advise on the revision of schemes and future tourism and travel training developments.

The schemes designed by City and Guilds and the ABTA National Training Board have considerable impact on new entrants to travel agency employment, and hence on the future skills balance of employees in the travel and tourism industry. Many of the larger travel agency chains will now only take on staff through the National Training Board Youth Training Scheme, where training is provided to COTAC level one standard, often through day release study at a

Further Education College which has been approved by the ABTA National Training Board.

One problem with the COTAC course is that the time constraint of one day a week in college prohibits extensive study of the use of IT outside the work environment. Patterns of use, whether efficient or inefficient, are perpetuated through the hands-on training in the work place. The training of new staff does not develop the positive aspects or full potential of the use of IT; rather COTAC shows them how a manual system used to operate in travel agents and how it has now been replaced by technology. This situation emphatically illustrates the point being made more and more frequently that developments in computer technology and associated IT are rapidly outdistancing the ability of management and staff to exploit them to the full. Although, as discussed in the first part of the chapter, they have an advisory as well as a sales role, travel agency staff require knowledge not so much of the product, for example of destination locations and facilities, as of marketing and customer care skills. Staff need to reinforce their role as experts, being able to understand not only the process of matching consumer needs and desires to available opportunities but also to guide consumers through the wide range of packages and other services which IT makes accessible to the consumer. This has advantages for the consumer, agent and tour operator. As Bruce and Kahn (1989) point out:

> The least attractive scenario exists where an employee is required to repeat continually the same tasks, sitting in front of a dedicated terminal. In this situation, customer relations are relatively poor. Getting the design of the job right is important ... recognising the effects of the technology on customer service which can also include aspects of customer relations and marketing. In sum, an approach to the management of technical change which is human-centred and market-orientated is likely to be more effective in the long run.

Problems which currently surround the use of IT in the UK are likely to be perpetuated through successive travel agency trainees. While the COTAC course is currently undergoing some revision, an increasing degree of skills-based competence testing of travel agency staff will in future be done in the work-place, and it is expected that this will form an increasingly important part of post-16 technical education through a system of National Vocational Qualifications.

The future might see the decline of the pre-packaged inclusive tour at the expense of 'tailor-made' packages, put together and booked through IT systems in travel agencies with the aid of further IT input in the form of decision support systems. This can only occur if there is a radical shift in the industry back towards a skills-led approach where the implementation of IT, and training for IT, is sympathetic to its role as an aid to sales staff. Long term benefits for both travel agents and consumers might result from such a shift.

Some concluding comments on the impact of IT on tour operators, travel agents and consumer choice

It was suggested earlier in this chapter that the UK tourism industry's product distribution system has not changed greatly and that the direct sell alternative

61

remains underdeveloped. However, the analysis of the structure of the UK industry in Chapter 4, together with this chapter's reference to the filtering of information supplied by the industry to consumers, suggests that although travel agents play a role in information exchange between consumers and producers, the major players, the large tour operators, manage to achieve a considerable degree of influence over both information gathering and transmission. Consequently they not only exercise control over consumers' decision-making and choice, but also consumers' perception of the structure and operation of holiday provision via the UK industry. Moreover, the ability of these large tour operators to use IT more effectively by dominating the flow of information into many consumers' perceived opportunity sets and onto the terminal screens of travel agents, has marginalised their competitors' marketing efforts. In this sense, it would appear that the use of IT is another strategy available to large tour operators, enabling them to achieve their commercial objectives.

The future

Speculation on the future of IT in the tourism industry provides a suitable conclusion to this chapter. One thing is certain: the future promises more change in both the market and IT. The move towards more independent and flexible holidays away from the conventionally rigid package holiday by charter, together with the emergence of an increasingly sophisticated and computer-literate generation, are providing new opportunities for IT and the tourism industry. In particular, developments in point-of-sale packaging will, potentially, enable travel agents to revert to their more traditional role of creating individual itineraries, thus enhancing their importance. In addition, expert systems in travel agencies would allow the consumer to undertake the first stage of the search for the 'right' product while counsellors using decision support systems would complete the process in identifying or putting together the final product.

In addition there are opportunities for the introduction of 'smart cards' which, as well as acting as a credit card, could eliminate the need for tickets and boarding passes. Interactive video, which has been described as 'a solution looking for a problem' (Bennett, 1990), has the potential to replace brochures. Indeed Transworld Airline's (TWA) Iris and Utell's Utellvision demonstrate that the technology is already available, thus rendering its development less futuristic. Ticket printing by the travel agent would benefit late bookers, enabling the agent to overprint stationery with the firm's own name and logo, so giving it greater prominence. Alternatively, remote ticketing would enable the agent to control the issue of the ticket from the outlet and print it at the travel departure point. Electronic Data Interchange (EDI) which is the 'transfer of structured data by agreed message standards from one computer system to another by electronic means' (Allen, 1990) could facilitate ticket printing and standardisation. Agents could also usurp some of the tour operators' marketing advantages by projecting their own format onto the screen and thus to the consumer. Ultimately this could strengthen the travel agents' position in the tourism industry, and so alter the power balance between them and tour operators.

However, not all developments would necessarily be so beneficial to the travel agent. Electronic funds transfer at the point-of-sale (EFTPOS), for example, could appear in two forms:

- between travel agent and principal;
- between consumer and principal.

It is the latter which could have a detrimental effect on the travel agent. If money is transferred directly to the principal then the implications for the travel agent are profound. Since the travel agent depends heavily on the interest gained from advance payments to earn revenue, if money is debited from the consumer directly to the principal the agent is by-passed and thus this form of income is lost.

Undoubtedly, IT's greatest impact on the tourism industry would be the disintermediation of the travel agent. Armchair retailing or electronic shopping between consumer and principal would cut out the agent altogether. Although there are a number of arguments favouring the introduction of this development, including a more computer-literate and travel-aware generation, the intangible nature of the tourism product and increased user-friendliness of IT, to name but a few, there are an equal number of factors constraining such a development, including the problem of obtaining critical mass, cost, the changing market and the perception of the travel agent's role. Of importance, too, is the human touch or personal service to counteract the more inhuman aspects of IT. Perhaps the most important factor is that of increased complexity in terms of both travel options and IT, a tendency which will be reinforced by 1992 and the liberalisation of the airways. Consequently, while armchair retailing will pose a threat to the travel agent, particularly in terms of standard or repeat bookings, disintermediation is unlikely. However, to counteract that threat, it is necessary for the travel agent to focus on and improve service levels.

A final point concerning the future is that of the issue of standardisation. It could be argued that a combination of competition and the economic climate, which is presently resulting in a reduction in the number of firms, could in turn lead to fewer systems. This would make the travel agents' role easier, enabling them to concentrate on service. It would also assist the consumer's decision-making process because the number of duplicated products available on the market would be reduced. However, while there may be attempts at improving standardisation of IT which would ultimately benefit both the travel agent and consumer, it is unlikely that this will ever emerge on a larger scale. In a survey of holiday intermediaries (Bennett, 1990), an employee of a multiple travel agency stated:

> I think that competition will always be there. I don't think there will be
> standardisation. I don't think airlines or principals will ever move to a form of
> standardisation because that is their way of hooking you onto their systems with
> the training that they give you, and that is the key – to hook you to one system, I
> suppose, in a roundabout way, to insist upon loyalty ... I think they'll make an
> attempt at standardisation but my personal impression is that they lay lip service
> to the word standardisation ... in practice it's a very bitter pill for them to
> swallow.

This statement epitomises the current situation in that the issues are 'political' rather than technical and until these are resolved, the problem of non-standardisation will remain.

The developments outlined in this section represent some of the future possibilities; there are undoubtedly many more. However, it should be acknowledged that some may never materialise while others may emerge in a different form.

Conclusion

Both currently and in the future, IT is having and will continue to have a profound effect on the tourism industry. The chapter has illustrated how IT is permeating a variety of functions throughout the different sectors of the industry, and, in turn, is increasing efficiency. However, it has also been shown that the benefits are not evenly distributed and that IT is tending to endorse the principal's competitive advantage over the travel agent. In addition, IT is found to be influencing consumer choice in a way which is not always in the latter's best interests. Speculation on the future has revealed that further changes in both IT and the market are probable, which will induce more change in terms of both the holiday choices available to consumers and the operations and structure of the industry. The final statement on IT concerns its functionality. To be adopted successfully, IT needs to serve a purpose. Its value should not be under-estimated. In the final analysis, the determinants of change will be social, economic and political factors associated with both the consumer and the industry, thus relegating IT to its rightful position of an enabling mechanism.

References

Allen, T. (1990) What is EDI?, *Systems,* Travel News, London, p. 22.

Bakos, Y.J. and Treacy, M.E. (1986) Information technology and corporate strategy: A research perspective. *MIS Quarterly,* 10 (2), June pp. 107–119.

Bennett, M.M. (1990) *Information Technology and Travel Agency: An Assessment of Present and Future Impact.* Unpublished PhD thesis, University of Reading.

Benton, P. (1986) Information for strategic advantage. In: Griffiths, P.M. (ed.) *Information Management: State of the Art Report.* Pergamon Infotech Ltd., Maidenhead, Berks, pp. 3–10.

Blois, K.J. (1987) IT and marketing strategies in service firms. *Service Industrial Journal,* 7 (1), 14–23.

Bruce, M. (1987) New technology and the future of tourism. *Tourism Management,* 8, 115–120.

Bruce, M. and Kahn, H. (1989) Effects of new technology on job motivation and job design of Travel Agent employees. In: Witt, S.F. and Moutinho, L. (eds), *Tourism Marketing and Management Handbook.* Prentice Hall, London, pp. 123–126.

Cullen, A. (1986) Electronic information services, an emerging market opportunity? *Telecommunications Policy,* 10, 299–312.

East, J. (1990) Tour operators and travel agents. In: Cameron, H. (ed.) *The Tourism Industry 1990–91*. Tourism Society, London, pp. 23–24.

English Tourist Board (1989) *Technology Now – Success at the Industry's Fingertips*. Marketing Systems Unit, ETB, London.

Forester, T. (1987) *High-tech Society*. Basil Blackwell, Oxford.

Foster, D. (1985) *Travel and Tourism Management*. Macmillan, Basingstoke.

Galliers, R.D. (1986) Information systems and technology planning within a competitive strategy framework. In: Griffiths, P.M. (ed.) *Information Management: State of the Art Report*. Pegamon Infotech Ltd, Maidenhead, Berks, pp. 37–51.

Goodall, B. (1988) Changing patterns and structure of European tourism. In: Goodall, B. and Ashworth G.J. (eds), *Marketing in the Tourism Industry*. Croom Helm, London, pp. 18–38.

Goodall, B. and Radburn, M. W. (1990) Marketing through travel agencies. In: Ashworth, G.J. and Goodall, B. (eds), *Marketing Tourism Places*. Routledge, London, pp. 237–255.

Griffiths, P.M. (ed.) (1986) *Information Management: State of the Art Report*. Pergamon Infotech Ltd., Maidenhead, Berks.

Holloway, J.C. (1985) *The Business of Tourism*, 2nd edn. Macdonald and Evans, Plymouth.

Keynote Report (1988) *Travel Agents and Overseas Tour Operators: An Industry Sector Overview*, 7th edn. ICC Information Group, London.

King, W.R., Grover, V. and Hufnagel, E. (1989) Seeking competitive advantage using information-intensive strategies: facilitators and inhibitors. In: Laudon, K.C. and Turner J.A. (eds), *Information Technology and Management Strategy*. Prentice Hall, Englewood Cliffs, New Jersey, pp. 50–63.

Lavery, P. (1987) *Travel and Tourism*. ELM Publication, Huntingdon.

McFarlan, F.W. (1984) Information technology changes the way you compete. *Harvard Business Review*, 62, 98–103.

Middleton, V.T.C. (1988) *Marketing in Travel and Tourism*. Heinemann, London.

Plant, R. (1988) Travel agents and tour operators. In: Cameron, H. (ed.), *The Tourism Industry 1988/89*. Tourism Society, London, p. 49.

Poon, A. (1988) Tourism and information technologies. *Annals of Tourism Research*, 15, 531–549.

Porter, M.E. and Millar, V.E. (1985) How information gives you competitive advantage. *Harvard Business Review*, 63, 149–160.

Price, S. (1988) Travel trade or direct sell? In: Cameron, H. (ed.), *The Tourism Industry 1988/89*. Tourism Society, London, pp. 47–48.

Rumble, D. (1986) Using communications for competitive advantage. In: Griffiths, P.M. (ed.), *Information Management: State of the Art Report*. Pergamon Infotech Ltd., Maidenhead, Berks, pp. 107–120.

Ward, J.M. (1986) An appraisal of the competitive benefits of IT. *Journal of Information Technology*, 1 (3), 1–13.

Wardell, D. (1987) Airline reservation systems in the USA. *Travel and Tourism Analyst*, January, The Economist Publications Ltd., pp. 45–56.

Chapter 4

Integration in the Tourism Industry: A Case Study Approach

Venancio Bote Gómez and M. Thea Sinclair

Introduction

The emergence of large firms dominating holiday 'production' is a relatively new feature of the tourism industry. Unlike the manufacturing sector, in which the actions and associated effects of large firms have generated a large literature (Schmalensee and Willig, 1989), there has been little analysis of the supply side of the tourism industry (Eadington and Redman, 1991; Sinclair, 1991). Research on the tourism has instead emphasized the demand for tourism and the associated income and employment generation effects (Fletcher and Archer, 1991; Hawkins and Ritchie, 1991; Sheldon, 1990). In addition, a range of country-based studies have been undertaken (for example, Hall, 1991; Williams and Shaw, 1991). Most studies have paid little attention to the cross-border integration of tourism firms which is an intrinsic feature of the international tourism industry. However, analyses of the tourism industry are incomplete without examination of the structure of large firms and the different forms of integration which characterise them.

Integration can take a variety of forms, ranging from total or partial ownership of 'production' activities to contractual arrangements between firms under separate ownership. In the context of tourism, integration occurs between travel agencies, tour operators, transportation companies and hotel chains. The extent and types of integration which occur are important because of their effects on both the tourist destination and origin countries. This chapter will focus on the supply side of tourism by using evidence for different European countries to examine the international structure of the tourism industry, including the ownership composition of large firms and contractual relationships between firms. Information relating to the United Kingdom and Spanish tourism industries, in particular, will be considered and reference will also be made to examples from Germany, France and Italy in order to indicate some of the differences and similarities between the tourism industries of these countries.

The first section of the chapter will outline the economic theories which have provided explanations of alternative types of integration. The following section will provide a context for the subsequent discussion by examining and comparing the ownership structures of the major firms in the UK and Spanish tourism industries, and identifying the main changes which have occurred in recent years. The emphasis will be on firms with the highest market shares in the tour operator, travel agency and charter airline sectors. The hotel sector will not be considered in detail but has been discussed by Go (1988; 1989), McGuffie (1987) and McVey (1986). The next section of the chapter will focus on the increasing internationalization of the tourism industry which has occurred as firms have invested to obtain total or partial ownership of different types of tourism activities abroad. Such foreign direct investment will be discussed with particular reference to Spain. The extent to which production activity in the tour operator, travel agency and charter airline sectors of the tourism industries within the UK, Spain and other European countries is dominated by a few large firms (the degree of concentration) will then be examined. Some possible explanations of integration in the forms of vertical ownership and contractual relationships between tourism enterprises at different stages of the 'production' process in the UK and Spain will be considered subsequently. Information obtained from interviews with participants in major firms in the tourism industries of Britain, Spain, France and Germany will be used to shed light on the nature and possible causes of alternative types of integration. The conclusion will discuss some implications of the preceding evidence and analysis for the strategies of large and small firms in the tourism industry, and for future research and policy making.

Explanations of integration

Horizontal and vertical integration are phenomena which, though increasingly important within the tourism industry, have received little detailed analysis (Buckley, 1987; Bull, 1991; Pearce, 1989; Sinclair, 1991). Horizontal integration is defined as occurring when two or more firms producing the same type of output (in the same industry) coordinate their production. Vertical integration entails the coordination of production by firms supplying different types of output within a production sequence, in which the outputs of some of the firms are the inputs of others. This 'effects-based' definition of integration, used by Casson (1987), will be used throughout this chapter, and has the advantage of encompassing the entire range of relationships which involve the coordination of economic activities. Such relationships include total and partial ownership, industrial collaboration, sales franchising, licensing and other contractual arrangements. A definition of integration based solely on common ownership, for example, might not involve the coordination of production as ownership is not always associated with control, so that common ownership of production activities might have no real economic effects. The chapter will concentrate on integration in the form of ownership and on contractual relationships, owing to the prevalence of these forms of integration within and between the large tour operators, travel agencies and charter airlines which are the main subjects of this study. Alternative forms of integration, including franchising and management contracts, are more common within the hotel sector of the tourism industry (United Nations Centre on Transnational Corporations, 1982).

Horizontal integration tends to increase industrial concentration and can take the form of changes in ownership via acquisitions (involving the purchase of one firm by another), mergers between willing partners and take-overs of an unwilling partner in the same industry. Internal growth of firms and exit from the industry also increase industrial concentration. Economic theories which attempt to explain mergers (and acquisitions and take-overs) involving firms producing the same types of output fall into two main categories. Traditional theories emphasize the role of mergers in increasing market power, prices and profitability – fulfilling shareholders' objectives if accompanied by a rise in the share valuation. Traditional theories also point to the potential effects of increasing efficiency and decreasing costs via economies of large-scale production and synergism, whereby the output of the combined firm exceeds that of the two individual firms. Empirical evidence concerning mergers in the manufacturing sector (Jacquemin and Slade, 1989, p. 437) has, however, shown that mergers have often been followed by similar or decreasing levels of profitability, that the size of the merged firm has often exceeded that necessary for full exploitation of scale economies, and that efficiency has sometimes decreased.

Alternative theories argue that the main function of mergers is to decrease uncertainty and increase the firm's control over its environment (Aaronovitch and Sawyer, 1975; Newbould, 1970). In a context in which firms are unable to decrease the costs of rivalry via the strategy of restrictive agreements, mergers may enable them to do so, although expenditure on advertising, research and development may be maintained as a means of deterring entry into the industry. The increase in concentration brought about by the merger may, at the same time, raise the likelihood of inter-firm collusion. A further explanation of mergers emphasizes their role as a strategy for meeting the preferences of managers (Marris, 1964) whose priorities are to maximise the firm's growth and market share, decrease risk and increase barriers to entry (by merging with a firm producing a differentiated product), increase the market valuation of the firm and obtain the easier access to finance which is available to large firms (Prais, 1976). Mergers are generally a means of achieving these objectives more rapidly than would occur via internal growth or the exit of competitors from the market.

Conglomerate mergers between firms in different industries may also be explained in terms of their possible effects on profitability and in relation to managerial objectives. The first explanation notes the function of mergers in meeting shareholders' preferences, and is based on the premise that earnings by firms in different industries and countries are less likely to be positively correlated than earnings by firms in the same industry and country. Conglomerate mergers between firms in different industries will therefore result in a decrease in the variability of profits, decreasing the risk attached to the earnings of shareholders and increasing the share valuation. Lewellen (1971) showed that conglomerate mergers can raise the merged firm's credit limit and decrease the cost of capital, also resulting in an increase in the value of shares. A further motive for undertaking conglomerate mergers is as a means of maintaining profitability in the case of firms with products in declining markets (Weston and Mansinghka, 1971).

While generally increasing the values of the firm's sales and assets, conglomerate mergers do not always result in rising profitability and share valuation. Hence the second explanation of conglomerate mergers emphasizes their function of fulfilling managers' objectives of increasing growth, decreasing risk and providing greater earnings stability. Conglomerate mergers may not have any economic significance if the managers of the merged firm choose to maintain the pre-merger allocation of resources.

Vertical integration between firms at different stages of the production process is interesting in the context of the tourism industry, within which production almost invariably takes place in different geographical locations. Like horizontal integration, vertical integration can take place via acquisitions, mergers and take-overs, and a number of the motives for vertical integration are similar to those for horizontal integration. Important differences occur, however, because vertical integration involves input suppliers and output purchasers at different stages of the production process, so that such motives as the attainment of economies of large-scale production lose relevance.

Explanations of vertical integration have been discussed by authors including Casson (1987), Perry (1989) and Bote *et al.* (1989). One important category of motives involves the objective of decreasing uncertainty and the avoidance of such contractual problems as contract-breaking (Klein *et al.*, 1978). Vertical integration can help to reduce uncertainty about future demand (Carlton, 1979), aiding information acquisition and facilitating the provision of inputs at known prices (Arrow, 1975; Oi and Hurter, 1965). A second important motive for vertical integration concerns improved synchronisation of operations, and a third involves increasing market power (Hymer, 1976). Overall, integration decreases the transactions costs which would occur if 'arm's length' contracts were made between firms under separate ownership (Coase, 1937). Foreign direct investment by multinational enterprises is a special case of vertical or horizontal integration across space, where the growth of multinational enterprises is underpinned by their ability to exploit proprietary knowledge, decrease transactions costs and increase quality.

Uncertainty about future demand is one of the most important characteristics of the international tourism industry. Although integration of tour operators and travel agencies does not reduce the uncertainty associated with political shocks or declines in economic activity, it may assist tour operators to decrease the level of uncertainty associated with holiday sales by such means as travel agents' preferential sales of their holidays. Integration between tour operators and foreign travel agencies can aid the synchronisation of tourists' local transportation, accommodation and entertainments provision, and is also a means of increasing tour operators' sales in a context in which the tourism product, unlike the products of the primary or secondary sectors, cannot be exported. Integration with travel agencies in a range of countries diversifies demand and is likely to decrease instability in total revenue, since decreases in demand in one country may be offset by increases in demand in another. Increasing sales may enable tour operators to achieve economies of scale which could not be achieved by sales to the domestic market alone.

The advantages of integration may, however, be outweighed by the disadvantages. For example, integration in the form of ownership involves an increase in fixed costs, foreign investment risk, reduced flexibility and 'dulled incentives', whereby ownership links may tie a firm to a producer which becomes inefficient or suffers decreasing quality of output, dulling the incentive for the firm to seek alternative producers. Vertical integration, particularly in the form of ownership, can also act as an exit barrier (Harrigan, 1985), hindering the firm from switching to the provision of an alternative product in such circumstances as a fall in the demand for an existing product, for example a particular tourist destination.

The structure of firms in the UK and Spanish tourism industries

This section will outline the ownership structure of the firms with the greatest market shares in the tourism industries in the UK and Spain; possible explanations of the changes in concentration and vertical integration which have occurred will be discussed in the following sections. The structure of firms in the UK and Spanish tourism industries is of interest, given the countries' positions as the most important tourist origin and destination countries for package holidays within the EC (Secretaría General de Turismo, 1989a). In 1987 out of a total of approximately 11 million package holidays in Spain, the UK was the source of 4.6 million, compared with 2.9 million from Germany. Spain is the most important destination for package holidays abroad organised by European tour operators, and holidays in Spain constituted approximately one-third of all package holidays abroad. Spain is also a growing origin market and between 1985 and 1988 the number of Spanish tourists and visitors abroad increased from 15.2 million to 23.3 million, while their expenditure rose from $1000 million to $3080 million at current prices (Secretaría General de Turismo, 1986; 1989b). In 1987 Spaniards purchased 2.9 million package holidays, of which 1.2 million were spent outside Spain (SGT, 1989a).

The UK tourism industry

The composition of the UK tourism industry has changed considerably over time and the structure of the major firms within the UK tourism industry varies greatly, as is illustrated by Table 4.1. For the purpose of identifying some of the main changes which have occurred and also for comparison with the data available for Spain, the information is provided for April 1988 and important changes which occurred subsequently are discussed. Table 4.1 concentrates on cases where one production activity is a subsidiary of or jointly owned with another, but does not include vertical integration in the form of contractual relationships, which are considered later.

British Airways and the International Thomson Organisation (now Thomson Corporation) are examples of firms embodying tour operators, travel agents, airlines and, in the case of British Airways, hotel chains. Cosmos is a smaller, independently owned tour operator which is under joint ownership with Monarch airline. Dan Air, owned in 1988 by Davies and Newman Holdings

71

Table 4.1 The structure of major companies in the United Kingdom tourism industry, 1988*

Parent company	International Thomson Organisation Ltd (Canada) (Communications)	International Leisure Group plc	Bass plc (Brewer)	British Airways plc (Scheduled Airline)	Sunmed (Tour Operator)	Cosmos (Tour Operator)	Owners Abroad Group plc (Tour Operator and Airline Seat Broker)	Midland Bank	National Freight Corporation (Road Freight)	Hogg Robinson plc (Finance & Property Services, Travel, Transport)	American Express (Bank)
Travel agency	Lunn Poly Ltd		Horizon Travel Centres Ltd	British Airways Holidays Ltd				Thomas Cook Ltd	Pickfords Travel Service Ltd	Hogg Robinson Ltd	American Express
Tour operator	Portland Holidays Ltd Skytours Ltd Thomson Holidays Ltd	Club 18-30 Ltd Global of London (Tours & Travel) Ltd Intasun España SA (Spain) Intasun Holidays Ltd Lancaster Holidays Ltd School Plan Tours Ltd	Blue Sky Holiday (International) Ltd, Horizon Holidays Ltd OSL Wings	Alta Holidays Ltd - Speedbird Overseas Air Travel Ltd - Poundstretcher - Dollarstretcher	Go Greek Go Turkey Go Ski Redwing (50% owned by Sunmed & 50% owned by British Airways) - Enterprise - Flair - Martin Rooks - Sovereign	Cosmos	Arrowsmith Ltd Falcon Leisure Group Ltd Owners Abroad Ltd Tjaereborg Ltd	Thomas Cook Ltd, Compass Tours Ltd Inter-Church Travel Ltd Rankin Kuhn Travel Ltd			
Transportation company	Britannia Airways Ltd (charter airline)	Air Europe Ltd (charter airline)	Orion Airways Ltd (charter airline)	British Airtours Ltd (charter airline) British Caledonian Airways (scheduled airline)		Monarch (charter airline)	Air 2000 Ltd (charter airline)				
Hotel chain			Bass Horizon Hotels Ltd, Bass Hotels and Holidays (UK-Crest Hotels) Holiday Inn Hotels Pontinental Española	Sovereign Group Hotels Ltd Kenya Safari Lodges & Hotels Ltd (A) Pegasus Hotels of Jamaica Ltd (A) Penta Hotels N.V. (Netherlands) (A) Sun Resorts Ltd (Mauritius)(A)							

* Important changes which occurred subsequently are discussed in the text. (A) = Associate firm. Source: Direct interviews; *Who Owns Whom 1988*, Dun & Bradstreet International.

(shipbrokers), and Pickfords Travel agents (owned by the National Freight Corporation until 1991, with subsequent ownership of business travel operations by Wagons Lits) are examples of participation in the tourism industry by major transportation firms. Such firms, along with Thomson, have the potential to offset decreases in revenue from tourism by revenue from non-tourism activities. Thomas Cook, Hogg Robinson and American Express illustrate links between tourism firms and the financial sector, and these travel agencies obtain a considerable amount of their revenue from business as well as holiday tourism. Since a substantial proportion of the transportation of their clients is undertaken by scheduled airlines, their incentive to form ownership linkages with charter airlines or coach companies is lower than that of agents dealing mainly in holiday tourism. The vertical composition of the major firms within the tourism industry in the UK thus ranges from specialization by firms in one form of tourism activity to firms embodying travel agencies, tour operators, transportation companies and hotel chains, providing the main range of tourism services.

A particularly important feature of the tourism industry during the 1980s was a high degree of instability in the form of ownership changes, entry into and exit from the industry. This was possible because of the relatively low costs of entry and low non-recoverable (sunk) costs. Barriers to entry into and exit from the industry were therefore low. Bass is an example of a major company which chose to invest in the industry and, 16 months later, in 1989, to sell its travel agencies and tour operators, as well as its charter airline to Thomson. A second major company, the International Leisure Group (ILG), went out of business during the 1991 recession and Gulf War. The Sunmed group merged with British Airways' unprofitable holiday companies in 1987 to form Redwing Holidays, half owned by Sunmed and half owned by BA, and sold to the Owners Abroad Group at the beginning of the 1990s.

In the airline sector, British Island Airways, Paramount Airways and Novair ceased operating at the beginning of the 1990s whereas Air 2000, belonging to the Owners Abroad Group, the second largest UK tour operator after the collapse of ILG, experienced rapid growth. Airtours, the third largest tour operator in 1991, established its own airline in the same year. Sheldon (1986) designated the international tour operator sector a contestable market (see Baumol, 1982; Gilbert, 1989, pp. 526-8), defined as a market in which equally efficient entrants are unable to set price and output combinations which provide sustained profits. The charter airline sector, with its highly competitive conditions, also demonstrates many of the characteristics of a contestable market.

The Spanish tourism industry

The structure of major firms within the tourism industry in Spain, also discussed by Bote *et al.* (1991), is indicated in Table 4.2; ownership linkages between tour operators, travel agencies, airlines and hotels in Spain and other countries are discussed in the following section. The degree of horizontal and vertical ownership has increased over time as Wagons Lits, together with the Banco Bilbao Vizcaya, purchased Viajes Ecuador in 1990. Such firms as Wagons Lits and Barceló now include travel agencies, tour operators, a hotel chain and, in the case of Wagons Lits, a transportation company. The association OTA

Table 4.2   The structure of major companies in the Spanish tourism industry, 1988*

Parent company/ Association	Meliá (1)	Viajes Ecuador	Viajes Iberia	Trapsa	Wagons Lits	VECISA	Barceló	Ultramar Express	Julia	OTA
Travel agency				Viajes Mas			Viajes Interopa Viajes Valdés		Central de Viajes	
Travel agency /Tour operator	Euroair Eurotour Tour Plan Viajes Meliá	Iberotour Viajes Ecuador Viajes Touring Club	Cyrasa Viajes Iberia	Libertur Viajes Internacional Expreso Viajes Marsans	Viajes Intersol Wagons Lits	Viajes El Corte Inglés	Viajes Barceló	Ambassador Expomundo Viajes Ultramar Express		
Tour operator			Iberojet	Trapsatur			Turavia		Viajes Julia	Central de Cruceros Club de Vacaciones Iberrail Pullmantur Tiempo Libre
Transportation company			Iberbus Mallorcabus	Spanair Universair	Wagons Lits				Autocares Julia	Trans-Mediterránea (Cruiseline) Spantax (2) (charter airline) RENFE (railway) Travel Bus Iberia (scheduled airline)
Hotel chain					Hoteles Pullman		Hoteles Hispanos	Iberotel		

* Important changes which occurred subsequently are discussed in the text.
(1) Travel agencies/tour operators acquired by SASEA and Interpart Holding (Comfinance), and hotel chain acquired by hotel chain Sol in 1987.
(2) Ceased operating in 1988.
Source: Direct interviews; *Directorio de Sociedades, Consejeros y Directivos*, INGRESA, 1989; *Fomento de la Producción*, 1989; *La Guía de Agencias de Viajes 1988, 1989*; Secretaría General de Turismo, 1988, 1989c.

(Operadores Turísticos Asociados) is unusual, having been established by the five mixed travel agencies and tour operators Viajes Ecuador, Marsans, Meliá, VIE and Wagons Lits, in collaboration with the transportation firms Iberia (scheduled airline), Spantax (charter airline), RENFE (railway), Travel Bus (coach) and Transmediterránea (cruise line). The tour operators which belong to OTA collaborate in such areas as marketing and specialise in different types of transportation. Iberia, Marsans, Meliá and Wagons Lits/Ecuador continued to collaborate via OTA at the beginning of the 1990s, although competition between them has increased.

Variations in the structures of the tourism industry between countries are associated with differences in national regulations. In Spain, for example, in addition to travel agencies and tour operators, there are 'mixed' travel agencies and tour operators, arising from the existence of regulations which allocate the three related types of licence. Although, as in the UK, tour operators in Spain are not permitted to sell directly to the public, mixed travel agencies and tour operators may do so. Thus there is greater overlap between the operations of these types of Spanish intermediaries than occurs in the UK. National regulations in other European countries are also associated with differences in operating functions; for example, travel agencies in Italy are permitted to operate as tour operators and vice versa.

As in the UK, there is conglomerate participation in the tourism industry in Spain. For example, the 'mixed' travel agency and tour operator Viajes El Corte Inglés (VECISA) is owned by the Corte Inglés chain of department stores. However, whereas the majority of the largest travel agencies and tour operators in the UK are part of groups which have considerable involvement in activities other than tourism, a minority of those in Spain formed part of firms whose main activity was other than tourism in 1990. Some common ownership of major tour operators, travel agencies, department stores and firms in the financial sector occurs in Germany, where the major tour operators, International Tourist Services (ITS), NUR Touristic and Touristik Union International (TUI) are totally or partially owned by major department stores in which the three major banks have a shareholding, the stores selling the tour operators' holidays (Drexl and Agel, 1987).

Some cross-country comparisons of the tourism industry

The vertical integration in the form of common ownership of tour operators and charter airlines which occurs in the UK and Spain differs from the case of Germany, where there is greater use of flights provided by scheduled airlines, with the exception of the tour operator holding company LTU Touristik (LTT), established in 1986 by the airline company Luft Transport Unternehmen (LTU). There is some common ownership of German tour operators and hotel chains. In Italy, the state airline Alitalia has a 65 per cent shareholding in the tour operator Italiatour SpA and the Ferrovia Dello Stato (Italian State Railway) has a 97 per cent holding in the country's largest travel agency, Compagnia Italiana Turismo (Economist Intelligence Unit, 1990). However, there are few ownership ties with the fragmented Italian hotel sector. Within the tourism industry in France there is some common ownership of tour operators, transport companies and accommodation, for example, in 1991, of Nouvelles Frontières, Air Corse and accommodation in France, Greece, Senegal and Tunisia, and of Club Méditerranée and Air Liberté and Minerve charter airlines. Air France owns the tour operators Sotair and Jet Tour and the hotel chain Société des Hotels Méridien.

Comparison of the ownership structures of the tourism industries in different European countries indicates both similarities and differences. In all the countries considered there are large firms characterised by ownership of activities which, together, range across most or all of the production chain, and there is also conglomerate participation in the industry. However there appears to be more common ownership of tour operators, travel agencies and domestic hotel chains in Spain than in the other countries, probably owing to the relatively low past demand by Spaniards for holidays abroad. The UK tourism industry has been characterised by a relatively high level of competition between firms in the industry in the context of both growth and decline in demand, together with a high level of entry into and exit from the industry. The more 'immature' Spanish tourism industry has experienced a high growth of demand and collaboration between the major tour operators and travel agents. Major tour operators and travel agents in all the countries considered have engaged in some investment in travel agencies abroad.

Foreign investment in the tourism industry

Foreign direct investment, resulting in the total or partial ownership of production activities abroad, is a special case of vertical or horizontal integration. The increasing internationalization of the tourism industry has received little attention in the literature to date, in contrast to the large volume of research on multinational involvement in the manufacturing sector. The following discussion will concentrate on foreign investment in the tourism industry in Spain, since Spain was the main west European destination for foreign investment inflows in the years prior to and following its EC membership. There is, however, considerable foreign involvement in the tourism industry in many countries. For example, foreign-based companies operating in the UK include Thomson Corporation (Canada), American Express and the Carlson Travel group (United States)(which purchased AT Mays and WH Smith's travel agencies in 1990 and 1991 respectively) and Cosmos (established by residents of Switzerland). Of the three largest travel agencies in Italy, two, Nouvelles Frontières and Wagons Lits, were French and Franco-Belgian respectively in 1991. The tourism industries in many developing countries are also characterised by foreign investment, the hotel sector in Kenya, discussed by Sinclair in Chapter 10, being but one example. The German charter airline, LTU, and Club Méditerranée also aim to invest in holiday camps in the Mediterranean and Caribbean, via a joint venture in which club Méditerranée will build and manage the camps and LTU will organise the marketing and transport.

Foreign investment in travel agencies and tour operators in Spain has occurred mainly for the purpose of gaining a share of the Spanish market and providing incoming tourists with reliable reception agents. The latter meet foreign tour operators' clients upon their arrival in Spain, organise local transportation and entertainments, and provide return travel to the airport. For example, Thomson established Viajes Cresta for airport transfer organisation and sales of excursions in Spain. Interviews with members of major firms in the Spanish tourism industry indicate that inward investment has also taken place with the objective of gaining a share of the growing Spanish holiday market. Examples of foreign investment include the German firm TUI's 77 per cent shareholding and the Holland International Travel Group's 10 per cent holding in the travel agency and tour operator Ultramar Express, and NUR Touristik's 25 per cent holding in Viajes Iberia. American Express, Nouvelles Frontières and Kuoni are examples of American, French and Swiss firms which have established travel agencies and tour operators in Spain.

Foreign investment has been particularly important in the largest travel agencies and tour operators in Spain. The Franco-Belgian Wagons Lits' 70 per cent investment holding in Viajes Ecuador created the largest travel agency and tour operator in Spain, and the acquisition of Meliá's travel agencies and tour operators by SASEA and Interpart Holding (Comfinance) with Italian capital, means that the second largest travel agency and tour operator also has majority foreign ownership. Among the nine most important travel agencies and tour operators in Spain in 1990, five (Wagons Lits/Ecuador, Meliá, Viajes Iberia and Ultramar Express) had foreign investment participation. Major companies which had total or partial ownership of hotel chains in Spain in 1990 include the UK's Trust House Forte, Bass (Holiday Inn) and the Ladbroke Group (Hilton International), the French groups Accor (Novotel) and Hotels Concorde, the German Maritim Hotels and TUI (Iberotel, Riu Hotels), and the Japanese leisure conglomerate Seibu Saison and Scandinavian Airlines System (Inter-Continental). Some of the most important travel agents and tour operators in Spain have, however, also engaged in investment outside Spain, examples being Wagons Lits'/Ecuador's and Trapsa's travel agencies in London, and Viajes Iberia's establishment of travel agencies and tour operators in London and the United States in collaboration with the UK firm International Group Service.

Charter airlines in Spain are characterised by considerable foreign ownership, as is shown in Table 4.3. For example, in 1989 Spanair embodied 49 per cent ownership by Scandinavian Airlines System (SAS), Viva Air included a 48 per cent holding by Lufthansa, and LTE International Airways involved 25 per cent ownership by the German airline company LTU. Nort-Jet has minority foreign ownership by Air Charter, which is part of the Air France group. The charter airline sector in Spain also includes considerable ownership by banks and savings banks (Caja Postal de Ahorros).

The tourism industry in Spain has thus been characterised by large inflows of foreign investment, as has occurred in other sectors of the Spanish economy. Foreign direct investment involving ownership of tour operators and travel agencies is likely to result from the investing firm's desire to decrease uncertainty and increase its control over the tourist destination environment, as well as to increase its sales in the growing Spanish market. Horizontal integration between charter airlines has the advantage of providing additional landing and take-off slots at airports. In the case of horizontal integration between hotels, foreign multinational hotel chains are able to take advantage of their specialist knowledge of hotel operations as well as to obtain greater overall earnings stability and a lower level of risk by spreading their investment portfolios across a wider range of countries (Sharpe, 1970). The extent of common vertical ownership of non-

Table 4.3 Spanish charter airlines, 1989

Airline	Number of employees	Sales value[1]	Capital value[1]	Market share[2]	Main Shareholders
Air Europa	836	21,500	600	35.7	BBV, Inservex & Bancaya (50%), Banco Crédito Balear e Inmobiliaria Mallorquina (25%), ILT (25%)
Spanair	370	11,283	750	10.0	Viajes Marsans (51%), SAS Leisure (49%)
Viva Air	379	8,000	1,750	4.9	Iberia (48%), Lufthansa (48%), Pankmer (2%) Cafivacasa (2%)
LAC (Linéas Aéreas Canarias)	190	7,500	1,350	8.8	Grupo Armas/Martinón (80%), Sadicán (5%) various individuals and tour operators (15%)
LTE International Airways	272	7,000	500	10.5	LTU (25%), Pedro Montaner e Iñigo Cotoner (75%)
Universair	150	4,720	617	2.2	Doliga (50%), Trapsa (50%)
Oasis International Airlines	138	4,500	400/600	2.2	Marenna (71%) Segatur (9%), Proturin (7%), Columbus (13%)
Air Sur (Canáfrica)	90	3,000	130	0.3	Private Spanish groups (100%)
Nort-Jet	180	3,000	500	n.a.	Air Charter (20%), Caja P. Ahorros Vitoria (10%), Caja P. Ahorros Alava (10%), others (60%)
Futura	150	-	600	n.a.	Aer Lingus (25%), Banco de Santander y Certidesa (60%), the Spanish management group Belton Air (15%)

[1]Million pesetas; [2]Percentage of passengers x kilometres flown by all Spanish charter airlines in 1988; figures for other Spanish charter airlines in 1988 are: Aviaco 2.4%; Hispania 20.4%; Spantax (subsequently ceased operating) 2.6%   n.a. = not available
Source: Casamayor, 1990; Dirección General de Aviación Civil, 1988.

Spanish tour operators and travel agencies and Spanish charter airlines and hotels decreased considerably with Bass and ILG's exit from the tourism industry. The low level of common ownership throughout the production chain may result from tour operators' and travel agents' desire to avoid the fixed costs associated with investment in hotels, in particular, and to preserve their flexibility to vary their portfolios of destinations in the short term.

Concentration in the tourism industry

The degree of concentration within the travel agency and tour operator sectors of the UK tourism industry increased considerably over a short period of time, as is demonstrated in Tables 4.4 and 4.5. The market share of the top five tour operators in the UK rose from 49.5 per cent in 1983 to 61 per cent in 1986 and 77.5 per cent in 1989, declining to 72 per cent in 1990. Whereas in 1986, the top five travel agencies owned 21.4 per cent of all Association of British Travel Agents (ABTA) outlets (Saltmarsh, 1986) and sold approximately 32 per cent of all summer holidays, by 1990 they sold 47 per cent. The percentage of all charter passengers carried by the top five charter airlines was 71.8 per cent in 1986, and remained high and fairly stable during the late 1980s, being 74.5 per cent in 1990, as is shown in Table 4.6.

Table 4.4 Major tour operators in the UK, 1983-1990

Tour operators	Market Shares							
	1983	1984	1985	1986	1987	1988	1989	1990
Thomson	17.0	19.0	20.0	27.5	31.5	33.0	38.0	30.5
International Leisure Group	11.0	13.0	15.5	18.0	18.0	19.0	19.0	16.5
Horizon Travel Group	6.0	6.5	5.0	7.0	8.0	6.0	–	–
British Airways (Redwing)	10.0	7.0	6.5	5.5	4.5	5.0	7.0	*
Cosmos	5.5	5.5	4.0	3.0	*	*	*	3.0
Owners Abroad Group	*	*	*	*	3.0	6.0	7.5	15.0**
Airtours	*	*	*	*	*	*	6.0	7.5
Percentage controlled by top five firms	49.5	51.0	51.0	61.0	65.0	69.0	77.5	72.0

*   Not in top five in these years
**   Includes Redwing
Source: *Annual Report and Accounts*, Thomson Travel Group

Table 4.5   Major travel agencies in the UK, 1986-1990

Travel agent	Estimates of summer market shares				
	1986	1987	1988	1989	1990
Thomas Cook	10.0	11.5	11.0	10.0	11.0
Pickfords Travel	6.0	7.0	8.0	7.0	7.0
Hogg Robinson	4.0	4.5	4.0	4.0	5.0
Lunn Poly (Thomson)	8.0	10.5	15.0	21.0	20.0
AT Mays	4.0	3.5	5.0	5.0	4.0
Percentage controlled by the top five firms	32.0	37.0	43.0	47.0	47.0

Source: *Annual Report and Accounts*, Thomson Travel Group

Table 4.6   UK charter airlines, 1986-1990

Charter airline	Percentage of charter passengers carried				
	1986	1987	1988	1989	1990
Britannia Airways (Thomson)	25.1	24.8	26.7	29.1*	25.8
Dan Air (Davies & Newman)	19.1	18.7	16.3	17.3	18.4
British Airtours/British Airways	11.8	11.8	7.7**	6.4**	5.5
Monarch Airlines (Cosmos)	9.5	9.5	9.9	9.3	11.3
Orion Air (Bass)	6.3	5.9	4.9	-	-
Air Europe (ILG)	5.3	5.9	7.8	8.8	10.2
Cal Air/Novair (Rank Organisation)	4.4	4.1	3.5	2.8	-
British Island Airways	n.a.	n.a.	3.8	4.0	-
Air 2000 (Owners Abroad Group)	n.a.	n.a.	3.6	5.8	8.8
Total:	81.5	80.7	84.2	83.5	80.0
Percentage controlled by the top five firms	71.8	70.7	68.4	70.9	74.5

* Includes Orion Air; ** Includes Caledonian Airways.

n.a. = not available

Source: *Annual Report and Accounts*, Thomson Travel Group

Although the degree of concentration of the travel agency sector is lower than that of the tour operator sector, it has increased via exits from the industry in the form of bankruptcies, internal growth and horizontal integration, mainly in the form of acquisitions. Carlson Travel's acquisition of AT Mays, WH Smith's travel agencies and negotiations to acquire Pickfords retail travel operations is but one example of ongoing concentration in the travel agency sector. The massive increase in concentration in the tour operator sector occurred in the context of the 1986-1987 'price war' between the major tour operators, the 1989 losses and the 1990-1991 recession. The largest tour operators also increased their market shares in the UK via acquisitions, mergers, internal growth and bankruptcies. The initially lower level of concentration is likely to have inhibited collusive agreements between firms within the industry, and acquisitions and mergers constituted attempts to increase growth and to decrease the high level of uncertainty associated with the actions of competitors. Thomson is an example of a company which appears to have pursued a strategy of maximising growth and market share while decreasing uncertainty by preventing rivals, for example the former ILG, from significant growth via acquisitions. Some horizontal integration occurred in the airline sector during the 1980s as Thomson purchased Orion Airways from Bass and British Airways purchased British Caledonian. Further concentration in the European airline sector is likely in the context of EC air liberalization (Wheatcroft and Lipman, 1990).

In Spain, in 1988, there were 1659 travel agencies, 210 'mixed' travel agencies and tour operators and 36 tour operators. The mean capital value of the mixed travel agencies and tour operators was estimated to be 26.6 million pesetas in 1986, compared with capital values of 16.0 million pesetas for tour operators and 6.7 million pesetas for travel agencies (Secretaría General de Turismo, 1987). Within each group there are considerable variations between the scale of operations of a small number of large firms and a large number of small firms, as is shown by Table 4.7. For example, of all tour operators, 10 per cent employed over 100 people compared with 85 per cent who employed less than 50. Of the mixed travel agencies and tour operators, 21 per cent employed over 100 and 83 per cent employed less than 50, and the corresponding figures for travel agencies were 1 per cent and 98 per cent.

Table 4.7 Tour operators and travel agencies in Spain, 1986

	Tour operators	Tour operators/ travel agencies	Travel agencies
Mean capital value [1]	16.0	26.6	6.7
Mean number of employees	56	60	8
Percentage of firms with:			
over 100 employees	10	21	1
50-100 employees	5	6	1
less than 50 employees	85	83	98

(1) Million pesetas.
Source: *La Encuesta sobre la Estructura Económico-Financiera de las Agencias de Viajes*, Secretaría General de Turismo, 1987.

The nine largest travel agencies and tour operators, shown in Table 4.8, had an estimated sales value approaching 262,000 million pesetas in 1988. They also owned approximately 15 per cent of all sales outlets, each with a considerably greater than average sales value, and 12 of the 14 most important holiday brand names. The main charter airlines based in Spain in 1989 are shown in Table 4.3. The top five firms accounted for 85 per cent of all domestic and international passenger kilometres flown with Spanish charter airlines in 1988.

Table 4.8 Major tour operators and travel agencies in Spain, 1988

Parent Company	Sales value [1]	No. employees	No. sales outlets	No. brands
Meliá	62,321	1,725	101	3
Viajes Ecuador	40,351	986	96	3
Viajes Iberia	29,300	1,130	44	1
Trapsa	26,270	729	97	17
Wagons Lits	25,030	3,045	81	6
VECISA	24,870	500	47	3
Barceló	23,950	1,038	55	4
Ultramar Express	20,455	483	51	4
Julia	9,400	225	20	2
Total	261,947	9,861	592	43

(1) Million pesetas
Source: Own calculations based on: *Directorio de Sociedades, Consejeros y Directivos*, INGRESA, *1989; Fomento de la Producción*, 1989; *La Guía de Agencias de Viajes 1988, 1989*, Secretaría General de Turismo, 1988, 1989c.

Although the data for the UK and Spain are not strictly comparable, available data indicate that the level of concentration in the travel agency and tour operator sectors in the UK has been higher than that in comparable sectors in Spain, probably owing to the more mature stage of development of the UK tourism industry. Moreover, it has been argued that an industrial structure consisting of a small number of large firms and a large number of small firms tends to occur, if for no other reason than that of random growth (Gibrat, 1931). Collaborative agreements between travel agents and tour operators in Spain have enabled some economies of scale to be achieved.

The phenomenon of increasing concentration in the tour operator and travel agency sectors in the UK and Spain is paralleled in some other European countries. In France three groups, Havas, Selectour and Wagons Lits, owned approximately 25 per cent of all travel agencies in 1988, and the tour operators Club Méditerranée, FRAM, Nouvelles Frontières and Sotair sold 56 per cent of all package holidays (Cazes, 1989; Leguevaques, 1989; Morandy, 1988). The German tour operators LTT, ITS, NUR Touristic and TUI sold 55 per cent of package holidays purchased by Germans in 1987 (Moran? four largest tour operators, Alpitour, Valtur, Aviatour and for over 25 per cent of package holidays sold in 1988 (largest travel agencies, the federally owned Compagnia I' Lits and Nouvelles Frontières, had a total market shar 1989. However, Alitalia and its subsidiary airlines acc 90 per cent of the internal air market.

Vertical ownership and contractual arrangements in the tourism industry

The tourism industries in the UK and Spain include a small number of large tour operators and travel agency chains and a large number of small firms. Charter airlines also vary between those with large fleets and the greater number with smaller fleets. The vertical composition of large firms in the tourism industry in the UK appears most commonly to entail travel agencies, tour operators and airlines, as was shown in Table 4.1, while most small firms specialise as travel agencies or tour operators. In the case of major firms in the Spanish tourism industry, included in Table 4.2, there is more common ownership of travel agencies, tour operators, hotel chains and companies providing road and rail transport, owing to Spain's geographical position within the European mainland and its relatively low level of income in the past.

Common ownership of major tour operators and transportation companies can decrease uncertainty about the future supply of the tour operator's inputs and demand for the transport company's output. By facilitating the purchase (sale) of seats, vertical ownership provides each activity within the production sequence with a source of inputs (market for output) and increased information about its associated expenditure (revenue). This is particularly advantageous in the case of airline seats, where the cost of the seat can constitute approximately 40 per cent of the total price of the holiday (Instituto de Estudios Turísticos/Consultores Turísticos, 1987). Common ownership provides tour operators with transportation during periods of high demand, and enables transport companies to raise their load factor, increasing the probability that they will cover their fixed as well as their variable costs during periods of low demand.

Airlines are also interested in decreasing the risk of shortfalls in demand by selling seats to a variety of clients, and large tour operators can negotiate favourable contractual arrangements with airlines under separate ownership. Such contractual arrangements vary greatly but can involve, for example, payment of a 5–15 per cent deposit upon agreement of the contract, and payment of the outstanding amount as late as two to three weeks before the flight. Thus tour operators which are commonly owned with a charter airline do not use the airline's entire annual capacity, but may use, for example, of the order of 60–80 per cent in a period of low demand. Both tour operators and airlines also negotiate contracts with separately owned firms.

Common ownership of tour operators and travel agencies occurs mainly within national boundaries, although there has been some investment in travel agencies abroad. Tour operators can avoid the fixed costs associated with ownership of travel agencies by paying travel agents commission for every

...ay sold. Moreover, large tour operators can ensure rapid receipt of holiday ...yments via a system of computerised direct debit, as was shown by Bennett and ...adburn in Chapter 3 of this book. Synchronisation of arrangements for tour operators' clients in destination countries is provided both by contracts with locally owned agents and by foreign ownership. Large tour operators may make agreements with travel agents which, even in the absence of ownership, result in preferential sales of their output. Such agreements can also be used to maintain their market power and profits via the imposition of barriers to entry into the market by competitors. For example, the International Leisure Group's attempt to enter the German market via the establishment of a local tour operator, Intasun Reisen, appeared to have been blocked by agreements between the major German tour operators and travel agents which precluded the sale by the agents of holidays supplied by the tour operators' main competitors, including Intasun Reisen.

There is little ownership by tour operators and travel agencies of hotel chains abroad, although the International Leisure Group owned the hotel chain Hoteles Globales in Spain, arguing that the chain supplied the minimum quantity of accommodation it required. A variety of reasons account for the general predominance of contracts rather than ownership, and include the high fixed costs which such ownership would involve. Decreases in flexibility to alter holiday supply and high foreign investment risk in a context of uncertainty about the future level of demand for different destinations are also relevant, as is uncertainty about the prices of accommodation in different destination countries over the long run. Tour operators can obtain accommodation via contracts with hoteliers which involve the tour operators in little or no advance expenditure, as also occurs for holidays in non-European destinations (Sinclair *et al.*, forthcoming). Most contracts are short term, made approximately twelve months in advance of the tourists' arrival, and can be changed from one year to the next. The prices which tour operators negotiate with hoteliers are often between 20 and 50 per cent below those charged to tourists on individually organised holidays. There is also a 'release back' system, whereby major tour operators can avoid payment for rooms by notifying the hotelier up to seven days prior to the tourists' arrival that they will require fewer beds than the number contracted.

Thus tour operators can contract an adequate supply of accommodation and catering well in advance of the tourists' arrival, and pay hoteliers upon receipt of an invoice, approximately one month after the tourists' departure. Over-booking problems sometimes arise as hoteliers contract over 100 per cent of their capacity in an attempt to avoid unused beds. Tour operators can make use of a variety of contractual arrangements with the aim of avoiding such problems. For example, Thomson's contractual arrangements with hotels in Spain have included an agreement whereby the Medplaya hotel chain has reserved 90 per cent of its bed-spaces for Thomson's clients, receives late bookings from Thomson and has not allocated bed spaces to any other UK tour operators. These types of contractual arrangements may be classified as 'vertical restraints', since payment to the hotelier depends upon variables other than the quantity of bed-nights purchased, (as well as on the latter) (Katz, 1989). Thomson has also made a small number of three year contracts with the owners of self-catering flats, for which there has been growing demand, and has occasionally provided advance payments to permit the owners to undertake improvements in the quality of the accommodation. Longer term contracts (of three to five years) are more common in contexts of high demand or excess demand for particular types of accommodation.

The quality of holiday provision was acknowledged by tour operators to be of considerably more importance by the end of the 1980s. Ownership of accommodation in a destination area is one means of guaranteeing known standards of provision as well as a known bed stock. However, ownership is accompanied by reduced flexibility in the form of pressure to use the accommodation, even if alternative provision is of better quality and/or cheaper. Therefore tour operators have generally pursued strategies for monitoring the quality of accommodation and catering provision which are more cost-effective than that of ownership. Contracts between tour operators and hoteliers may include specified standards of provision, such as apply to Thomson's 'Sun Hotels', and tour operators may also ask tourists to complete questionnaires at the end of their holidays. Tour operators engage in repeat business (via regular annual contracts) with a core of hotels of consistent quality, and the general absence of ownership of hotels has enabled major tour operators to decrease their use of smaller, older hotels which do not meet rising quality requirements.

Summary and conclusions

Generalisations concerning the similarities and differences between the tourism industries in European countries are impeded by the considerable changes which have accompanied the growth of international tourism in the recent past. The tourism industries of the UK and Spain, for example, were characterised by major changes in their composition and ownership structures during the 1980s. Concentration in the UK tour operator and travel agency sectors appears to be explained, at least in part, by theories which emphasize the maximisation of the firm's growth and market share and managerial preferences for lower levels of uncertainty. Acquisitions, mergers and collaborative agreements between some of the most important travel agents and tour operators in Spain have permitted the attainment of marketing and other economies, and traditional theories which point to increasing profitability and economies of scale may be relevant in this context. Further increases in the level of concentration among UK travel agencies and Spanish tour operators and travel agencies are likely, via internal growth, acquisitions, mergers, take-overs and exit from the industry.

The extent of ownership of vertically related activities by firms in the tourism industries of different European countries varies greatly, ranging from firms specializing in one sector to large, highly vertically integrated firms involving travel agencies, tour operators, transportation and hotels. Banks and savings banks appear to have significant involvement in the tourism industry, as was illustrated in Tables 4.1 and 4.3. There is considerable foreign ownership of major tourism firms in the UK and Spain, and the largest travel agencies and tour operators in both countries, and two of the three largest travel agencies in Italy, are part of companies whose headquarters are located abroad. However firms in all five countries considered have also invested in tourism enterprises abroad.

The relative importance of integration in the form of ownership and contractual relationships is a generally unexplored area within the literature on the tourism industry. It varies between different sectors of the tourism industry and is likely to vary according to differing macroeconomic contexts of high or low demand, and to changes in the distribution of demand between alternative destinations. Total or partial ownership involves the potential disadvantages of fixed costs, foreign investment risk, reduced flexibility and dulled incentives to search for more efficient sources of supply or more profitable markets. Large firms are able to cover the fixed costs of ownership and can limit foreign exchange risk by means of a low ratio of foreign to domestic ownership. Their strategy of contracting with firms under separate ownership, in addition to undertaking purchases from and/or sales to jointly owned activities, reduces the risk of inflexibility and dulled incentives. The strategy also enables them to decrease their uncertainty concerning the availability of inputs or the sale of output, while retaining the incentive to increase profitability by purchasing from or selling to firms under separate ownership.

Large firms thus take advantage of a variety of forms of integration, including ownership and contractual relationships. It is difficult for small firms, which are unable to meet the fixed costs associated with ownership, to challenge the large firms' dominant position in the market. Small firms can attempt to achieve economies of scale by specialising in particular activities and types of holiday or business tourism which do not involve high fixed costs of ownership. Small firms may also attempt to compensate for higher costs of production which result from less favourable contractual terms by specialising in new products, for example innovatory forms of 'green tourism', and/or in products for which there is an inelastic demand and for which high prices may be charged to particular market segments (a strategy of 'niche marketing', also discussed by Goodall and Bergsma in Chapter 5).

This chapter has drawn together recent evidence concerning the ownership structures of major firms in the tourism industry, the levels of concentration in different sectors and the types of vertical integration between them, and has suggested theories which are consistent with the main changes which have occurred. The chapter thus forms the necessary basis for further, more detailed research on the explanations and effects of horizontal and vertical integration in the tourism industry. Such research is important because of the effects of different forms of integration on, for example, the level of holiday output, the prices charged to consumers of tourism, the profits received by producers and the number of employees in the industry. The research could encompass the effects of firms' internal characteristics, for example different types of ownership structure and degrees of specialisation, as well as external variables including the proportion of sales outside the domestic market and the changes in national regulatory frameworks which occur as tourism regulations are aligned at the EC level.

Research on the relevance of non-traditional theories of integration as a means of decreasing uncertainty, as well as of meeting managerial preferences for maximising the firm's growth and market share and stabilising earnings, would be useful. Such research would be particularly apposite given the relative 'immaturity' and instability of the tourism industry. Exploration of the relationships between different forms of integration, profitability and risk is a further topic of interest. Although it is frequently difficult to measure the causes and consequences of such phenomena as persistent profitability, unobservable variables, as well as the dynamics of the process of competition, could be taken into account by using the reduced form of a structural model (Geroski and Jacquemin, 1988).

The research topics proposed are relevant to the attainment of a single European market for the tourism industry and firms' conduct within it. A single market implies the absence of barriers to inter-country purchases and sales, the elimination of preferential subsidies to national producers and the harmonization of taxation. In this context, purchases of inputs (for example transportation and accommodation) and final products (for example package holidays) would be made from the cheapest supplier of the product in question. 'Imperfections' in the market could, however, prevent this outcome from occurring. Monopolistic firms could supply a lower level of output (such as holidays) and charge higher prices than would occur within a competitive market. Monopolies could result from acquisitions, mergers or take-overs. The EC aims to avoid anti-competitive outcomes which could result from ownership integration by means of its competition policy which, in some cases, prevents the acquisition, merger or take-over from taking place.

This chapter has shown that integration can also occur in the form of contractual relationships, so that the coordination of economic activities and economic control can take place in the absence of common ownership. Some contractual terms can impede competition among holiday producers, for example contracts between travel agents and tour operators which involve preferential sales of the tour operator's holidays. It is more difficult to monitor contractual arrangements than integration in the form of ownership. However, the economic effects of contracts may be equally if not more important than those of ownership. Examination of all the different forms of integration within and between the tourism industries of different countries is thus a prerequisite for the formulation and implementation of policies designed to promote effective competition at the international level.

Acknowledgements

The authors would like to thank Stephen Page and Mike Stabler for helpful comments on this chapter. The support of the British Council and Spanish National Research Plan is gratefully acknowledged. The views expressed in the chapter are the sole responsibility of the authors.

References

Aaronovitch, S. and Sawyer, M. (1975) *Big Business*. Macmillan, London.
Arrow, K.J. (1975) Vertical integration and communication. *Bell Journal of Economics*, 6, 173–183.
Baumol, W.J. (1982) Contestable markets: an uprising in the theory of industry structure. *American Economic Review*, 72, 1–15.

Bote Gómez, V., Huescar, A. and Vogeler, C. (1991) Concentración e integración de las agencias de viajes españolas ante el Acta Unica Europea. *Papers de Turisme*, No.5, 5–43. Instituto Turístico Valenciano, Valencia.

Bote Gómez, V., Sinclair, M.T., Sutcliffe, C.M.S. and Valenzuela Rubio, M. (1989) Vertical integration in the British/Spanish tourism industry. In: *Leisure, Labour and Lifestyles: International Comparisons. Tourism and Leisure. Models and Theories*. Proceedings of the Leisure Studies Association 2nd International Conference, Conference Papers No. 39, Vol. 8, Leisure Studies Association, Eastbourne, pp. 80–96.

Buckley, P.J. (1987) Tourism - An economic transactions analysis. *Tourism Management*, 8, 190–204.

Bull, A. (1991) *The Economics of Travel and Tourism*. Pitman, Longman Cheshire, Melbourne.

Carlton, D.W. (1979) Vertical integration in competitive markets under uncertainty. *Journal of Industrial Economics*, 27, 189–209.

Casamayor, R. (1989) Un trozo de cielo. In: El País de los Negocios, *Diario El País*, Madrid, 21 January.

Casson, M.C. (1987) *The Firm and the Market*. Basil Blackwell, Oxford.

Cazes, G. (1989) *Le Tourisme International. Mirage ou Stratégie d'Avenir*. Hatier, Paris.

Coase, R.H. (1937) The nature of the firm. *Economica* (New Series), 4, 386–405.

Dirección General de Aviación Civil (1988) *Anuario Estadístico del Transporte Aéreo. España 1988*. Dirección General de Aviación Civil, Madrid.

Drexl, C. and Agel, P. (1987) Tour operators in West Germany: survey of the package tour market, the operators and how they sell. *Travel and Tourism Analyst*, May, 29–43.

Dun & Bradstreet International (1988-1990) *Who Owns Whom*. Dun & Bradstreet Ltd., High Wycombe.

Eadington, W.R. and Redman, M. (1991) Economics and tourism. *Annals of Tourism Research*, 18, 41–56.

Economist Intelligence Unit (1990) Travel and Tourism Analyst database. The travel and tourism industry in Italy. *Travel and Tourism Analyst*, No. 4, 74–8.

Fletcher, J.E. and Archer, B.H. (1991) The development and application of multiplier analysis. In: Cooper, C.P (ed.), *Progress in Tourism, Recreation and Hospitality Management*, Vol. 3. Belhaven, London.

Fomento de la Producción (1989) *España 25000*. Fomento de la Producción, Barcelona.

Geroski, P.A. and Jacquemin, A. (1988) The persistence of profits: a European comparison. *Economic Journal*, 98, 375–389.

Gibrat, R. (1931) *Les inégalités économiques*. Paris.

Gilbert, R.J. (1989) Mobility barriers and the value of incumbency. In: Schmalensee, R. and Willig, R.D. (eds) *Handbook of Industrial Organisation, Vol. 1*. North-Holland, Amsterdam, pp. 475–535.

Go, F. (1988) Key problems and prospects in the international hotel industry. *Travel and Tourism Analyst*, No. 1, 27–49.

Go, F. (1989) International hotel industry – capitalizing on change. *Tourism Management,* 10, 195–200.

Hall, D.H. (ed.) (1991) *Tourism, Eastern Europe and the Soviet Union.* Belhaven, London.

Harrigan, K.R. (1985) Exit barriers and vertical integration. *Academy of Management Journal,* 28, 686–97.

Hawkins, D. and Ritchie, J.R. Brent (eds) (1991) *World Travel and Tourism Review; Indicators, Trends and Forecasts. Vol. 1. 1991.* CAB International, Wallingford.

Hymer, S.H. (1976) *The International Operations of National Firms: A Study of Direct Investment.* MIT Press, Cambridge, Mass.

INGRESA (1989) *Directorio de Sociedades, Consejeros y Directivos.* INGRESA, Madrid.

Instituto de Estudios Turísticos/Consultores Turísticos S.A. (1987) El gasto turístico. Análisis del escandallo de los paquetes turísticos. Distribución por tipologías y nacionalidades. *Estudios Turísticos,* No. 93, 3–26.

Jacquemin, A. and Slade, M.E. (1989) Cartels, collusion and horizontal merger. In: Schmalensee, R. and Willig, R.D. (eds), *Handbook of Industrial Organization, Vol. 1.* North-Holland, Amsterdam, pp. 415–73.

Katz, M.L. (1989) Vertical contractual relations. In: Schmalensee, R. and Willig, R.D. (eds), *Handbook of Industrial Organization, Vol. 1.* North-Holland, Amsterdam, pp. 655–721.

Klein, B., Crawford, R.G. and Alchian, A.A. (1978) Vertical integration, appropriable rents and the competitive contracting process. *Journal of Law and Economics,* 21, 297–326.

Leguevaques, M. (1989) Les tour operators européens et la destination à France. In: *Collection Hotellerie et Tourisme.* Assemblée Permanente des Chambres de Commerce et d'Industrie, Centre d'Etude de la Commercialisation et de la Distribution, Paris.

Lewellen, W.G. (1971) A pure financial rationale for the conglomerate merger. *Journal of Finance,* Papers and Proceedings, 26, 521–37.

Marris, R. (1964) *The Economic Theory of 'Managerial' Capitalism.* Macmillan, London.

McGuffie, J. (1987) UK hotel industry: revival for the chains at home and abroad. *Travel and Tourism Analyst,* September, 15–31.

McVey, M. (1986) International hotel chains in Europe: survey of expansion plans as Europe is 'rediscovered'. *Travel and Tourism Analyst,* September, 3–23.

Morandy, G. (1988) Les tour operators en Europe. In: *Collection Analyses de Secteurs.* Eurostaf Dafsa, Paris.

Newbould, G. (1970) *Management and Merger Activity.* Guthstead, Liverpool.

Oi, W.Y. and Hurter, A.P. (1965) *Economics of Private Truck Transportation.* William C. Brown, Dubuque, Iowa.

Pearce, D. G. (1989) *Tourist Development.* Longman, Harlow.

Perry, M.K. (1989) Vertical integration: determinants and effects. In: Schmalensee, R. and Willig, R.D. (eds), *Handbook of Industrial Organization, Vol. 1.* North-Holland, Amsterdam, pp. 182–260.

Prais, S.J. (1976) *The Evolution of Giant Firms in Britain.* National Institute of Economic and Social Research, Economic and Social Studies, 30. Cambridge University Press, Cambridge.

Saltmarsh, G. (1986) Travel retailing in the UK: survey of the agents, their costs, markets and mergers. *Travel and Tourism Analyst*, September, 49–62.

Schmalensee, R. and Willig, R.D. (eds) (1989) *Handbook of Industrial Organization, Vols. 1 and 2.* North-Holland, Amsterdam.

Secretaría General de Turismo (1986, 1989b) *Anuario de Estadísticas de Turismo.* Ministerio de Transportes, Turismo y Comunicaciones, Madrid.

Secretaría General de Turismo (1987) *La Encuesta sobre la Estructura Económico-Financiera de las Agencias de Viajes.* Ministerio de Transportes, Turismo y Comunicaciones, Madrid.

Secretaría General de Turismo (1988, 1989c) *La Guía de Agencias de Viajes 1988, 1989.* Ministerio de Transportes, Turismo y Comunicaciones, Madrid.

Secretaría General de Turismo (1989a) *Plan de Marketing del Turismo.* Ministerio de Transportes, Turismo y Comunicaciones, Madrid.

Sharpe, W.F. (1970) *Portfolio Theory and Capital Markets.* McGraw-Hill, New York.

Sheldon, P.J. (1986) The tour operator industry: an analysis. *Annals of Tourism Research*, 13, 349–65.

Sheldon, P.J. (1990) A review of tourism expenditure research. In: Cooper, C.P. (ed.), *Progress in Tourism, Recreation and Hospitality Management*, Volume Two. Belhaven, London, pp. 28–49.

Sinclair, M.T. (1991) The economics of tourism. In: Cooper, C.P. (ed.), *Progress in Tourism, Recreation and Hospitality Management*, Vol. 3. Belhaven, London.

Sinclair, M.T., Alizadeh, P. and Atieno Adero Onunga, E. (forthcoming 1992) The structure of international tourism and tourism development in Kenya. In: Harrison, D. (ed.), *International Tourism and the Less Developed Countries.* Belhaven, London.

Thomson Travel Group (1986–1991) *Annual Report and Accounts.* Thomson Travel Group, London.

United Nations Centre on Transnational Corporations (1982) *Transnational Corporations in International Tourism.* Research project undertaken by J.H. Dunning and M. McQueen. UNCTC, New York.

Weston, J.F. and Mansinghka, S.K. (1971) Tests of the efficiency performance of conglomerate firms. *Journal of Finance*, 26, 919–36.

Wheatcroft, S. and Lipman, G. (1990) *European Liberalisation and World Air Transport.* Economist Intelligence Unit, London.

Williams, A.M. and Shaw, G. (eds) (1991) *Tourism and Economic Development. Western European Experiences*, 2nd edn. Belhaven, London.

Chapter 5

Tour Operators' Strategies: A Cross–Country Comparison

Brian Goodall and J. R. Bergsma

Tour operators

This chapter maintains the focus on the intermediaries in the tourism industry by both expanding on and illustrating the issues raised in the three previous chapters. First, it demonstrates, in the context of package skiing holidays, the application of the suggested conceptual framework of opportunity sets introduced in Chapter 2. Second, by examining the product as developed by the industry and the way it is marketed and promoted, it underpins the earlier analysis of the use of information technology (IT) and changing strategies of mass market tour operators. It indicates how such tour operators have responded to technical change, in particular their turning of the application of IT to their advantage by increasing the differentiation of the tourism product and segmentation of the market and facilitating flexibility, for example, late availability of package holidays. Accordingly it complements the discussion of the role of travel agents and IT in Chapter 3. Third, the chapter also illustrates, through the case study of United Kingdom and Dutch tour operators' strategies, the growing internationalisation of and concentration in the tourism industry examined in Chapter 4.

Tourists may buy each component – transport, accommodation and other services and activities – of a holiday separately. However, tour operators, in purchasing or reserving the separate components in bulk, not only act as wholesalers but, in combining these components into an inclusive tour, also become producers, since a new product, the inclusive tour or package holiday (PH) is created. Their success depends on their ability to organize and supply such holidays, selling them either directly or indirectly, through travel agents, to potential tourists.

Tour operators may be based in destination areas, i.e. inbound or incoming tour operators selling PHs to a given destination in many different (overseas) markets. Advantages, however, attach to a market location, so most tour operators are based in tourist-generating areas, i.e. outbound tour operators selling PHs to a variety of destinations in a single (national) market. This is possible because the destination visited matters little to some tourists. For example, in the case of summer holidays what is of most importance is the promise of reliable sunshine, warm temperatures, a sandy beach to lie on, warm water to swim in, clean and comfortable hotels and restaurants serving familiar foods and offering facilities the tourists would find at home. Many destinations can provide these characteristics. Thus the PH appears as a standardized, homogeneous product which can be sold to consumers with no prior knowledge of or experience of the resorts on offer. It is also a feature of market-oriented tour operators that, with few exceptions, their marketing activities are confined to their national market and that they do not normally compete in other tourist-generating countries.

As shown in the previous chapter, horizontal integration has led to increasing concentration in the structure of the industry within tourist-generating countries. For example, in the United Kingdom, although there are now over 800 tour operators, the top three firms account for about 50 per cent and the top 30 for over 80 per cent of the supply of overseas PHs. Catering for the mass market are the larger tour operators with PH portfolios covering all the standardized parts of the market, for example summer sun, winter sun, skiing holidays. The more numerous specialist or independent tour operators target a particular segment of the holiday market. Specialisation may be based upon destination, accommodation (e.g. self-catering villas, camping), activities (e.g. golf holidays, art tours, wine-tasting), and age (e.g. school parties).

The foreign package holiday became established in Western Europe in the 1960s, bringing both a substantial reduction in the real price of overseas holidays and a significant extension of the season. Tour operation is the dominating feature of the holiday market not only in the United Kingdom but in most tourist-generating countries (Burkart and Medlik, 1981). Although, as stated earlier, the PH appears as a standardized, total tourism product (Middleton, 1988), in the portfolio of an individual tour operator, especially a mass market one, it can demonstrate variety in terms of product depth, for example summer sun, winter sun, winter sports and short-break PHs, and of product width, including summer sun PHs with a choice of destinations, accommodation type and travel mode. The extent and structure of tour operators' PH portfolios is therefore critical to their success in such a highly competitive market. These portfolios and the total tourism market structure have been made possible and are sustained by the advent and development of information technology.

The PH portfolio, which differs between tour operators within and between tourist-generating countries, is central to marketing strategy, since its product depth and width, allied to product differentiation via 'branding', is a reflection of the tour operator's assessment of the size and segmentation of the holiday market in the country in which it operates. Each tour operator determines a portfolio whose PH capacity and competitive prices is expected to appeal to holidaymakers and to generate profits for the firm. Mass-market tour operators will have the most extensive portfolios in terms of product depth, but they will be more than rivalled in terms of the width of a particular product line by the most successful specialist tour operators. Generally, within any tourist-generating country, the larger and more segmented the holiday market the greater is the product depth of mass-market tour operator portfolios, and the more extensive the product width of all tour operator portfolios. Differences between PH portfolios of tour operators in different tourist-generating countries not only reflect size of market but are also tempered by other factors, such as differential economies of transport options available to move holidaymakers to destinations.

Skiing holidays via inclusive tours

A comparison of skiing holidays offered by UK and Dutch mass market tour operators can be used to illustrate the similarities and contrasts in tour operators' strategies in developing their PH portfolios. Skiing has been a leisure phenomenon for 50 years, but only in the last 25 years has it become a multibillion value industry in western Europe. It accounts for about one-fifth of the overall European holiday market but, as yet, skiing holidays have not been packaged to the same extent as summer and winter sun holidays. Thus it is estimated that, of the total skiing holidays, only half are booked as PHs through travel agents: the rest are accounted for by school parties, direct sales and independent holidays. Four out of every five persons taking a skiing holiday are 'regular' skiers and the market therefore relies heavily upon repeat business, as well as on younger persons, since nearly three-quarters are under 35 years of age. Europe's ageing population is not yet seen as a constraint on skiing holidays, which are predicted to grow in number by at least five per cent per annum (*Travel Trade Gazette*, 1986).

It is against this background that the packaging of skiing holidays since the 1960s has opened up an opportunity to a new generation of skiers to participate in large numbers. The PH skiing market has expanded in Europe to the extent that there are PHs offering a broad selection of options for those with differing levels of competence, to suit all tastes and wallets. In both the United Kingdom and The Netherlands, packages are available throughout the winter season (pre-Christmas to Easter) encompassing the full range of accommodation possibilities, offering alternative modes of transport to include a widening range of resorts with associated services and facilities in an increasing number of countries. The basic skiing PH is, however, being increasingly standardized, i.e. packaged to include travel, accommodation, equipment hire, lift pass, ski instruction, aprés-ski and excursions, or any combination thereof. It is made 'repeatable' irrespective of destination. Whilst considerable variation exists between ski resorts, especially the smaller ones, in the extent of their skiing terrain, the main resorts offer roughly comparable skiing and some package holiday skiers, like their summer sun counterparts, are indifferent as to the country in which the resort is located. The skier's preference for one resort may be due to factors other than the physical challenge of the skiing, for example ease of transfer from the airport or accessibility by car, quality of the aprés-ski, or even the tour operators who offer holidays there.

Skiing holidays have therefore been fully embraced by the mass market in tourism, and all tour operators in this mass market, in both The Netherlands and the United Kingdom are represented in the sector. It is to be expected that such tour operators will increase their share of the winter holiday market as a consequence of the sheer magnitude of their capacity and the pricing advantages they possess. In all major segments of the overall holiday market, package programmes are an important feature, including a sizeable winter holiday segment. In the United Kingdom Cosmos entered the skiing market in 1986–1987 with a coaching-only programme and Olympic Holidays diversified into skiing by taking over Ski Mac G and Ski-Plan. This has been primarily at the expense of medium-sized tour operators since small specialist operators are still doing well because their market niche is based on giving more choice and flexible departures. Nevertheless there is a trend towards the concentration of skiing opportunities in mass-market tour operator programmes which goes hand in hand with the standardization of the product. Competition between these tour operators rests on the way they 'brand' their packages via their brochures (Burkart and Medlik, 1981), and this represents a breadth of choice which is more apparent than real.

A comparative analysis of the winter skiing portfolios offered during the 1986–1987 season, by mass-market tour operators in The Netherlands and the United Kingdom, reveals that the Dutch tour operators have more extensive portfolios in terms of product width than their UK counterparts, despite catering for a market less than a quarter of the size of the UK market. The analysis uses the concept of opportunity sets (Goodall *et al.*, 1988; Stabler, 1990), also discussed in Chapter 2, to identify overlaps and contrasts between the resorts, accommodation types and travel modes offered in the skiing programmes of the tour operators in the two countries.

Information for the 1986–1987 winter holiday season, especially skiing brochures, was obtained from all the mass-market tour operators supplying skiing PHs in the United Kingdom and The Netherlands. In analysing the skiing holidays marketed in the skier's country of origin, emphasis is placed on the role of the tour operators since they shoulder some of the risks inherent in formulating and marketing a programme of inclusive tours. The aggregate programme of all such skiing holidays available from all tour operators (specialist as well as mass market) in a single country for a given season would comprise the 'industry' or 'PH' opportunity set (and the potential skier will have to choose from this set or act independently).

The skiing PH opportunity set may be disaggregated into 'company' opportunity sets, which contain the skiing PHs offered by each company. Varying degrees of overlap exist between company opportunity sets and this can best be explored by an analysis of the resorts in which individual tour operators base their skiing holidays. The analysis concentrates on skiing holidays offered by mass-market tour operators in European ski resorts, and is based on information obtained from travel trade guides, particularly tour operators' skiing brochures. The latter provide details not only on resorts but also on the means of transport, holiday duration, accommodation and meals, price and extras, booking conditions and insurance, as well as skiing equipment hire, skiing instruction, lift systems, lengths and gradings of pistes, and so on.

For the United Kingdom analysis, 12 mass-market tour operators were surveyed and for The Netherlands seven, representing a 100 per cent coverage of such tour operators in the two countries. The PH opportunity set of the 19 tour operators surveyed offered skiing holidays to a total of 340 resorts in 10 European countries.

Skiing PHs from the United Kingdom via mass-market tour operators

Tour operators formulate their PH programmes to appeal to the widest possible market. Even so there are considerable differences in the size and range of individual tour operator programmes. This may be demonstrated by examining the number of countries and skiing resorts contained in the United Kingdom mass-market tour operator PH skiing programmes. Table 5.1 indicates that these operators have company opportunity sets which normally offer the choice of a skiing PH from at least four countries (including the traditional ones of Austria, Switzerland, plus France) and from at least 20 resorts.

Table 5.1 Numbers of European countries and skiing resorts offered by UK mass-market tour operators in 1987

Countries		Resorts	
Number	Number of tour operators	Number	Number of tour operators
1	-	less than10	1
2	2	10 to19	3
3	-	20 to 29	2
4	3	30 to 39	4
5	2	40 or more	2
6 or more	5		

Which were the most popular countries and resorts represented in United Kingdom mass-market operators' company opportunity sets in 1987? Measured simply in terms of the presence or absence of at least one resort in a country represented in a tour operator's brochure, skiing holidays were most commonly offered in Austria, France, Italy and Switzerland. This is clear from Table 5.2, which also shows that mass-market tour operators feature certain innovative destinations in countries such as Andorra, Bulgaria and Spain.

Whilst Table 5.2 points to the popularity of Austria and France in particular, it may be misleading since no account is taken of either the number of resorts in each country appearing in tour operators' company opportunity sets, or the popularity of individual resorts. As the summary list of resorts, which occur most frequently in the United Kingdom ski tour operators' programmes presented in Table 5.3, shows, Austria and France dominate the scene, with 14 of the top 15 ski resorts located in either of those two countries. The nine resorts located in Austria are representative of the traditional first and second generation village skiing resorts, whilst the five located in France represent the third generation of new functional ski stations. It is possible that skiing PHs in Austrian resorts appeal to a different segment of the market than those in French

Table 5.2 The top countries offered by UK mass-market tour operators, 1987

Country	Number of tour operators	Representation (%)
Austria	12	100
France	11	92
Italy	10	83
Switzerland	9	75
Andorra	5	42
Spain	5	42
Bulgaria	3	25
Yugoslavia	2	17
Romania	2	17
Liechtenstein	1	8

Table 5.3 The top fifteen resorts, in rank order, offered by UK mass-market tour operators in 1987

Resort	Number of times offered
Kitzbühel (A)	10
Mayrhofen (A), Zell am See (A)	9
Söll (A), Westendorf (A), Avoriaz (F),	8
Niederau (A), Obergurgl (A), Seefeld (A),	
Sölden (A), Les Arcs (F), Meribel (F), Val d'Isère (F),	
Val Thorens (F), Cervinia (I)	7

(Based on the number of times a resort is offered by separate tour operators: A = Austria; F = France; I = Italy)

resorts, and this appears to be confirmed when the accommodation aspect of the PH is examined (see below).

Table 5.4 presents information on the number and popularity of resorts in each country (based on the frequency of their appearance in brochures) and demonstrates that the mass-market tour operators' PH opportunity set is dominated by Austria. This dominance is greatest for the top resorts, and Austria's popularity declines in relative terms as more resorts are considered. Nevertheless, when all the resorts in the United Kingdom mass-market tour operator PH opportunity set are considered, Austrian destinations are nearly twice as popular as resorts in France, the next most popular country. Together,

Table 5.4 The top countries offered by UK mass-market tour operators, 1987

Resorts	In top 5 (%)	In top 20 (%)	In top 40 (%)	All (%)
Andorra	.	.	2.5	3.0
Austria	83.0	60.0	50.0	39.0
Bulgaria	.	.	.	1.0
France	17.0	30.0	25.0	21.0
Italy	.	10.0	12.5	12.0
Liechtenstein	.	.	.	0.5
Romania	.	.	.	0.5
Spain	.	.	.	4.0
Switzerland	.	.	10.0	17.0
Yugoslavia	.	.	.	1.0
Total	100.0	100.0	100.0	100.0

Austria and France account for over two-thirds of all destinations in this opportunity set, with Italy and Switzerland the only other countries where the number of resorts exceeds 10 per cent of the PH opportunity set.

The explanation of these patterns lies in the diversity of the UK skiing market. Mass-market tour operators cater for the highest proportion of first-time skiers, who are likely to have an image of a traditional ski resort and a preference for serviced accommodation – hence the popularity of Austria. The fact that Switzerland does not match Austria is probably both a function of the strength of the Swiss franc compared to the Austrian schilling against the pound sterling, and greater marketing activity on the part of Austrian tourism organizations. Swiss-based PHs are relatively more expensive. Other countries, such as Spain and Bulgaria, are at an access/distance disadvantage which, although offset by the availability of cheap serviced accommodation, cannot compensate (as yet) for their not having an established skiing image in the UK market: they therefore remain a minority segment of that market.

From what has been said above it is obvious that the UK skiing PH opportunity set is not homogeneous. It may be disaggregated in a number of ways, for example, the simple division between serviced and self-catering accommodation, the latter being a relatively recent but increasingly popular form of accommodation. Table 5.5 shows that whilst serviced accommodation is available in virtually every resort (97 per cent) of the PH opportunity set, self-catering PHs are only found in just two-fifths (40 per cent). The figures highlight France as the innovator of self-catering skiing opportunities, since France is the only country in which more resorts offer self-catering than serviced PHs. Andorra is the only other country involved in self-catering possibilities in a big way.

Table 5.5 Type of accommodation available, by country, in UK mass-market tour operator programmes in 1987

	Serviced accommodation (%)	Self-catering (%)
Andorra	80	80
Austria	100	8
Bulgaria	100	-
France	90	92
Italy	100	42
Liechtenstein	100	-
Romania	100	-
Spain	100	29
Switzerland	100	38
Yugoslavia	100	100
Total	97	40

The skier may also exercise choice with respect to the mode of transport used to reach the ski destination. Table 5.6 reflects the importance of air travel, both charter and scheduled flights, for the mass-market tour operators since only one resort in the PH opportunity is not accessible by air. In an attempt to broaden the market, self-drive options are now common to most mass-market tour operator company opportunity sets. Only eight resorts in the PH opportunity set are not accessible in this way (these resorts are the most distant ones, especially in Bulgaria and Romania). Particularly striking is the fact that no UK mass-market tour operator offered rail travel as an option, except for the very special case of either the outward or return journey via the Orient Express.

The UK mass-market tour operator skiing PH opportunity set comprises some 162 resorts, of which the tour operator offering the widest choice of resorts has a company opportunity set covering 59 per cent of the national set, and the tour operator offering the least choice, covers just 5 per cent. Company opportunity sets differ considerably in the extent and content of their resort portfolios. Whilst certain resorts, based on their popularity ratings in Table 5.3, must appear in the majority of mass-market tour operator company opportunity sets, most firms seek to offer some resorts in which few or no other competitors operate. In the case of mass-market tour operators this may be because they are testing the appeal of a new resort. However, it also reflects the fact that each company is trying to appeal to as wide a spectrum of the market as possible as well as catering for particular segments, for example beginners on tight budgets.

Table 5.6 Choice of transport in UK mass-market tour operator programmes in 1987

| | Transport mode | | | |
	Air (%)	Coach (%)	Rail (%)	Self-drive (%)
Andorra	100	60	-	100
Austria	100	62	-	95
Bulgaria	100	-	-	-
France	100	46	-	95
Italy	95	16	-	95
Liechtenstein	100	-	-	100
Romania	100	-	-	-
Spain	100	43	-	100
Switzerland	100	3	-	100
Yugoslavia	100	-	-	100
Total	97	40	-	95

Skiing PHs from The Netherlands via mass-market tour operators

In the case of The Netherlands the programmes of mass-market tour operators, as Table 5.7 shows, are extensive and varied. Indeed, in terms of the number of resorts included, they are more extensive than those of their UK counterparts. Again the most popular countries and resorts amongst Dutch mass-market tour operator skiing PHs can be illustrated, in the first instance, in terms of presence or absence of at least one resort in a country represented in a company's brochure (Table 5.8) and by the frequency with which individual ski resorts are used by the tour operators (Table 5.9).

It is very clear from Tables 5.8 and 5.9 that Austrian destinations also dominate the skiing PHs offered by Dutch mass-market ski tour operators, with five of the seven tour operators having over 70 per cent of their packages based on Austrian ski resorts, and with resorts in that country accounting for 61 per cent of all resorts, as shown in Table 5.10. Again the explanation is likely to be Austria's preferred image as a traditional country, allied to the better purchasing power of the Dutch guilder against the Austrian schilling relative to the Swiss franc or the Deutschmark. Resorts in countries such as France and Italy are at a distance disadvantage compared to those in Austria, Switzerland and West Germany in serving the Dutch market. This factor, in conjunction with the transport mode used, explains why these other countries account for only 12.5 per cent of the skiing PHs available on the Dutch market.

Table 5.7 Numbers of European countries and skiing resorts offered by Dutch mass-market tour operators in 1987

Countries		Resorts	
Number	Number of tour operators	Number	Number of tour operators
1	-	less than 40	1
2	1	40-59	1
3	-	60-79	1
4	-	80-99	3
5	4	100 or more	1
6 or more	2		

Table 5.8 The top countries offered by Dutch mass-market tour operators, 1987

Country	Number of tour operators	Representation (%)
Austria	7	100
Italy	6	86
Switzerland	6	86
W. Germany	6	86
France	4	57
Yugoslavia	3	43
Andorra	1	14
Romania	1	14

The PHs offered by Dutch mass-market ski tour operators also contain a choice regarding type of accommodation (Table 5.11) and mode of transport (Table 5.12). Table 5.11 confirms the growing importance of self-catering, (approximately two out of every five skiing PHs), and also suggests significant differences between countries, with France again showing as the only country in which self-catering skiing PHs are more common than ones using serviced accommodation. Land-based transport, particularly road, dominates access to resorts, as Table 5.12 demonstrates, whilst the option of air travel is insignificant.

Table 5.9 The top 15 resorts offered by Dutch mass-market operators in 1987

Resort	Number of times offered
Kirchberg, Lermoos, Maurach, St. Johann im Pongau	7
Zell am See, Gerlos, Hinterglemm, Kaprun, Pertisau, Seefeld	6
Ehrwald, Ellmau, Fügen, Mayrhofen, Nauders, Oberau, Söll, Westendorf	5

Resorts (all Austria)
(Based on the number of times a resort is offered by individual tour operators.)

Table 5.10 The top countries offered by Dutch mass-market tour operators in 1987

	Resorts			
	In top 5 (%)	In top 20 (18) (%)	In top 40 (37) (%)	All (%)
Andorra	-	-	-	1
Austria	100	100	95	61
France	-	-	-	5
Italy	-	-	2.5	5
Romania	-	-	-	0.5
Switzerland	-	-	2.5	15
W. Germany	-	-	-	11
Yugoslavia	-	-	-	1
Total	100	100	100	100

Weighted by resort frequencies

The Dutch mass-market skiing PH opportunity set comprises some 260 resorts, of which the tour operator with the widest choice of resorts has a company opportunity set covering 45 per cent of the national set, and the tour operator offering the least choice, 13 per cent. Whilst there are noticeable differences between company opportunity sets in terms of choice of accommodation and transport (with at least one mass-market tour operator offering packages using only serviced accommodation and coach travel), all the sets are dominated by Austrian resorts. The most popular Austrian resorts (top 40) appear in the company opportunity sets of at least five of the Dutch mass-market tour

Table 5.11 Type of accommodation available, by country, in Dutch mass-market tour operator programmes in 1987

	Serviced Accommodation (%)	Self-catering (%)
Andorra	100	100
Austria	88	35
France	21	100
Italy	92	46
Romania	100	-
Switzerland	45	83
W. Germany	62	97
Yugoslavia	100	50
Total	75	54

operators. However, each tour operator also tries to offer something different, since at least one in every five resorts in their brochures is unique to that tour operator. Overall, 55 per cent of the resorts in the national PH opportunity set are offered by just a single tour operator.

Comparison of United Kingdom and Dutch mass-market tour operator programmes

In general, Dutch mass-market tour operators offer more extensive skiing holiday portfolios than their UK counterparts: the average Dutch brochure contains 76 resorts against only 34 in the UK case. This would appear at first sight unexpected since the Dutch market is considerably smaller than the UK market for skiing holidays. The explanation lies in large part with the influence of the transport factor on the selection of resorts to be included in each mass-market tour operator's brochure. For Dutch skiers resorts in Austria, Switzerland, and especially West Germany, are within convenient day-driving distance, even when winter road conditions are allowed for. Because crossing the Channel necessitates use of two surface transport modes and distances to the nearest ski resorts are greater than from The Netherlands, UK mass-market tour operators make much greater use of air travel, which is up to ten times more important. Once committed to air travel, especially charter flights, it is essential that such tour operators achieve a very high seat occupancy ratio. Compared to the Dutch situation, limiting the number of resorts offered in their individual company opportunity sets is therefore an important means of ensuring high occupancy ratios on charter flights.

Table 5.12 Choice of transport in Dutch mass-market tour operator programmes in 1987: proportion (%) of resorts accessible by each transport mode

	Air	Coach	Rail	Self-drive
		Transport mode		
Andorra	-	-	100	100
Austria	13	95	48	86
France	-	43	21	86
Italy	-	69	69	85
Romania	100	-	-	-
Switzerland	3	50	53	65
W. Germany	-	90	48	100
Yugoslavia	100	100	100	100
Total	9	82	49	84

In considering the composition of the mass-market tour operator skiing PHs offered in brochures in the two countries, it is clear that Austrian skiing holidays, as pointed out above, dominate the company and national opportunity sets. Table 5.13 attempts a comparison by destination country and gives an indication of the extent to which UK and Dutch mass-market tour operators have penetrated the destination area opportunity set. It is acknowledged, however, that this analysis ignores resorts which do not figure in such tour operators' programmes. Whilst confirming the dominance of Austrian resorts in relation to the total number of resorts, Table 5.13 also suggests that Dutch mass-market tour operator company opportunity sets are much more concentrated on one or two countries than the sets of their UK counterparts. Dutch tour operators have also penetrated the Swiss, as well as the Austrian, destination opportunity set to a much greater degree. On the other hand, UK tour operators' portfolios demonstrate greater product width in terms of the number of destination countries used. They have penetrated destination opportunity sets to a greater extent in France, Andorra and Italy. Furthermore, they have pioneered destinations in Bulgaria and Spain not represented in the Dutch mass-market PH opportunity set.

These differences again reflect an underlying distance–decay phenomenon, as modified by travel mode considerations. The Netherlands is nearer to Austrian and Swiss skiing resorts than the French Alpine and Pyrennean (Andorra and Spain) ones, whereas the reverse is the case for the UK market. Austria remains the most important destination for UK mass-market tour operators because journey times by air are around two and a half hours, and Austrian resorts have a traditional skiing image plus a reputation for good instruction.

Table 5.13 Comparative use of European ski resorts by UK and Dutch mass-market tour operators (TOs)

Country	Resorts served			Penetration (%)	
	UK TOs only	Dutch TOs only	Both UK & Dutch TOs	UK TOs	Dutch TOs
Andorra	3	-	2	100	40
Austria	11	113	51	35	88
Bulgaria	2	-	-	100	-
France	21	1	13	97	40
Italy	17	11	2	63	43
Liechtenstein	1	-	-	100	-
Romania	-	-	1	100	100
Spain	7	-	-	100	-
Switzerland	12	23	17	56	77
W. Germany	-	29	-	-	100
Yugoslavia	1	1	1	67	67

Do UK and Dutch mass-market tour operators use the same ski resorts? Perhaps surprisingly, only just over a quarter of all resorts in the PH opportunity set are common to both the UK and Dutch sets. This applies at the level of the main destination countries, since it is only with the 'minority' destinations of Romania and Yugoslavia that resort profiles are identical. This relative lack of resorts in common is confirmed when they are analysed according to their frequency of occurrence in company opportunity sets. Austrian resorts are the only ones popular in both national mass market tour operator PH opportunity sets. Only a quarter of resorts in the top 20, and a fifth of those in the top 40, in each country are common to both sets. The limited overlap of company opportunity sets within a country can be explained by tour operators' actions in differentiating their sets, in terms of specific destinations, in order to avoid competition. Overlap was not anticipated to the same extent between countries since tour operation is primarily a function of tourist-origin country-based firms, i.e. mass-market tour operators based in The Netherlands are not competing for markets with those based in the UK. Further research is necessary to ascertain whether this limited overlap of UK and Dutch tour operator company opportunity sets is related to destination area characteristics, such as a restricted amount of accommodation being available in small village resorts or the existence of skiing instruction in the skier's own language.

Conclusion

The skiing market is small, relative to overall holiday demand in both The Netherlands and the UK, but it is a growing market and one in which increased disposable income is likely to have more effect than for summer sun holidays. It is of a size, however, where it has attracted the attention of the mass-market tour operators. As a consequence skiing holidays have been packaged as inclusive tours so that a standardized and repeatable product is now available. Individual tour operators, keen to be represented in all important segments of the market, have attempted to develop PH skiing portfolios of extensive product width, as the opportunity set analysis demonstrated. Whilst resorts undoubtedly differ, for reasons other than the quality of the skiing they offer, on the basis of the analysis of skiing PHs supplied by UK and Dutch mass-market tour operators many other aspects were similar.

Skiing being a highly competitive and mass market, tour operators compete in it not simply in the extent of their company opportunity sets but also by including certain resorts unique to their programme, in the hope of mitigating the severity of the competition in parts of the market. Increasingly, however, the distinctions between mass-market tour operators rest not so much on the range of resorts and their skiing and non-skiing characteristics, as on the brochure images conveyed of the 'product brand' and on the prices asked. Potential skiers have increasing difficulty in comparing resorts within and between company opportunity sets. Thus to throw light on this difficulty the current analysis has been extended to include variation in the design and content of skiing brochures (Goodall and Bergsma, 1990). This research showed tour operators to be selective in the information they presented in their brochures about skiing resorts. Often it was the information not given, for example snow records, which would be of more value in assisting choice. Even where the same 'vital statistics' were used, individual tour operators' 'suitability ratings' differed for skiers of a given level of competence.

At the international level there is likely to be increased concentration in the tour operator sector of the industry. Whilst this is already evident at a national level in tourist-origin countries, it may be anticipated that, with a European market from 1992, multinational tour operators will appear since there will be some scale advantages in preparing company opportunity sets and in accommodation use, although not in transport. Indeed this may already be happening in The Netherlands, where one mass-market tour operator is part of an even larger German organization. This in turn is likely to hold implications for other sectors of the tourism industry such as couriers and hoteliers and, in particular, travel agents.

References

Burkart, A.J. and Medlik, S. (1981) *Tourism: Past, Present and Future*, 2nd edn. Heinemann, London.

Goodall, B. and Bergsma, J. (1990) Destinations: as marketed in tour operators' brochures. In: Ashworth, G.J. and Goodall, B. (eds), *Marketing Tourism Places*. Routledge, London, pp. 170–192.

Goodall, B. Radburn, M.R. and Stabler, M.J. (1988) *Market Opportunity Sets for Tourism. Geographical Paper No. 100 (Tourism Series No. 1)*, Department of Geography, University of Reading, Reading.

Middleton, V.T.C. (1988) *Marketing in Travel and Tourism*. Heinemann, London.

Stabler, M.J. (1990) The concept of opportunity sets as a methodological framework for the analysis of selling tourism places: the industry view. In: Ashworth, G.J. and Goodall, B. (eds), *Marketing Tourism Places*. Routledge, London, pp. 23–41.

Travel Trade Gazette (1986) Operators get together on the slopes, 11 Sept., pp. 44–5.

Chapter 6

Changing Styles of Sports Tourism: Industry/Consumer Interactions in Canada, the USA and Europe

G. Redmond

Introduction

An American book entitled *Commercial Recreation* (Ellis and Norton, 1988) offers one of the most succinct definitions of tourism: '[Tourism] ... comprises destinations, activities, and travel facilitation'. On the page opposite this definition is a photograph, with a caption stating that 'A destination resort must cater to all the needs of its guests'; the photograph depicts four guests on the 18th green of the golf course at a Marriott's Tan-Tar – a resort in the USA. This is but one small example, from literally hundreds that could be given, of the symbiotic relationship that now exists between sport and tourism in our modern world – a world in which the 'needs' of tourists are increasingly identified by the international provision of sporting facilities and experiences. Another British publication summarised the key tourism features of each continent, and concluded:

> Tourism is one of the world's growing industries, generating 340
> million arrivals and expenditure of US $15 billion in 1986.
> Developments to supply this demand are burgeoning across the
> world as tourism searches out ever-distant and unusual destinations
> at the same time the more popular holiday formulae, such as
> Mediterranean summer sun, are continually developing,
> particularly by adding in activity and sporting ingredients.
>
> (Cooper, 1988)

'Activity and sporting ingredients' predominate, as the obvious relationship between sport and tourism continues to develop in significant ways. Certainly no international analysis of the tourism industry can properly ignore the contributing factor of sport.

Since sport may be regarded as the world's largest social phenomenon (Arlott, 1975; Loy *et al.*, 1981; Mandell, 1984) and tourism is predicted to become the world's biggest industry early in the next century by futurist Herman

Kahn and many others (Bonciolini, 1988), it would be strange if such a relationship did not exist. The mutual benefits of an economic 'marriage of convenience' are clearly perceptible. In recent years the points of contact between sport and tourism have increased dramatically – a trend that is likely to continue well into the next century. In fact, the relationship is so compatible and seemingly enduring that the term 'sports tourism' has been coined to describe it.

Sport and tourism both have enduring pedigrees, and first merged long ago in their histories. The numerous multi-sport festivals of the ancient Greek and Roman civilisations, for example, of which the Olympic Games are probably best-known, attracted their share of tourists over many centuries (Harris, 1972). Many factors have contributed to the dimensions of sports tourism in the modern world, an obvious manifestation of which has been the emergence of a worldwide recreation-and-leisure industry, replete with specialised paraphernalia, catering for a well-advertised and expanding market (Jackson and Burton, 1989). New facilities, allied with government-sponsored programmes, have assisted in the promotion of fitness and 'sport for all' movements for a largely materialistic and narcissistic international society (Lasch, 1979; Skinner, 1988). Modern technology has served to create an international sporting playground for the reasonably affluent athletic tourist (Cooper, 1988; Martin and Mason, 1984; Vickerman, 1975). It is not possible in a single chapter to analyse the changing styles of international sports tourism in comprehensive detail, but a brief examination of key areas where the interaction between sport and tourism has intensified in recent years, with examples drawn mainly from Europe and North America, should be sufficient to sustain conviction of its significant contemporary status. These areas involve the development of sports resorts and sport vacations (including cruises); the growth of sports museums, the plethora of multi-sport festivals and world championships, such as the Olympic Games and World Cup; and sports facilities in national parks. Let us begin by elaborating upon the resort example introduced in the first paragraph.

New facilities for the athletic tourist: hotels, resorts and spas

Most dictionary definitions of the word 'resort' refer to a vacation centre with facilities for recreation. Increasingly, the facilities provided are those which offer participation in various sports – not only the perennial favourite of golf, but also tennis courts, swimming pools, racquetball and squash courts, jogging trails, and the like. Indeed, such amenities are mandatory nowadays to qualify for the title of 'resort'. This is obvious from the mass advertising of tourism today. Demanding and health-conscious tourists expect such facilities to be included, and hosts around the world in the hotel business are hastening as never before to cater to them.

One typical advertisement for The Breakers resort in Florida refers to it as a 'Playground for the World', where 'Golfers can test one of the two 18-hole courses. Tennis buffs will find 19 courts; the fitness-minded, a health club complete with Nautilus and Keiser exercise equipment'. Another one for Jumby

Bay in the West Indies, claims that 'Sports buffs can keep busy and healthy from dawn to dusk' with a wide variety of activities. Although these two quotes must suffice to illustrate the point here, similar statements are legion in thousands of magazine advertisements and brochures for such establishments. They are common in practically all well known journals of quality with a large circulation, such as *The Illustrated London News*, or *Time*, but naturally most prominent in both the well established and recent travel-and-tourist magazines which are now in vogue, such as *Travel & Leisure, Travel-Holiday, European Travel & Life, Traveler*, and *Trips*, among many others. Behind the obvious hyperbole and rhetoric which is characteristic of these expensive advertisements, is the very real and pragmatic investment in sports facilities for tourists everywhere, considered to be necessary today by the owners, backers and planners of such resorts.

Beyond the proliferation of such amenities, it is also essential for resorts to be able to stress their quality. Two or three golf courses may be impressive, but increasingly the emphasis is upon possession of 'championship' golf courses, preferably those laid out by a well-known designer or a famous player (Nicklaus, 1989). Although the possibilities for tennis court design are obviously more limited, even here adjectives and phrases stress quality beyond mere provision; hence the Makena Resort in Hawaii refers to its 'championship golf, and award-winning tennis facilities', while Rancho Bernardo Inn in San Diego offers 'unlimited golf and tennis on our tournament quality facilities' (*Travel & Leisure*, 1988). Perhaps the ultimate example of this 'quality philosophy' can be found on the Monterey Peninsula in California, where millions of dollars were spent on landscaping alone to replicate conditions similar to British Open Championship courses.

The developments discussed briefly here are not confined to affluent western industrialized nations; with regard to sporting facilities, international tourists are being enticed wherever airlines, automobiles, cruise ships or railways take them. Among many examples which could be given, the US$400 million international tourist resort developed by British-managed Hainan Island Development Company in China is one of the most interesting. Included in its many recreational facilities are 'a premier tennis centre' and a 'golf complex', comprising two 18-hole courses, two 9-hole courses, a clubhouse and a practice range. These will be designed and developed by Golfconsult International, which has undertaken projects in nearly 50 other countries. Another international luxury sports development is on a ten-acre site near Marbella, in Spain, where 'all racquet sports will be catered for' – but of course it also features heated swimming pools, a fitness centre and jogging track, bowling green and ten-pin bowling centre, a pistol range, golf and several other sports facilities (*Leisure Management*, 1988a).

The emergence of health clubs and fitness equipment has been concomitant with the provision of sports facilities as a feature of the leisure industry in recent years, largely because of what has been documented as an international health-and-fitness movement, or even an industry (Green, 1986; Grover, 1989; *Life*, 1987; Skinner, 1988). Fitness and sport are largely synonymous, and tourists now expect both elements to be provided for. Comprehensive health and sports facilities are becoming mandatory for any resort worthy of the title, and urban hotels which are restricted by space considerations from providing the extensive sports facilities necessary for qualification as a fully-fledged resort, are nevertheless now providing exercise facilities far beyond what would have been expected a few years ago. It is significant that in London alone, the famous Claridge's and Ritz hotels have just provided luxurious fitness clubs for their clientele. An article on this trend referred to an explosion in the hotel industry in the area of health facilities, concluding that:

> ... as long as the general interest in fitness remains at its current
> high level, and as long as at least one hotel can claim some
> advantages by providing this very expensive amenity, fitness
> facilities in hotels will be an important consideration for any hotel
> with an eye to capturing the business.
> (Travelling on Business, 1987).

This statement is borne out by the specific renovations of all the major hotel chains around the world in recent years. From the many examples which could be given, consider the thorough renovation undergone at the fashionable Villa d'Este on the shores of Lake Como in Italy, to provide it with impressive facilities for a large number of sports (*European Travel & Life*, 1988); or the similar and very expensive developments at Tudor Park Hotel in Maidstone, Kent. The English example is a product of Country Club Hotels (a division of Whitbread) and in 1988 the organization's Director of Leisure, Patrick Henchoz, stated: 'As market leaders in leisure-based hotels, we believe that leisure, and within that, health and fitness, form very important aspects of the total package offered to customers' (*Leisure Management*, 1988b). It is a statement that is now applicable to the international hotel industry as a whole, as the competition in the 'leisure market' has intensified.

A significant part of developments everywhere has been the reemergence and renewed popularity of the 'spa', within the leisure industry. All the magazines mentioned have included articles on spas recently, as did many others not mentioned (Harding, 1987; Williams, 1988), and 'the first comprehensive catalogue of spas, fitness resorts, and retreats ... at home and abroad' was published for 1987–1988, included a 'spa world map', and was entitled *The Spa Finder*, a confirmation of their international renaissance. Historically, in Europe, the famous spa towns were based on natural springs whose waters were believed to have therapeutic, almost magical powers, and 'taking the waters' became very popular for those who could afford it in the late seventeenth and eighteenth centuries (Wechsberg, 1979). The curative beliefs underlying such spas were subsequently eroded by advances in medical knowledge and the widespread provision of health services, but they have now made a comeback in revised form. Peter Sargent (1987) has noted that: 'The former medical function has gone forever ... but we live in a new age of health consciousness and exercise which could easily revive on the same scale as the Georgian desire for 'the cure' '. For example, Intra Travel began its worldwide travel guide annual issue for 1989 with a chapter entitled: 'The Vacation of the 90s: Spas!' (*Intrigue*, 1989). A guide to 'The Top Spas of Europe', describing 23 such establishments in nine countries, was provided in the early 1980s, and a distinction has already been made between the 'healing' variety traditional to

Europe and 'the athletic and/or pampering variety found in America' (Michael, 1984). For the tourists of today the words 'resort' and 'spa' have both been re-defined in terms of contemporary society. Perhaps the ultimate yardstick of this fashion, for the next few years at least, may well be the new US$38 million King Ranch Health Spa and Fitness Resort on 177 acres north of Toronto, Canada, developed by Adam Kouffler of Four Seasons Hotels fame. Genuine modern spas can now be found in many countries and are still increasing in number. The shape of the future can be seen in a new travel guide entitled Select Spas, which has comprehensive descriptions of the top 10 spas in North America for ... 'Executive Renewal', 'Weight Loss', 'Bargains', 'Families', 'Corporate Groups', 'Fitness', 'Pampering', 'Romantic Retreats', and 'Speciality Programs' such as 'Quit Smoking', 'Skiing', 'Golf', 'Tennis' and 'Lifestyle Management Programs' (Harding, 1989).

Sport vacations

The different kinds of `spa holidays' now available, along with the plethora of offerings in various other fields of specific interest, may be placed under the rubric of special interest tourism, a term of increasing relevance in recent years. In fact, partly because of the development of resorts and spas briefly outlined, sports vacations represent probably the largest and fastest growing segment within special interest tourism. Major sports (and even some minor ones) are the focus of special interest tourists' vacations in most parts of the world. These range from summer sport camps, (Goldsmith *et al.*, 1983) through different sport tours and sport vacations, to sports cruises of a surprising range and variety. Recreational sport, of course, has been a part of holidaymakers' enjoyment for many years. The British holiday camp, for example, from its origins at the turn of the century through to the golden era of Butlin's, Pontin's and Warner camps in the 1950s and 1960s, offered various sporting activities in its recipe for total family fun (Read, 1986; Ward and Hardy, 1986). However, nothing in the past matches the specific nature and variety of contemporary international vacations, of which sport is the focus.

One of the most obvious and popular manifestations of this focus is Club Med, a 40-year old concept which has grown into a US$1.3 billion empire, with 110 villages in 33 countries on five continents, whose boast is: 'Whatever you fancy, we've got the sport'. Its formula of 'beautiful locations' plus numerous activities organised by congenial hosts, allied with interesting and varied cuisine, has proved to be one of the most successful offerings in international tourism (Lang, 1990; Rand, 1983). Not being an organization to rest upon its laurels, Club Med has recently felt obliged to enter the sports cruise business with its new ship Club Med 1 (the title suggests other ships to follow, in a Club Med fleet of the future). Advertised as the world's largest sailing vessel, 610 feet long, with five masts and computer-controlled sails, this represents a significant entry into a lucrative and rapidly growing marketplace, heralded in the 'Cruise News' column of *Travel & Leisure* magazine a few years ago:

> The competition among cruise liners to attract passengers has
> generated a new marketing twist: sports cruises. Travellers are
> lured on board by the opportunity to play golf at exotic locations,
> attend tennis clinics run by world-class players and mingle with
> Olympic gold-medal runners or skiers at shipboard cocktail
> parties'.
>
> (Friedland, 1987)

In fact, Cunard has run sports theme cruises for over a dozen years, during which time several other cruise lines have followed suit.

The leader in the sports cruising stakes at present might well be the Norwegian Cruise Line (NCL), which advertised that: 'On selected weeks, famous sports figures gather with NCL to host cruises on just about every sport under the sun' (Norwegian Cruise Line, 1988). Apart from specific sports cruises, however, the cruise ships themselves – like the Royal Caribbean Cruise Lines' 74,000 ton Sovereign of the Seas, or the Royal Viking Line's Seaborne Pride, among many others – are, in effect, sea-going resorts which 'offer all the amenities and more than most resorts on terra firma provide, with the exception of an attached 18-hole golf course or set of tennis courts' (*Edmonton Journal*, 1989). The transformation on land of hotels with limited amenities into resorts with multi-sport facilities, has been replicated on sea, as the 'floating palaces' of yesteryear with their swimming-pools, deck-tennis and shuffle board routines have been superseded by the opulent cruise liners of today, with their much more lavishly-equipped sports facilities (Bannerman, 1982; Owen, 1979; Ward, 1986). A study of the world cruise market for 1989 showed that it topped US $6 billion in gross revenues (of which North America generated US $5.21 billion), and continued significant growth was forecast (*Tourism Intelligence Bulletin*, 1990a).

The growing diversity of offerings in the sports cruise market is matched on terra firma. For many years, all kinds of vacations have been available for such major sports as golf, skiing and tennis. These are increasing at a tremendous rate, as numerous tourism enterprises now offer such vacations. Major sports have their own magazines devoted to them; many of these now have several pages of advertisements detailing numerous vacations available for their devotees (see, for but one typical example, the regular and comprehensive 'Holidays' section in the British monthly magazine *Golf World*). Specialist companies have emerged in significant numbers to cater for this demand, such as SporTours Inc. in North America, which advertises itself as 'The Ultimate in Sport Travel'. The sport of golf is undergoing a tremendous surge in popularity around the world, and there now exist a large number of firms, such as Inter Golf Inc. and Golf Pac Inc., which organise golf holidays for tourists in countries wherever the sport is played. Not surprisingly, as golf's 'mecca' and home of The Royal and Ancient Club, arbiter of the sport, the town of St. Andrew's in Scotland is perhaps the most popular stop on the golfing tourist's itinerary, which brings us to the plethora of sports museums today.

Sports halls of fame and museums

In 1990, a new US$3 million British Golf Museum was opened in St. Andrew's, behind the famous clubhouse, the latest in a growing number of such establishments in the United Kingdom. It joined the Cricket Museum at Lords ground in London, the National Horseracing Museum at Newmarket, and the Lawn Tennis Museum at Wimbledon, among several others. Museums can be found at other arenas and stadiums, such as the Scottish Rugby Football Union Museum in Edinburgh. There are also many smaller sports museums scattered throughout the UK, such as the Cenarth Fishing Museum in rural Wales. In a pub at Heckmondwike, in North Yorkshire, there is even a small Rugby League 'hall of fame' operated by the enthusiastic proprietors (*In Britain*, 1990).

The growth of sports museums in Britain is part of an international trend. Museums have long been recognized as one of the most enduring and popular of tourist attractions (Alexander, 1979), and the emergence of specialist sports museums underlines the contemporary recognition of the cultural status of sport. Part of this recognition is economically motivated, using the high profile of sport to attract the tourist dollar, but much of it is also culturally driven, to allow sport its place within the heritage interpretation movement. Most of the initial impressive rise of sports museums in this century derives from the United States, and from the 'hall of fame' concept in particular.

Since The Hall of Fame for Great Americans was established in 1901, the idea has permeated American culture to such an extent that there are now halls of fame for practically every field of human endeavour, and the phrase has firmly entered the English language. A pioneer work featured 50 such institutions (Lewis and Redmond, 1971), to be followed in 1977 by a more comprehensive work giving details of nearly 200, with a statement that: 'New halls of fame are opening at the rate of approximately one every month' and that probably 'a hundred or more new or smaller halls' had escaped the editors' attention (Soderberg *et al.*, 1977). In 1978 it was claimed that no less than three out of five halls of fame in the United States were sports halls of fame (Thurmond, 1978). By 1990, more than 400 such institutions existed throughout North America, from small one- or two-room enterprises to impressive edifices costing millions of dollars, with many more being planned.

Although there has been some antipathy to the hall of fame concept in some traditional museum quarters, this has not prevented their international spread and recognition as tourist attractions. Here a clarification should be made between the terms 'hall of fame' and 'museum'. The *raison d'être* of a sports hall of fame is the celebration of sporting heritage, in which the noun 'fame' is all-important. It exists to glorify the deeds of athletes considered significant enough to qualify for 'enshrinement', and the eligibility rules and procedures involved ensure admission only to the elite. A museum, on the other hand, will exhibit items because of their intrinsic historical interest – and so old golf clubs, bicycles and footballs will have their place regardless of whether any famous athlete wielded, rode or kicked them. There are institutions which are exclusively sports halls of fame, and others which are specifically sports museums, but there is a trend towards fulfilling both functions within the same institution. By adding 'museum' to its role and title, a sports hall of fame may become eligible for government funds and private museum grants; by embracing a 'hall of fame' function, a sports museum may attract more fans as visitors. Thus titles such as The Aquatic Hall of Fame and Museum of Canada, at Winnipeg; or The National Lawn Tennis Hall of Fame and Tennis Museum, at Newport, RI, have become more common in recent years.

The label 'National' and the phrase 'of Canada' point to a patriotic trend behind many of the new sports museums which have been established, and one which is cognisant of their worth as tourist attractions. Although the adjective 'national' is often applied to single-sport museums, as with The National Horseracing Museum at Newmarket and other examples mentioned, it is also used in a collective sense to embrace the sporting heritage of a whole country. To date there is still no national 'British Museum of Sport', but a passionate plea was made for the same through the *In Corpore Sano* column of the Times Educational Supplement (1966) no less than 25 years ago. The writer pointed out that the Polish government had financed a national Museum of Physical Culture and Tourism to the tune of more than 3 million zlotys (then about 70,000 pounds sterling), that sports museums already existed in many other countries, and the lack of such a facility in the United Kingdom was strongly deplored.

A similar argument was presented in Australia in 1975, where the famous Melbourne Cricket Ground already housed a museum which celebrated all the sports played there. It was stated in a Report of the Australian Sports Institute Study Group, completed for the Department of Tourism and Recreation that:

> ... the time is ripe for consideration to be given to a National
> Museum devoted to preserving, researching and educating about
> the remarkable sporting heritage of this country...Such
> institutions are increasing rapidly in Canada and the United States,
> and public support there shows that there is a fast need and demand
> for this display of an important aspect of the history of these
> countries. Similar institutions also exist in European countries.
> One of the most impressive because of its detail, completeness and
> imaginative arrangement is the Polish Museum in Warsaw.
> (Australian Sports Institute Study Group, 1975)

There followed the establishment of The Australian National Gallery of Sport in Melbourne, described in its brochure as 'this country's first national multi-sport museum'. Canada's Sports Hall of Fame and Hockey Hall of Fame occupy a building in the famous Canadian National Exhibition Grounds in Toronto, a magnet for visitors to this cosmopolitan city. Among European examples is the National Museum of Sport (Museu Nacional do Desporto) in the Portuguese capital city of Lisbon.

Portugal can also boast of other sports museums, including an Olympic Museum, the Museum of the Portuguese Olympic Committee. This is but one of several museums around the world devoted to the Olympic Games. Perhaps the best-known of these at present is the Museum of the Olympic Games at Olympia, in Greece, while what is billed as 'The World's largest Olympic Museum' is to be found in Calgary, Alberta, host city of the 1988 Winter Olympics (and the site of the 1990 Conference of The International Association of Sports Museums and Halls of Fame, formed in 1971). This Canadian guardian of Olympism may well be superseded in size, however, by the new Olympic Museum being built on the shores of Lake Geneva at Lausanne, Switzerland (headquarters of the International Olympic Committee), and scheduled for completion in 1992. The active promotion of Olympic Museums by the International Olympic Committee (IOC) is recognition of their worth as tourist attractions, now and in the future.

Multi-sport festivals and world championships

The modern Olympic Games represent the largest of the world's multi-sport festivals, and have been increasingly acknowledged as significant tourist entertainment, particularly since the advent of mass international air travel (Mill and Morrison, 1985; Turner and Ash, 1975). It was reported that the 1988 Winter Olympics in Calgary, for example, bore most responsibility for the record number of 595,000 visitors who entered Canada during February of that year, (*Edmonton Sun*, 1988). It has been calculated that the 1992 Summer Olympic Games to be held in Barcelona, Spain, should attract 'about 600,000 visitors' (Livesey, 1990).

These are impressive figures, and these two examples alone indicate the ability of the Olympic Games, and other major sporting events, to harness international attention and commitment with ease and to attract large numbers of visitors. Olympic statistics are but the tip of an iceberg, for the Olympic Games have spawned many similar festivals, such as the Commonwealth Games, Pan-American Games, Goodwill Games, or World Student Games, among many others, which also regularly attract thousands (Zeigler, 1988). Since the Summer Olympics began at Athens in 1896, and the Winter Olympics in 1924 at Chamonix, there have been several kinds of imitations based on geographical regions (such as the African Games, Asian Games, or Mediterranean Games); religious affiliation (Maccabiah Games); political motivation (Games of the New Emerging Forces); physical disabilities (Special Olympics, World Games for the Deaf); career or profession (such as the Law Enforcement Olympics) – and even sexual orientation, as the Gay Games III were held in Vancouver, Canada, in 1990, where there were 'an estimated 30,000 homosexual visitors in town, competing or watching the Games' (Preston, 1990).

Canada, because of a peculiar mixture of history and geography and some political factors, probably qualifies as one of the foremost 'games nations' of modern times, and one which readily accepts their value within the tourism industry. With the recent disappearance of the German Democratic Republic (East Germany), Canada now has the most direct government involvement in sport, and concomitant bureaucracy, of any nation (Macintosh *et al.*, 1987). The United States and Mexico, for example, may host and enter the Olympics, but do not qualify politically like Canada for the (British) Commonwealth Games. Similarly, Australia or England participate in the Commonwealth Games, but are not eligible geographically (like Canada, Mexico and the US) for the Pan-American Games. In fact, the Commonwealth Games actually began in Canada

115

in 1930. Since the First British Empire Games at Hamilton, Ontario, in 1930, Canada's record in hosting international multi-sport festivals is unique, and includes the fifth British Empire and Commonwealth Games, fifth Pan-American Games, eighteenth Summer Olympic Games, eleventh Commonwealth Games, ninth World University Games, and the fifteenth Winter Olympic Games. This list does not include several other international multi-sport festivals hosted in Canada during this period, such as the 1976 Olympics for the Physically Disabled, in Toronto, or the Law Enforcement Olympics (sometimes known as Police Games) held in Edmonton in 1990.

Canada's unmatched internal investment in games festivals contributes to its unique status. Inter-provincial 'Canada Games' are held every two years at different cities. There are also national Canadian games for special groups, such as mentally and physically disabled athletes and senior citizens. In addition, each provincial government has established its own provincial games, such as the Alberta Games, Quebec Games, summer and winter variety, as well as those for special groups in the provincial population. All of these different kinds of games, i.e. multi-sport festivals, are recognized by the various levels of government in Canada – and elsewhere – as significant and regular tourist attractions, and advertised widely as such by the local hosts and organizers of each event (Redmond, 1988).

But even multi-sport festivals may not represent the biggest sporting and tourist attraction. It is debatable whether the Olympic Games or the World Cup in Association Football (Soccer) is the world's largest single sports event. World Championships in single sports, are noteworthy attractions too, whether they be the World Series (Baseball) or Superbowl (American Football) in the United States; the America's Cup in Yachting; the Tour de France Cycling Race; or the Lawn Tennis Championship at Wimbledon. There are diverse other sporting events that are less well known in an international capacity, from the Calgary Stampede (rodeo) to the Hong Kong Dragon Boat Races, which consistently attract devotees in their thousands. Travel to hundreds of sports events worldwide is eagerly arranged by tour operators; witness this recent extravagant example advertised in *Golf* magazine for the 1991 British Open Golf Championship:

> An ultra-luxurious eight-night British Open tour departing New York July 14 via British Airways Concorde to Liverpool features transportation by vintage Rolls-Royce to Shrigley Hall, a Regency-style country house set in a 262-acre estate; a two-day tournament at Shrigley's Golf course; admission to the Open at Royal Birkdale (including use of a chandeliered tent); sightseeing tours; all meals and a gala farewell dinner;...
>
> (*Golf*, 1991)

This succinctly illustrates how many of the pleasures of the modern tourist are organised around a single sporting event, how sport is now part of the core of the tourism industry.

National parks

The 1988 Winter Olympic Games in Calgary were preceded by vigorous attempts to secure them for 1968 and 1972, in Banff National Park. These efforts failed for various reasons, including the growing opposition of conservationists. They argued that such games and their associated facilities were contrary to the original purpose of national parks, a doubtful proposition in view of the variety of recreational amenities introduced in this park since its establishment in the 1880s (Nelson and Scace, 1968).

This Canadian example indicates an international dichotomy of function in the modern world, between parks as 'playgrounds for people' and/or as places to be preserved largely untouched for posterity. The rise of recreation and sport, aided by the mass social mobility afforded by the car, aeroplane, bus and train, has intruded upon parks' space everywhere. Many of the developments described in this chapter, such as the proliferation of sports resorts or the increase in sports vacations, have taken place within the boundaries of national parks, whether they be in Canada, England, or several such areas in the United States. To conservationists, this is a deplorable trend which must be reversed; to others, especially some developers and athletic tourists, it is natural and desirable growth.

In the Canadian context, national parks have been actively promoted for profitable tourism, a promotion in which sport played no small part. Bella (1987) has convincingly demonstrated the historical tension between the use of parks for preservation and/or profit. Throughout her analysis she mentions various sports and explains how even low budgets did not prevent the development of sporting facilities in parks. Under the 1939 National Forestry Programme, for example, workers were used to build athletic grounds, golf courses and ski slopes. Earlier, in 1917, the Parks Branch obtained the Canadian Pacific Railway (CPR) golf course in Banff, in order to enlarge it, a move readily supported by the Banff Board of Trade. The Premier of Newfoundland, where Terra Nova National Park was established in 1957, actively intervened in developments to ensure that they had: 'all the recreation facilities available in the national parks in the other Canadian provinces – such as golf courses, tennis courts and swimming pools'. Delegates to a national conference on conservation held in 1961 heard that: 'More intensive use of and greater return from resources devoted to recreational purposes' was still needed. By the early 1980s: 'hang-gliders, bicyclists, snowmobilers, hostellers, hikers, riders, campers and cavers', as well as golfers and skiers, were all seeking policy changes to increase their opportunities. Some of the world's best-known ski resorts are in Banff National Park and Jasper National Park, including Canada's largest such facility at Lake Louise; and Alberta Tourism has recently launched a $250,000 'Treasure of the Rockies' advertising campaign to promote them, as well as Kananaskis Provincial Park and Canadian Pacific Hotels and Resorts (*Tourism Intelligence Bulletin*, 1990b).

The philosophy and role of parks, is a broad and complex issue which cannot be adequately addressed here but the Canadian model illustrates that the almost insatiable appetite of tourists everywhere for recreational and sporting experiences now presents one of the biggest challenges within the tourism industry. It is one of the issues increasingly debated at the growing number of conferences on tourism worldwide. Many presenters at these conferences are employed in various capacities within the tourism industry, some directly related to sport. The growth of sports tourism has meant that more 'traditional' roles, from parks wardens or ski instructors to swimming pool managers, have been expanded or joined by positions specifically related to sports tourism. All the developments briefly mentioned in the chapter are offering new kinds of employment opportunities – whether it be on the staff in a National Park, in one of the growing number of sports museums, an instructor on a sports cruise, one of the organizers of sports festival, or the leisure director of new hotel resort and/or spa.

Conclusion

Sports tourism is a vast and growing enterprise whose significance is not yet matched in the related literature of tourism, or sport. The often over-used term 'cutting edge' may be appropriately applied to contemporary developments within this high profile segment of the tourism industry. This will no doubt change in the future as more research is focused upon all its components, and not just those discussed here. It is hoped, however, that the examples given indicate the international importance of sports tourism. Ministers of tourism in many countries are already heavily involved in sport at several different levels, a commitment likely to become a permanent responsibility everywhere.

References

Alexander, E.P. (1979) *Museums in Motion: An Introduction to the History and Functions of Museums.* American Association for State and Local History, Nashville.

Arlott, J. (ed.) (1975) *The Oxford Companion to Sports and Games.* Oxford University Press, London, New York and Toronto.

Bannerman, G. (1982) *Cruise Ships: The Inside Story.* Collins, Toronto.

Bella, L. (1987) *Parks for Profit.* Harvest House, Montreal.

Bonciolini, L. (1988) National tourism week: tourism works in America. *Travelhost,* March 27, N2–3.

Cooper, C. (1988) Global tourism: a 1988 perspective. *Leisure Management,* March, 36–38.

Edmonton Journal (1988) May 28, F1.

Edmonton Journal (1989) September 30, F4.

Edmonton Sun (1988) April 6, 51.

Ellis, T. and Norton, R.L. (1988) *Commercial Recreation.* Times Mirror/Mosby College, St. Louis.

European Travel & Life (1988) April, 90–91.

Friedland, L. (1987) Cruise news. *Travel and Leisure,* May, 78–79.

Goldsmith, A., Lansing, A., and Levy, L. (1983) *Summer Camps and Programs.* Harmony Books, New York.

Golf (1991) January.

Green, H. (1986) *Fit for America: Health, Fitness, Sport and American Society.* Pantheon, New York.

Grover, K. (ed) (1989) *Fitness in American Culture.* University of Massachusetts, Amherst.

Harding, A. (1987) Bargain spas. *Chatelaine.* July, 38, 123–127.

Harding, A. (1989) *Select Spas.* Harding, Toronto.

Harris, H. A. (1972) *Sport in Greece and Rome.* Cornell University Press, Ithaca, NY.

In Britain, (1990) March, Diary, 52.

Intrigue (1989) Intra Travel Corporation, Toronto, pp.9–13

Jackson, E.L. and Burton, T.L. (eds) (1989) *Understanding Leisure and Recreation: Mapping the Past, Charting the Future.* Venture Publishing Inc., State College, PA 16803.

Lang, G. (1990) Family plan. *Travel & Leisure,* July, 1990, 82–90, 131.

Lasch, C. (1979) *The Culture of Narcissism.* Warner, New York.

Leisure Management, (1988a) April 29, 4–5.

Leisure Management, (1988b) March, 9.

Lewis, G. and Redmond, G. (1971) *Sporting Heritage: A Guide to Halls of Fame, Special Collections and Museums in the United States and Canada.* A.S. Barnes, New York.

Life (1987) February.

Livesey, H.B. (1990) Barcelona rising to new heights. *Travel & Leisure,* June, 136–160.

Loy, J., Jr., Kenyon, G.S. and McPherson, B.D. (eds) (1981) *Sport, Culture and Society,* 2nd edn. Lea and Febiger, Philadelphia.

Macintosh, D., Bedecki, T. and Franks, C.E.S. (1987) *Sport and Politics in Canada.* McGill-Queen's University, Kingston and Montreal.

Mandell, R.D. (1984) *Sport: A Cultural History.* Columbia University Press, New York.

Martin, W. and Mason, S. (1984) The Economic Impact of Leisure. *World Leisure and Recreation,* December, 54–60.

Michael, J.W. (1984) The top spas of Europe. *Town and Country,* April, 126–134.

Mill, R.C. and Morrison, A.M. (1985) *The Tourism System: An Introductory Text.* Prentice-Hall, Inc., Englewood Cliffs, New Jersey.

Nelson, J.G. and Scace, R.C. (eds) (1968) *Canadian Parks in Perspective.* University of Calgary, Calgary.

Nicklaus, J. (1989) *The Golf Courses of Jack Nicklaus.* Bison, London.

Norwegian Cruise Line (1988) *Voyages,* Canada, pp.12–13.

Observer (1989) 16 April, 20.

Owen, C. (1979) *The Grand Days of Travel.* Windward/Webb & Bower, Exeter.

Preston, B. (1990) The pursuit of happiness. *West,* November, 26–34.

Rand, A. (1983) The widening world of Club Med. *Travel & Leisure,* February, 69–73, 82.

Read, S. (1986) *Hello Campers!* Bantam Press, London.

Redmond, G. (1988) A Plethora of Games: Multi-sport-Festivals in the Modern World. Paper presented at The First World Congress on Free Time, Culture and Society, Chateau Lake Louise, May 16–22.

Sargent, P. (1987) Taking the waters: British spas. *Leisure Management,* March, 35–38.

Skinner, J.S. (1988) The fitness industry. In: Malina, R.M. and Eckert, H.M. (eds), *Physical Activity in Early and Modern Populations.* Human Kinetics, Champaign, IL 61820, pp. 67–72.

Soderberg, P., Washington, H. and Press, J.C. (eds) (1977) *The Big Book of Halls of Fame in the United States and Canada.* RR Bowker, New York and London.

Sports Institute Study Group (1975) *Report of the Australian Sports Institute Study Group.* Department of Tourism and Recreation, Canberra.

The Spa Finder. (1988) Jeffrey Joseph, New York.

Thurmond, R.C. (1978) Sports Museums, Halls of Fame, Libraries and America's Passion for Sport History. Paper presented at The North American Society for Sport History (NASSH) Convention, University of Maryland, May 25–28.

Times Educational Supplement (1966) October 14, *In Corpore Sano.*

Tourism Intelligence Bulletin (1990a) September.

Tourism Intelligence Bulletin (1990b) November.

Travel & Leisure (1988) June, pp.49,192.

Travelling on Business (1987) March, 3, 5–6.

Turner, L. and Ash, J. (1975) *The Golden Hordes. International Tourism and the Pleasure Periphery.* Constable, London.

Vickerman, R.W. (1975) *The Economics of Leisure and Recreation.* Macmillan, London.

Ward, C. and Hardy, D. (1986) *Goodnight Campers! The History of the British Holiday Camp.* Mansell, London.

Ward, D. (1986) *Complete Handbook to Cruising.* Berlitz, Lausanne, Switzerland.

Wechsberg, J. (1979) *The Lost World of the Great Spas.* Harper and Row, London and New York.

Williams, B. (1988) Stressed to kill. *Destinations,* June 7–9.

Zeigler, E.F. (ed.) (1988) *History of Physical Education and Sport.* Stipes, Champaign, Illinois.

Chapter 7

Products, Places and Promotion: Destination Images in the Analysis of the Tourism Industry

G.J.Ashworth

Marketing as an analytical framework for tourism

The three main components of a holiday, namely the tourist, the holiday 'product' (consisting of a set of facilities, activities or experiences), and the industry, can be related together in many different ways. The nomenclature attached to these components by researchers investigating tourism normally betrays the approach being applied to the relationship between the components. Among the possible ways of considering this relationship is the industrial approach, as in the preceding chapters, or behavioural or spatial planning and development approaches, as in the following chapters. However, it is the contention here that marketing science offers a similar relational approach which, because it possesses a more integrated analytical framework, is in some ways superior for it is derived from, and is logically based upon, both the industrial and behavioural approaches. Its advantage is that it juxtaposes the various components in a way which allows studies of quite different aspects of tourism, utilising different disciplinary techniques of analysis, to be incorporated into the same process model.

A marketing approach confers two benefits. First, it provides a holistic framework of analysis within which the various, and otherwise extremely diverse, components of tourism can be incorporated, and thereby the relations between them examined. This not only encourages new insights into the relations between the individual components and the system as a whole, but also allows strategies for intervention at any point in the model to be devised and its effects on the system to be monitored. Second, within such a framework the accent is placed very firmly upon the means by which supply and demand are brought together. This is the central process of marketing: a set of deliberate actions designed to influence the system so as to achieve certain predetermined goals for the organisation or individual engaging in such actions. In other words, strategy is not an afterthought or modifier acting upon an existing situation, it is an integral requirement of the operation of the system itself.

Both the activity of tourism, and the marketing approach need to be subject to simplifying assumptions so that analysis remains manageable. The argument presented here depends upon two basic axioms: first, to paraphrase the idea of 'hedonic utility' derived from consumer economics (Lancaster, 1966) and applied to tourism (Stabler, 1988; Sinclair *et al.*, 1990), that the demand for holidays emanates from a consumer reaction to perceptions of anticipated tourism experiences which are inextricably place-bound; second, that the tourism product is a set of such experiences packaged as a destination place and marketed largely through images of that place. Both statements represent particular and partial views of tourism. However, they provide a focus upon places and images. The first is a means of integrating both supply and demand variables; the second offers the most obvious and effective means of manipulating the system.

A precondition for the successful use of this approach is the redefinition of the tourism components in marketing terms, and thus the incorporation into the model of the marketing concepts that underpin them. Once this has been achieved the active component, marketing, can be isolated, and image promotion as one instrument of this intervention placed within its proper context of the marketing process as a whole.

It should be stressed that marketing science is not being applied to tourism here as a set of sales techniques (for which a number of handbooks exist, such as Holloway and Plant, 1988; Middleton, 1988, or Jefferson and Lickorish, 1988). Nor is it being suggested that it is a method of management of industrial organisations (Mill and Morrison, 1985) and still less a synonym for the exercise of such political–economic policies as either commercialisation or privatisation. It is offered as a means of structuring, and thereby understanding, the important relationships between otherwise extremely diverse phenomena, which in turn allows the exercise of deliberate influence upon them, for whatever reasons.

If marketing as an explanatory structure is to be devised from the industrial analogy, which forms the core explanatory framework of this book, then a number of tasks are necessary. First, the various elements that comprise the marketing process must be identified within the tourism industry, and the central function of place images within this process isolated. Second, the characteristics, variety, origin and malleability of such images can best be demonstrated through a range of case studies. From these illustrations the use of place images when intervention in the market occurs, and the necessary steps in moving from analysis to strategy, can be outlined.

The elements of place marketing as applied to tourism

At its simplest, place marketing is the manipulation of up to four main components within a particular context. The application of this approach to tourism poses three basic questions:

- which components?
- within what context?
- how manipulated?

The same questions are posed in any marketing situation but here two additional features, each of which introduces distinctive peculiarities, have to be incorporated. These are, first, the application specifically to tourism and, second, the assumption that the place, in this case the tourism destination, is the product. Each of these features necessitates modification to the basic marketing model.

The components

The three fundamental components of tourism referred to earlier, the tourist, the product and the industry, re-emerge somewhat transformed, as three elements in the marketing process. To these three can be added goals to make a fourth element. The transformation is essentially that if the industry component encompasses marketing intervention, perhaps reflecting different goals, then that intervention should be designed to bring the tourist (consumer) and product satisfactorily to the point of exchange within the market. Established analyses of the consumer and industry generally are relatively easily applied to tourism, but consideration of the product is likely to cause problems, which in practice have often been either ignored, thus rendering the marketing process ineffective, or regarded as an unsurmountable reason for not applying it in the first place. These components or elements are examined in turn. Figure 7.1 indicates the relationship between these components in the marketing process.

The tourism consumer

The tourist can be treated in much the same way as the consumer of most other services, the difficulties that arise being practical rather than conceptual. The problem is that the consumer of the tourism place-product is identifiable only through the motivation and behaviour of the customer at the point of consumption, rather than in terms of any prior classification. Thus 'tourists' are not a species of consumer fundamentally different from 'residents' or other groups, but are only definable in terms of their relation to the product. From this juncture the segmentation of the market, a necessary preliminary to the targeting of the marketing effort, through various aspects of purchasing behaviour rather than through more general demographic, social or economic categorisations, can proceed.

The market intervention

By market intervention is meant the marketing measures through which the consumer is brought to the point of consumption, which in tourism is also the location of production, itself an unusual occurrence, and these measures include all those generally found in the marketing of other commercial goods and services. It has been argued that the marketing of place products, in particular, presents an opportunity for a wider rather than narrower range of measures to be included in the marketing mix (Ashworth and Voogd, 1988). This is because a series of strictly physical design features can be added to the more conventional measures. In any event, image promotion is likely to be both the most employed and the most effective of such measures. Marketing measures are instruments for the attainment of predetermined goals, themselves expressed through marketing strategies. The measures are not goals in themselves although often mistakenly treated as such.

The product

The discussion of what is the tourism product can yield a number of widely different answers, depending upon the definition of who is the producer. From the viewpoint of the consumer the product is necessarily the individual internalised holiday experience, assembled from a variety of components available and produced, therefore, by him or her as the holidaymaker. To the industry intermediaries the product is the package of services assembled and sold, while to the component suppliers at the destination, who may also term themselves the 'industry', it is a particular activity, facility, good or service sold or hired to holidaymakers or the intermediaries. In effect the destination is taken to be the product.

This in turn raises a myriad of practical and conceptual difficulties, arising from the intrinsic characteristics of places. The attributes of spatial scale and hierarchy, multifunctionality and consequent multi-selling of the same physical space as different products in different markets, have been described in Ashworth and Voogd (1990). Some of the consequences of these attributes, however, will become apparent below.

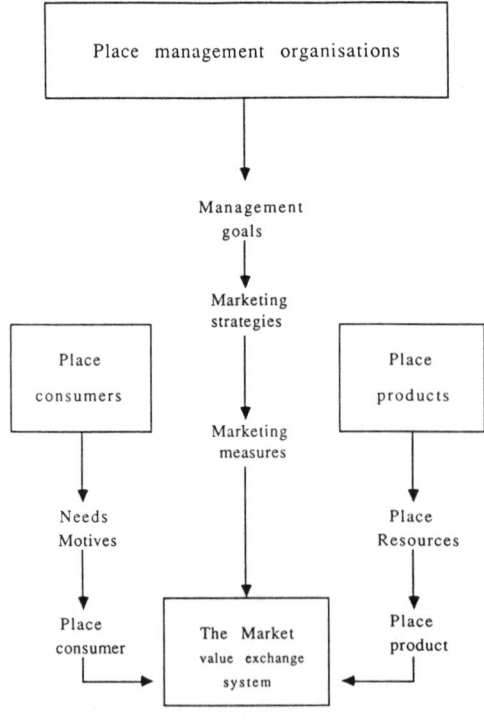

Figure 7.1 Elements in a place marketing system

Goals

The significance of the fourth component, the goals of the organisation, only becomes apparent in place marketing. All marketing, by definition, is a goal-directed and not a purposeless activity. Thus all organisations engaging in marketing have specified goals which direct the exercise. However, in most commercial marketing of goods and services the goal of profit maximisation can be taken to be so simple and measurable as to need no further comment. Place marketing, in contrast, is more usually pursued as part of much broader place management, which in addition is likely to be undertaken for collective rather than individual benefit. Whether the organisations engaging in place marketing for tourism are themselves part of the private or public sectors is irrelevant; the important question is the nature of the objectives of the organisation. Place management objectives are likely to be vague, difficult to monitor, long term rather than immediate, and multifarious rather than simple. This does not mean that they are less important, only that they are more difficult to incorporate into the marketing model.

The pursuit of these goals is undertaken through marketing strategies. The assumption must not be made that the goals and the resulting strategies of the marketing exercise are self-evident. Table 7.1, for example, gives a list of some possible tourism place marketing strategies, each stemming from quite different place management objectives, in different demand situations.

Table 7.1   Tourism place marketing strategies in relation to types of demand and stage in a product life-cycle (loosely after Kotler, 1975)

Phase in product life cycle	Type of demand	Possible marketing strategy
Introduction	No demand	Stimulational marketing
Development	Latent demand	Developmental marketing
Growth	Full demand	Maintenance marketing
Saturation	Over full demand	Demarketing
Decline	Faltering demand	Remarketing
Relaunch	Negative demand	Conversional marketing

The context

The context within which these elements are combined is the market which is both an abstract concept derived from a set of ideal and unobtainable assumptions, as well as a mechanism governing the interrelationships between the elements. The exchange concept, which lies at the heart of the general theory of marketing, requires that the consumer has a free choice of alternatives, the producer free access to potential consumers, and that a free exchange of product for value occurs. The obvious imperfections in such a scenario are not in themselves critical. Indeed it is only the existence of such imperfections that allows the development of interventional strategy, whether on the part of the consumer, maximising product choice, or the producer, maximising customer exposure, which is the essence of marketing. The relevant difficulty here lies in the application of such a concept to tourism place-products. Put more accurately, it is the problem of the way the distinctive attributes of both tourism as an activity and holiday destinations as places result in the development of quite distinctive markets for such products, which consequently require specialised marketing.

The mechanism

The means through which the components interact within markets is quite simply the price mechanism. It is action through this mechanism that provides the opportunity for manipulation. Without pricing neither the producer nor the consumer can pursue their various optimisation strategies. Without pricing there is no competitive market and no exchange principle can operate. Tourism place marketing is not, however, 'marketing without markets', an obvious contradiction; it is marketing in a system where pricing is frequently indirect in terms of who pays, when, and how much. Such payment may be calculated in non-monetary units and be difficult to account for. This in turn often makes the process of tourism place marketing difficult, indirect, and gives rise to a sluggish response. It does not, however, make it impossible. Again it should not be concluded that because pricing is difficult it is necessarily unimportant and so can be ignored. Such a reaction makes impossible the essential monitoring of the effectiveness of marketing and thus renders the exercise largely futile.

The special function of place images in marketing

Place-product images can be most easily analysed through the use of a simple radio analogy as shown in Figure 7.2. The complex amalgam of ideas, preconceptions, intentions, promises, expectations that comprise the tourism image of a place can be approached from the side of the product or the potential consumer. Images can be conceived of as being projected, whether consciously in the form of promotion or not; they are then transmitted through various channels of communication, which themselves influence or distort the nature of the message, the strength, effectiveness or credibility of its transmission and the accuracy of the targeting of its reception. Finally from the many such messages received, a set of images is assembled by consumers in accordance with their own predisposed constructs, and their behaviour is thereby influenced. Exactly how such projection, transmission and reception occurs and how the process can be most effectively influenced to attain predetermined behavioural results, is the concern of social-psychologists (Pearce, 1981), semiologists (Burgess and Wood, 1988) or advertising executives (Wertheim, 1988). The obvious, but largely ignored, implication of importance here is that the study of any isolated part of this whole continuous process will be misleadingly incomplete. Yet this is precisely what has happened in most tourism research on these topics. 'Market research' is usually restricted to that part of the whole marketing process concerned with the received images of latent customers. Alternatively, projected images are usually analysed in the form of officially promoted images without

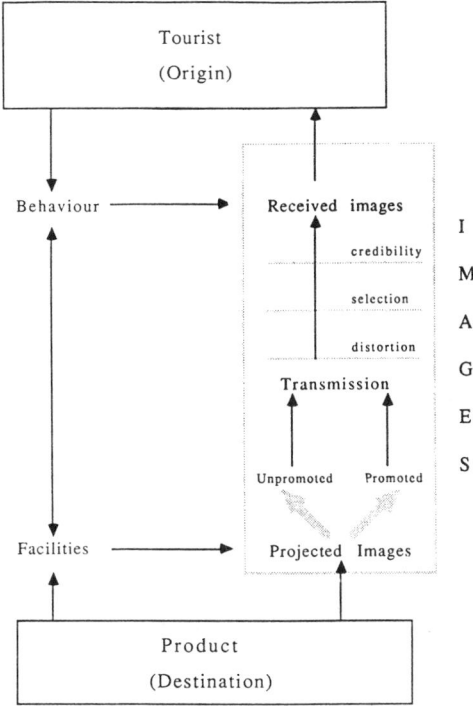

Figure 7.2   Tourism place images in a simple system

reference to either transmission or reception. In this field of marketing, where the very definition of the product depends upon its appreciation by the customer, such an approach without reference to demand is in serious danger of being meaningless. Part of the explanation for the absence of complete studies of place imaging lies in the restricted goals and requirements of the research commissioning agencies, but in part can also be related to the nature of the research design required to obtain information on the different stages of image projection, transmission and reception. The need to employ different research techniques makes it difficult to relate results and thus trace the whole process, however desirable that might be.

A second and even wider integrative use of place imaging is to relate work on images to parallel studies on both the supply and demand sides of tourism destinations. Projected images are ultimately derived from the structure of tourism supply, while received images, if not directly stemming from, at least have an intimate relationship with actual or anticipated tourism behaviour. Both facility supply and visitor behaviour have been extensively researched in many types of destination, but have only rarely been linked to image research in the same locations. The practical dangers of basing policy upon such disintegrated studies, where promotion loses contact with the nature of the product being promoted and where visitors' perceptions are not related to their actual behaviour, are obvious. Again, the more serious loss is not to the short term efficiency of

127

promotional exercises, or even to the quality of the individual holiday experience, it is the missed opportunity of using marketing analysis as an instrument for understanding the functioning of tourism places as a whole.

Tourism place marketing images in the Mediterranean

The selection of a range of case studies from the Mediterranean with which to illustrate place marketing as a means of analysing tourism has a number of advantages. A simple but clear general tourism image of the Mediterranean as a holiday experience is widely held and has been diffused throughout the main markets. This has occurred regardless of the considerable differences that exist between its various destinations in physical and man-made endowment, and variations in the history of tourism development. From the viewpoint both of a large proportion of customers and of producers, the geographical area defines a single 'choice opportunity set' (Stabler, 1989). Thus considerable variety of place-products exists within what is largely a single competitive market. In particular the main distinguishing variable appears to be the history of tourism development, with a continuous series of 'new' place-products appearing on the market needing to compete with those already existing. Something of the context for the following case studies of images can be appreciated in Figure 7.3, which introduces some of the participants, and Figure 7.4 which arrays some of the competing destinations along a product development curve.

Tour operator images of Turkey

Turkey is a relative newcomer to the fiercely competitive market for Mediterranean beach package holidays offered principally to north west European consumers. Developing in the early 1980s, it had attracted almost four million holiday packages by 1988 (Figure 7.5). This relatively late development of large-scale foreign tourism on the base of a very limited pre-existing domestic tourism, has resulted in some problems, some distinctive characteristics, and some reactive strategies on the part of the producers.

The producers in this context were principally tour operators based in the major markets of north western Europe, who played the initiating role in developing Turkish tourism, both by assembling the elements of the package and marketing it. These operators were, at least initially, predominantly small, independent firms who identified an increasing market division in the 1980s between a mass market seeking low cost packages, needing a high volume of sales on low profit margins, and a more discerning specialised market requiring a more diversified and higher priced product.

The role played by the Turkish governmental agencies in the destination resorts was largely permissive and on occasion supportive, through subsidies and fiscal concessions (coordinated through the Tourism Encouragement Act of 1986 which established favoured tourism development areas within which such support would be concentrated), rather than initiatory, even in the field of national image marketing (Uysal and Crompton, 1984). The aims of the Turkish government were principally national economic, with foreign tourism earnings contributing up to a quarter of total export earnings, and national political. The political objectives, which were necessarily vaguely delineated and expressed, were

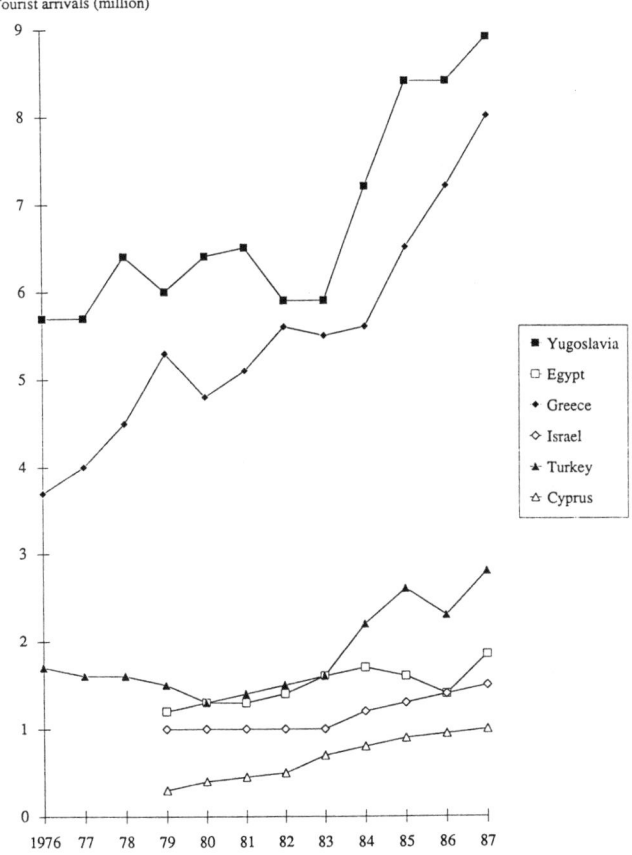

Tourist arrivals (million)

Yugoslavia
Egypt
Greece
Israel
Turkey
Cyprus

Figure 7.3 A comparison of tourism arrivals in some eastern Mediterranean destinations

essentially concerned with the reinforcing of an image among citizens of West European countries of Turkey as a western secular state. This was seen as aiding foreign policy objectives in relation to the European Community and, to a lesser extent, the long-standing political disputes with Greece in the Aegean and Cyprus. The introduction of political motives alongside the economic in national image building obviously complicates the establishment of goals, and thus marketing strategies and measures.

However, it must be remembered that Turkish tourism was to a high degree demand-led, originating mainly from the countries of north western Europe, with the authorities in the destination places playing only a reactive, enabling and occasionally obstructive role. In some ways the more significant Turkish contribution emanated from tour operators, some of which had developed links with Turkey as a consequence of the travel demands of Turkish resident workers in western Europe, and some of whose personnel were of Turkish origin.

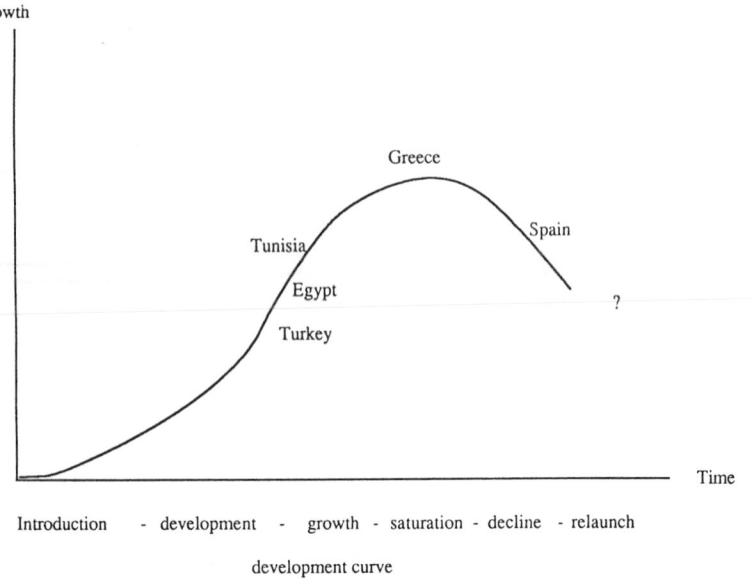

Figure 7.4 Some Mediterranean place products on a product development curve

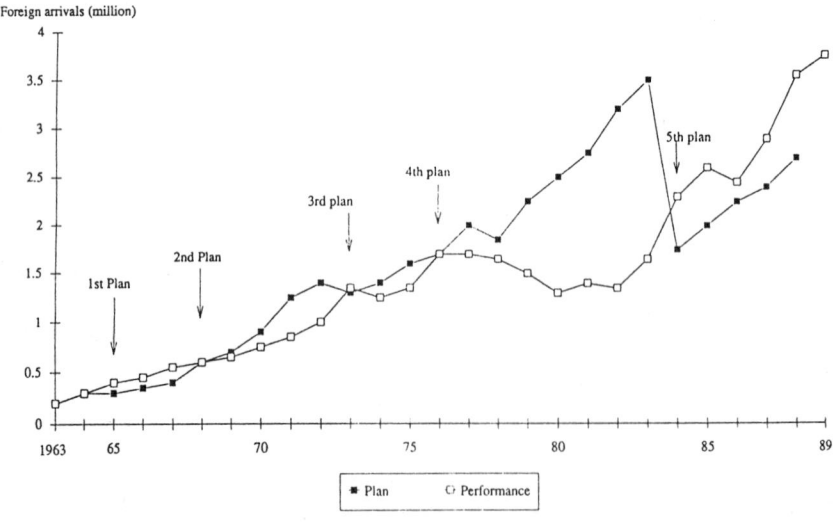

Figure 7.5 Turkey: a comparison of projected and actual foreign tourist arrivals

Clearly a new entrant has to shape and project a place image that is both different from established competitors and a reaction to them. In the case of Turkey, the fundamental dilemma faced by those promoting the destination image strategy could be summarised as, on the one hand, the need to emulate existing competitors, especially the market leaders in this particular product line, particularly, given both proximity and the political situation, Greece. On the other hand there was a need to present a local distinctiveness that highlighted its superiority over the role models. The three most important place resources identified by Seekings (1989) related to the coast (in particular its suitability for beach tourism in terms of quality, variety and shore length), sets of historical associations, recognisable in western markets, and a certain eastern exoticism as a result of its Asiatic associations. Only the last could be said to be distinctive, in competition with Greece.

The market segment being targeted was that established in Mediterranean beach packages in general, and which had already been successfully sold as an eastern Mediterranean beach destination image. The strategy was to present the Turkish product as a variant on the established Greek one, with the early phase in the product life-cycle being presented so as to give the competitive advantage of an 'unspoilt' thus implying a less crowded and cheaper destination, with the added esteem of pioneer status.

The way the key suppliers, the tour operators, saw Turkey as a destination and subsequently promoted it through their brochures was investigated by Laban (1989) in a case study of all firms operating in the Dutch market. Figure 7.6 summarises the importance attached to the various components of the image of Turkey as a holiday destination. The tour operators stated that recognition of important elements and those actually promoted in the holiday brochures issued by them were broadly similar.

A number of difficulties were implicit in this strategy, of which the most fundamental and long term were those relating to image content. First the obvious dualism between the promotion of the beach product and the heritage product has created tension, although not necessarily for the visitor: the beach and heritage tourism markets are largely socially, demographically and spatially separate. The former concentrates on the central and southern Aegean coast and the bay of Antalya on the south coast, while the latter is both more concentrated in the western cities and dispersed through Anatolia. The joint promotion of 'sun' and 'history' images was not necessarily discordant. To the beach holidaymaker, heritage was a background feature and day-excursion attraction, while to the heritage visitor the beach element was simply irrelevant. The problem lay in a certain vacillation of national government policy towards these quite different destination products, partly as a reaction to the quite different patterns of economic and spatial distribution that resulted. The concentration of beach package tourism (Figure 7.7) had both advantages and disadvantages in terms of regional policy, while heritage tourism offered the possibilities both of moving 'upmarket' as well as opening up the central and eastern districts of the country.

The content of the heritage image itself raised a political difficulty, stemming from the different uses of heritage. As has been stressed elsewhere (Ashworth and Tunbridge, 1990), heritage by definition is customer-defined, and

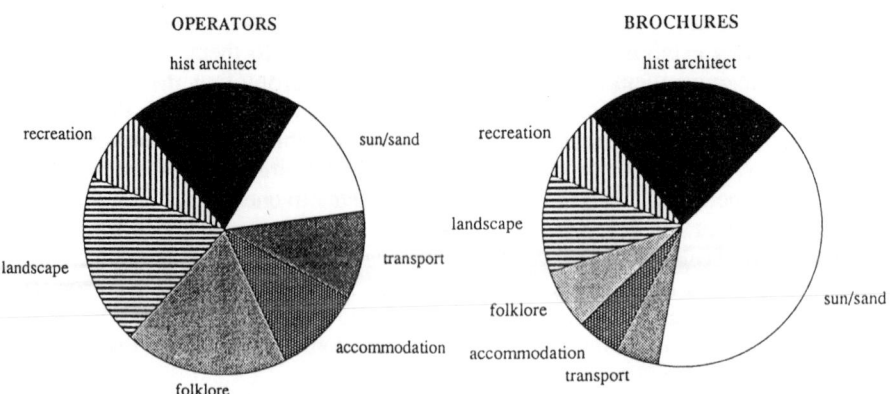

Figure 7.6 Elements in the tourism image held of Turkey held by tour operators and presented in brochures

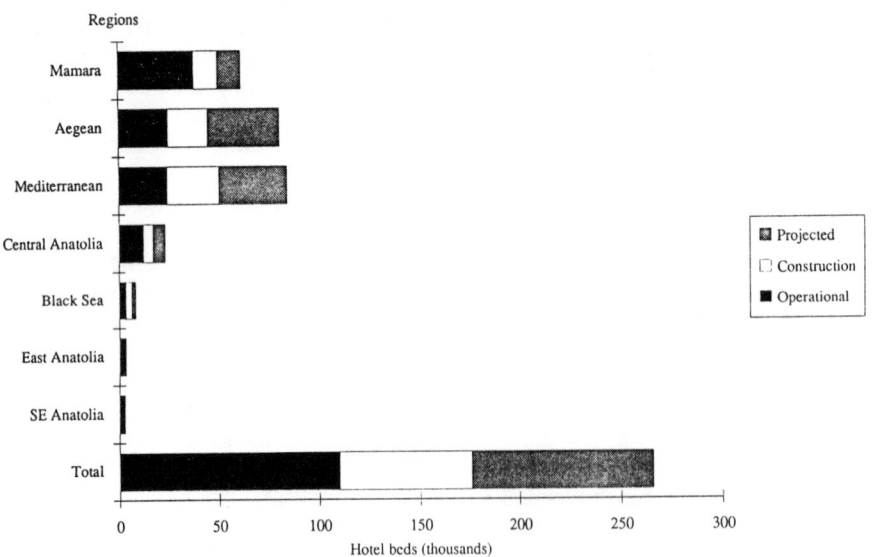

Figure 7.7 Licences for hotel development in Turkey

the attempt to use it simultaneously to satisfy two distinct purposes may create tensions. In this case heritage was being promoted to western visitors as a tourism resource and to Turks as a reinforcement to nation building. Two quite distinct heritage product lines were therefore on offer. The visitor's heritage was necessarily principally classical and early Christian, while the heritage 'sold' domestically and used as part of nation building is Turanian and Kemalist; Ephesus, Homer and St. Paul on the one side, and Bursa, Ottoman sultans, and Ataturk on the other. Even many of those limited aspects of Turkish heritage that have an appeal to visitors tend to be flavoured with an eastern exoticism (such as Ottoman decadence, Topkapi harems, or dancing dervishes at Konya) which is contrary to the secular, western-oriented republicanism upon which the state is based. The combination of 'culture' and 'tourism' in the same central government ministry, as well as the coincidence of the timing of the growth of western tourism, with the rise in a number of external and internal perceived threats to the integrity and character of the Turkish state, such as Islamic fundamentalism, ethnic minority unrest, political polarisation, and the hostility of western liberals, all compounded the problem.

The more short term difficulty which took on the dimensions of a crisis by the end of the 1980s was equally implicit in the original image promotion strategy. The use of the 'unspoilt Greece' image was an obviously wasting asset, as well as a competitive advantage that could also be exploited by subsequent new entrants to the market in the eastern Mediterranean. In any event 'unspoilt' often also meant unprepared, especially in terms of public utilities, and trained manpower to staff tourism facilities, a problem highlighted by the Turkish association of travel organisations (TURKSAB) (Laban, 1989). Poor-quality infrastructure, soaring costs, a reputation for poor service and even visa restrictions in some important western markets, arising from political frictions with some western governments, resulted, by the end of the 1980s, in a clear set-back to tourism development and the introduction of a number of negative elements in the received image of Turkey as a beach package destination. Undoubtedly much of the 'stimulational marketing' of the 1980s could be classified as 'premature marketing', i.e. promotion that outstripped product development, and needs now to be replaced by 'conversional' strategies aimed at image correction rather than image creation.

Comparative customer images of Egypt and Tunisia

The study of the Turkish case stressed the role of tour operators and destination governments in promotional images, whereas that of Dijk (1989), of Egypt and Tunisia in the context of other Mediterranean destinations, examined the received images of actual and potential Dutch visitors to a range of destinations. The Dutch market has many of the typical economic, social and holiday experience characteristics of west European consumers. In the study potential customers, making personal enquiries at the travel office of the main Dutch travel association (ANWB), were questioned about their image of Egypt and Tunisia as possible holiday destinations. The general content of these customer images can be summarised as simple, vague and comparative. The simplicity stemmed from the limited number of dimensions used (principally sun, beach quality, well known heritage attractions, together with shopping and catering possibilities).

133

G.J. Ashworth

The vagueness reflected a single image, not only of an entire country, regardless of any differences in its nature, but also of whole groups of countries. Both Tunisia and Egypt were frequently included in a wider north African or even Islamic Middle Eastern image. Somewhat in contrast, but not necessarily in contradiction to this, potential customers placed particular destinations in a comparative context, whether this was requested or not, often in the form of the product development curve considered earlier (Figure 7.4). Thus countries were assigned positions on such a developmental curve and thereby were seen to possess advantages or disadvantages in relation to competitors. Different respondents could of course regard the same position as either attractive or repellent. For example, 'unspoilt' could also be 'underdeveloped' and 'crowded' seen as 'lively'.

The most significant consumer characteristic affecting the nature of the image held of destinations was previous holiday experience, either of a particular destination or of other eastern Mediterranean tourism destinations. The 'mental souvenirs' (Pearce, 1981) acquired by such experience led generally to more positive, or at least less negative, images. Such experience need not necessarily be at a particular destination to affect the image of it. Experience of any one east Mediterranean destination was diffused over images of its neighbours, especially in removing impeding characteristics. Of particular importance in this context are the negative elements among the images of potential visitors, that act as barriers to the eventual purchase of a holiday. These tend to relate to practical aspects of the preconceived holiday, such as costs, the standard of hotels, and the quality and characteristics of the catering, rather than contact with a broader but unfamiliar culture. Thus Dijk found that the Arabic, Islamic countries were not particularly disadvantaged in this respect compared with southern European destinations.

Government sponsored images of Malta and Cyprus

The role of governments, in particular, and local political factors, in general, in the shaping of the image of the tourism place-product can be put alongside the creative intermediary of the Turkish example, and the customer in the case of Egypt and Tunisia. Although destination governments have substantial powers of image projection, they also have wider responsibilities for the management of places than for tourism alone. Thus the main difficulty that arises is that tourism place images are only one form of image, and may be in competition with others which have simultaneously been devised and projected for quite different purposes.

In the case of Malta, a tourism product based upon traditional Mediterranean beach characteristics has been successfully sold, overwhelmingly on the British inclusive package tour market, in the last ten years. This tourism is principally concentrated in a string of north coast resorts from Sliema to St. Paul's Bay. The use of heritage elements in the destination image, however, presents a number of dilemmas, similar in some respects but more subtle than those described for Turkey. Malta's peculiar dependence on British imperial policy for 150 years has endowed it with a substantial heritage of direct relevance to its major foreign tourism market. Linguistic and culinary familiarity has been a major element in this particular market penetration. There are growing arguments for a broader and more explicit marketing of a heritage product. These include a policy of

134

augmenting economic benefits without increasing actual tourist numbers and thus perceived environmental and congestion costs (a 'ceiling' of two million annual visitors has been proposed as an optimum capacity) achievable by attracting higher spending heritage tourists, including a higher proportion from continental European markets. Such a product would require the further development of a heritage product based principally upon Malta's past colonial roles, whether under British, French or Knights Hospitaller rule (such as the great sieges of 1563 and 1940–1942).

A difficulty here is the simultaneous use of local history to reinforce a distinctly national post-independence identity. A heritage image for local consumption stresses linguistic and historic distinctiveness, which is at best irrelevant to the visitor and at worst conflicting. These differences are reflected in such factors as public statutory policy, and local street name changes as well as a sharply vacillating government foreign policy, and attitude towards tourism development. The possibility of spatial segregation, open in the Turkish case, is rendered next to impossible by the small size of the country, so that local destination place images are difficult to distinguish from those of the nation-state as a whole.

The Cyprus case is particularly interesting because of the direct and important involvement of a range of national political factors in tourism. In terms of place product definition, beach package tourism to Cyprus has much in common with the history of development in Turkey. A similar mix of beach and heritage components was combined and sold on west European markets, although earlier than Turkey (Figure 7.8) and with a much stronger involvement of local entrepreneurs in the management of the destination facilities, although the tour operators were largely market-based (Lockhart, 1990).

The Turkish invasion and subsequent political division of the island in 1974 left the major coastal tourism developments around Famagusta and Kyrenia in the Turkish-controlled sector of north Cyprus. Both the heritage image and, more immediately important, local tourism management, were essentially Greek Cypriot, but the Turkish authorities had little interest in re-establishing either. The result has been a physical relocation of the industry to Limassol, Larnaca and Paphos rather than its remarketing *in situ*.

Despite its unique political circumstance, Cyprus shares the more general dilemma of Malta and other Mediterreanan destinations. The quantitative success of the sea/sun package must be set against growing misgivings about the accompanying costs and resulting economic and spatial distortions (World Bank, 1987). A recent reappraisal of strategy (Lockhart, 1990) favours market and product diversification with the aim of increasing incomes, lowering costs and spreading impacts in time and space. Both parts of Cyprus therefore have the difficult task of modifying an existing well-entrenched image in an attempt to reposition the product.

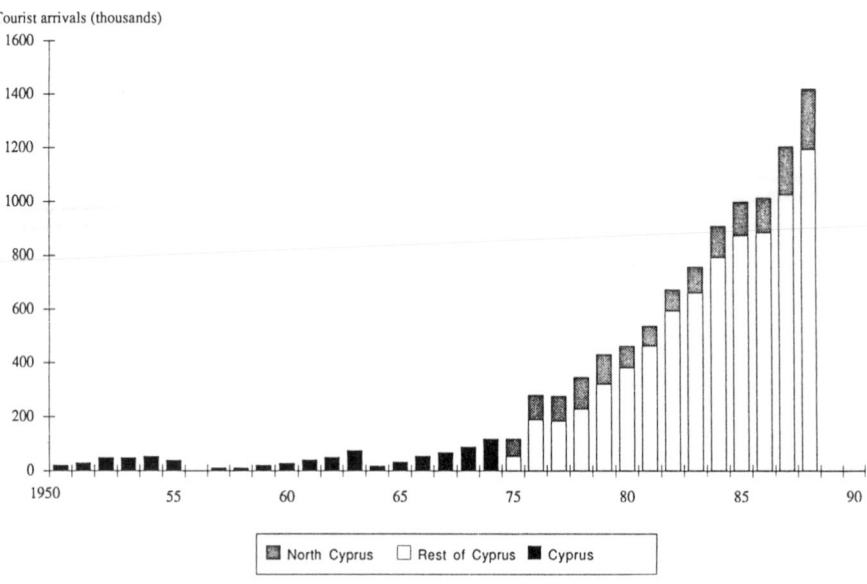

Tourist arrivals (thousands)

Figure 7.8 Tourist arrivals in Cyprus (After Lockhart, 1990)

A synthesis and comparison of images of the Languedoc coast

The 200 km stretch of the Mediterranean coast of France between the Rhône and the Pyrenees has generated a substantial body of published work on tourism development (Miossec, 1976; CPREE, 1977; Pearce, 1978; Lozato, 1985; Murphy, 1985). Its use in this context is particularly appropriate. On the one hand it shares the well-established generalised image of the Mediterranean as a beach tourism destination, while on the other it is quite different, in terms of its natural endowment, facilities and patterns of tourism development from other resort regions of the western Mediterranean developed earlier.

Promotional images were especially important for two reasons. First the region was the subject of large-scale, central government directed and funded tourism development, completed in the late 1970s (Racine, 1980). It was therefore necessary to establish a distinctive tourism image for the region as a whole, in comparison with other developed Mediterranean competitors. Second, each of the constituent resorts needed to differentiate its particular product for its specific market within the region. These two necessities were potentially, but not inevitably, contradictory.

A detailed study of 12 resorts in the region examined images both locally promoted and those held by existing visitors. It also considered the local facility supply and holidaymaking behaviour (Ashworth and de Haan, 1987; Ashworth, 1989). The intention was to allow comparisons between images and the other elements to be drawn at the resort level. The most important of these comparative conclusions are summarised below.

Promoted and received images
The resorts in general are projected strongly as beach and active sport-oriented centres, although considerable variations exist between the individual resorts in this respect as it is at the resort level that most promoted images are created. In contrast, the visitors see the resorts as pleasant, peaceful and unpretentious places. They are neither seen by visitors nor projected as sophisticated and exciting places full of cultural, gastronomic or nightlife attractions. The discrepancy between the extensive use of the wider regional context of Languedoc in the promoted images, with a stress on the natural landscapes and fauna of the resort hinterlands, and the almost total absence of this dimension in images held by visitors, is interesting.

Image and behaviour
The type of visit could be a major influence upon the expectations, experience and thus received image of visitors. Certainly day visitors, who have less time but visit more frequently, have a clearer objective for the visit than long-stay visitors. The place of origin of visitors revealed some differences in the way the resorts were viewed, although the French/foreign distinction was more important than the intra/extra regional one. Foreigners tended to see the resorts as part of broader Mediterranean images, while the French were more discriminating between resorts.

A major general discrepancy was found between the projected images of the resorts and the way visitors actually used them. The distinctive pattern of visitor activity throughout the coast was uniformly characterised by a relatively simple and unvarying pattern of activities. In order of importance, the beach activities of sitting, watching, playing informal games and swimming, dominated daylight hours. The only other facilities used frequently by visitors were the food shops and catering establishments. Such a pattern of behaviour accords well with the pleasant, peaceful, unexciting, received images of the resorts, but contrasts markedly with the promoted images of active water-associated sports.

Image and facility supply
The actual facility endowment of each of the resorts varied enormously. First there are the new, mainly purpose-built, monofunctional resorts of La Grande Motte, Cap d'Agde, Gruissan, Port Camargue. Second, there are the older resorts of Grau du Roi, Carnon, Palavas, Grau d'Agde, Valras, Narbonne Plage, with new tourism facilities grafted on to pre-existing settlements. These have more varied shopping and catering facilities and a physical structure of a more varied age. Third, there are the tourist-historic towns of Sete and Agde with conserved urban morphologies and well developed tourism, shopping and catering sectors but with little accommodation. A comparison of these actual facility characteristics with the promoted images reveals the obvious point that it is the new Mission resorts, with their visually spectacular harbour and associated

137

developments, rather than the older established resorts, that have shaped the regional image.

Discrepancies in image transmission
The clearest discrepancy in the transmission of regional images lay in the quite different media considered as important in promotion and reception respectively. Local promotion depended almost exclusively upon printed material and local information centres, while the received images had been shaped largely by personal experience and those of acquaintances and professional advisors. This difference was not only a matter of access to information sources but, more critically, the valuation and credibility placed on such sources. The effectiveness of the marketing measures has obvious implications for pursuing marketing strategies.

Images and marketing
The aspects of existing or potential disharmony between the three identified components of the tourism industry, at the resort destination level, i.e. facilities, behaviour and images, can be related back to the place of images within the wider marketing model. These disharmonies can be traced to differences in spatial scale, and specifically to the relationship between the individual resort and the region in which it is set. The centrally directed regional development focus (the 'Mission') was attempting to use tourism as part of a broader economic strategy dependent upon extra-regional public or private investment. This, together with the more immediate need of a new area to capture a share of the tourism market from existing competitors, encouraged the use of a strong and homogeneous regional image projected to national and international markets. Variations in local facility endowment, past resort development, and even local government structure encouraged a quite different spatial scale of image promotion, i.e. at regional and local level, which was heterogeneous and frequently aimed only at local markets. The promoted images, as marketing measures, reflected quite different strategies, which in turn can be related to the goals of the place management organisations engaged in the marketing exercises.

From analysis to strategy

As has been stressed above, marketing is essentially interventionist in that the analysis has the inherent purpose of describing, in this case the tourism system, in such a way that intervention to influence the outcome and operation of the system at various points, is not merely permitted but is assumed to occur, whether in a conscious and goal-directed manner or not. The move from descriptive analysis to the examination of how strategy is devised and implemented is thus inevitable.

However, it is equally apparent, from the selected cases described above, that arriving at a strategy is not as self-evident a process as is frequently assumed. There is clearly a wide variety of possible interventionist strategies, using various aspects of promoted images in different ways in order to achieve equally diverse possible goals. Quite simply, a large number of conscious decisions have to be made. Before this point is reached, however, an even more fundamental exercise, particularly important in tourism, must be undertaken. The possible intervenors, that is those who have the will and ability to intervene and thus devise such interventionist strategies, must be identified. The tourism industry is notoriously fragmented, as has been demonstrated in different guises in the preceding chapters. The assumption in most place-promotion analysis is that public sector agencies play the main initiating and coordinating roles. But even if this assumption is generally valid, the role of private sector tour operators (as in Turkey) and other private intermediaries may be critical. In addition, public authorities will differ widely in their spatial jurisdiction and portfolios of responsibilities (as in Languedoc), so that many such agencies may be promoting distinctive place images for different purposes to segmented markets.

The main sets of strategic decisions can be summarised under four headings:

- scale;
- product positioning and market segmentation;
- the place management context of tourism marketing strategies;
- image promotion and consumer behaviour.

Scale

A number of the discrepancies identified above can be traced to differences in spatial scale and the relationships between the various nesting levels of resort, region, national and international scales. In terms of projected images the goals of authorities with jurisdictions at different spatial scales can result in the promotion of distinctly different images. Equally the scale of the received place image may be quite different from that promoted. The place being bought by the consumer is on a smaller scale from that being sold by the industry or public authorities, a curious marketing phenomenon in itself. The correspondence between the projected and received place image scale and the product being developed (here principally measurable in terms of facility supply) and the consumption experience of visitors (principally measurable in terms of their holiday behaviour patterns), is critical. If there is a lack of correspondence, such spatial scale discrepancies do not necessarily create problems but they can, on occasion, do so, and this possibility is an important factor in the devising of strategies.

Product positioning and market segmentation

The two phases in the marketing process which offer the widest opportunity for strategic intervention are product positioning and market segmentation. The first defines the relationship of the place product to others within its competitive context. The second is the identification of differences in the market in terms of the behaviour of consumers towards the product, in such a way that measurable, accessible, and profitable groups of consumers can subsequently be targeted. Both of these processes are to a large extent influenced by the manipulation of place images.

139

The place management context of tourism marketing strategies

As stated earlier, place images are promoted in the pursuit of a variety of goals and the attainment of tourism objectives may not be the only, or even the most important of such goals. In the Maltese, and more subtly the Turkish cases, different national objectives led to potentially conflicting images being promoted. But even in the pursuit of tourism objectives, quite different strategies are not only possible but are likely to be derived by place management authorities at different levels in the jurisdictional hierarchy, reacting to local demand and local management goals.

Image promotion and consumer behaviour

Place image promotion is only one means of influencing consumer behaviour and, in the cases of Egypt and Tunisia, not a notably effective one. It should only be undertaken as part of a wider series of measures, including product development. Image promotion that loses touch with changes in either the product or the market is at best futile and at worst counter-productive, which, given the essentially volatile nature of both market requirements and product positioning, necessitates flexible and responsive marketing strategies. The difficulty is that place images may prove particularly unresponsive to change once established, and existing received images often impede the implementation of just such a flexible response.

Thus the use of image promotion as an integral part of a wider marketing method, offers both a means of analysis and strategy implemention opportunities as part of an industrial approach to tourism. It is equally clear, however, that the exploitation of the opportunities presented by such a method are neither automatic nor inevitable, but are dependent upon a number of preconditions. The three most important of these are:

- a redefinition of the terms, and thereby the underlying concepts, of marketing specifically for application in tourism; in this case to a tourism system where the destination is regarded as the place-product;
- a translation of this analysis into appropriate strategy by executive agencies in pursuit of predetermined objectives;
- identifying organisations capable of implementing and operating such strategies.

None of these preconditions has as yet been fully met in the cases discussed but their attainment provides a challenge for the development of tourism, in the Mediterranean and elsewhere, in the service of many place management objectives.

References

Ashworth, G.J. (1989) The projection and reception of destination images: promotion and reality in Languedoc. In: Stabler, M. (ed.), *Leisure, Labour and Lifestyles: International Comparisons.Tourism and leisure: models and theories.* Leisure Studies Association Second International Conference Proceedings, No. 39, Vol. 8, pp. 1–17.

Ashworth, G.J. and de Haan, T.Z. (1987) *Regionalising the resort system: Languedoc.* Field Studies 12. Fac. Ruimtelijk Wetenschap. Groningen.

Ashworth, G.J. and Tunbridge, J.E. (1990) *The Tourist-Historic City.* Belhaven, London.

Ashworth G.J. and Voogd, H. (1988) Marketing the City: concepts, processes and Dutch applications. *Town Planning Review,* 59 (1), 65–80.

Ashworth, G.J. and Voogd, H. (1990) Can places be sold for tourism? In: Ashworth, G.J. and Goodall, B. (eds), *Marketing Tourism Places.* Routledge, London, pp. 1–16.

Burgess, J. and Wood, P. (1988) Decoding Docklands: place advertising and decision making strategies for the small firm. In: Eyles, J. and Smith, D.M. (eds), *Qualitative Methods in Human Geography.* Polity Press, London, pp. 94–117.

CPREE (Centre Regionale de productivite et études économiques) (1977) *Tourisme et croissance urbaine.* Montpellier.

Dijk, R. (1989) *Het toeristisches imago van Egypt.* Faculteit. Ruimtelijk Wetenschappen. Groningen.

Holloway J.C. and Plant, R.V. (1988) *Marketing for Tourism.* Pitman, London.

Jefferson, A. and Lickorish, L. (1988) *Marketing Tourism: a Practical Guide.* Longman, London.

Kotler, P. (1975) *Marketing for Non-profit Organisations.* Prentice Hall, Englewood Cliffs, New Jersey.

Laban, G.P. (1989) *Marketing van Turkije als toeristische bestemming.* Faculteit Ruimtelijk Wetenschappen. Groningen.

Lancaster, K.J. (1966) A new approach to consumer theory. *Journal of Political Economy,* 84, 132–157.

Lockhart, D.G. (1990) Tourism development in Cyprus since 1950, Commonwealth Geographical Bureau, Conference on Small Island Development, University of Malta.

Lozato, J.P. (1985) *Geographie du tourisme.* Masson, Paris.

Middleton, V.T.C. (1988) *Marketing in Travel and Tourism.* Heinemann, London.

Mill, R.C., and Morrison, A.M. (1985) *The Tourism System.* Prentice Hall, Englewood Cliffs, New Jersey.

Miossec, J.M. (1976) *Eléments pour une théorie de l'espace touristique.* Les Cahiers du Tourisme C–36, C.H.E.T., Aix-en-Provence.

Murphy, P.E., (1985) *Tourism: A Community Approach.* Methuen, London.

Pearce, D.G., (1978) Form and function in French Resorts. *Annals of Tourism Research,* 5(1), 142–156.

Pearce, P.L. (1981) *A Social-Psychology of Tourism.* Oxford University Press, Oxford.

Racine, P. (1980) *Le mission impossible?* Midi Libre, Montpellier.

Seekings, J. (1989) 'Turkey'. In: *Economist Intelligence Unit, International Tourism Reports 1*, London.

Sinclair, M.T., Clewer, A. and Pack, A. (1990) Hedonic prices and the marketing of package holidays. In: Ashworth, G.J. and Goodall, B. (eds), *Marketing Tourism Places*. Routledge, London. pp. 85–103.

Stabler, M.J., (1988) The image of destination regions, theoretical and empirical aspects. In: Goodall, B. and Ashworth, G.J. (eds), *Marketing in the Tourism Industry*. Croom Helm, Beckenham. pp. 133–161.

Stabler, M.J. (1989) Modelling the tourist industry: the concept of opportunity sets. In: Stabler M.J. (ed.), *Leisure, Labour and Lifestyles: International Comparisons. Tourism and leisure: models and theories*. Leisure Studies Association Second International Conference Proceedings, No. 39, Vol. 8, pp. 60–79.

Uysal, M and Crompton, J.L. (1984) Determinents of demand for international tourist flows to Turkey. *Tourism Management*, 4, 288–297.

Wertheim, M. (1988) Using market research. In: *The Tourism Industry*. The Tourism Society, London, pp. 41–43.

World Bank (1987) *Cyprus: a Long-term Development Perspective*. World Bank, Washington DC.

Chapter 8

Guest–host Perceptions of Rural Tourism in England and Portugal

J. Edwards

Introduction

Rural areas have long been a location for tourism in particular countries or regions and have become increasingly important both for day-trip excursions and longer stay residential visits as transport networks have developed. The considerable growth of rural tourism in Europe, the USA and Canada has not, however, been accompanied by research into the relative attractiveness of the characteristics of countryside accommodation and of the rural areas themselves, or the extent to which perceptions of attractiveness on the part of the providers of accommodation coincide or contrast with those of their tourist guests. Mismatch in the supply of and demand for accommodation and related facilities can constrain the growth of rural tourism and limit the associated increases in income and employment generation. Examination of tourist guests' and their rural hosts' perceptions of the relative importance of key characteristics of rural tourism is therefore important.

This chapter provides new information about hosts' and guests' perceptions of rural tourism based on survey work undertaken in south west England and northern Portugal. Firstly the context for the development of rural tourism in the two areas is discussed. Subsequent sections of the chapter examine the information which the survey provided about hosts' and guests' prioritisation of key characteristics relating to accommodation and to the rural areas. Hosts' and guests' rankings of the criteria are compared for each area in order to indicate the degree of overlap or mismatch between the supply and demand characteristics in each region. Finally, given the context of increasing intra-European tourism, an overall comparison of perceptions of rural tourism by hosts and guests in both south west England and northern Portugal is undertaken.

The development of rural tourism in south west England and northern Portugal

South west England was one of the first areas in the United Kingdom to develop commercial tourism as an important economic activity. Facilities catering for visitors, particularly the provision of accommodation, developed in the nineteenth century, initially in association with the expansion of the railway network. The subsequent development of tourism in the late nineteenth and early twentieth centuries was hampered by inadequate public transport. However the rapid increase in car ownership in the period following the second World War resulted in the exploitation of the south west by tourists, with particular emphasis on beach locations. Williams (1975) demonstrated that between 1960 and 1973 the region not only maintained but improved its position as the UK's leading domestic holiday region. By 1976 the area accounted for 25 per cent of the UK domestic holiday market. However, the period 1978–1981 saw a sharp fall in the number of tourists. Whilst in some measure due to the recession, there is no doubt that the increasing attractiveness of overseas destinations for long stay holidays adversely affected the growth in domestic tourism. Elsewhere in England the short stay two to three night visit increased in importance, but this increase in domestic tourism was of little benefit to the south west due to poor communications with the rest of the country. Poor communications with major airports have also been given as part of the reason for the relatively low share, four per cent, of international tourists in this area (Devon County Council, 1985).

In Portugal the development of a rural tourism industry, as distinct from providing for friends and family, only occurred in the 1970s and 1980s. Centres of tourism in mainland Portugal were initially confined to developments in the Algarve and on the Estoril coast as far as Cascais. These developments have been associated with international visitors. Survey work (Portuguese National Plan for Tourism 1985–1988, RPNPTI, 1985) suggests that only 41 per cent of the indigenous population over 15 years of age are holidaymakers. The Algarve and to a lesser extent the Costa Verde in the north have been favoured destinations for domestic tourism. The northern provinces of Portugal have not experienced much development of international tourism (O'Flanagan, 1984). As with south west England, poor communications have inhibited the development of rural areas of Portugal. Whilst a start has been made on the North–South motorway linking the major centres of Lisbon and Oporto, the road system does not offer the desired conditions for growth. The rail system is old, deficient and inadequate for tourism, as are the inland and coastal waterways. Notwithstanding that the three major airports (Lisbon, Faro, Oporto) have been upgraded, only very recently have there been improvements in internal flight schedules.

There have been fewer analyses of Portugal than of south west England, but it is widely acknowledged (Goldey, 1981; Unwin, 1985; Belo Moreira, 1986) that the northern region is the most underdeveloped rural area in western Europe, although by contrast to south west England its population density is high. Both areas are of high landscape quality, as is demonstrated by National Park status having been given to their granitic landscapes, i.e. the Dartmoor and Exmoor

National Parks in England and the Peneda Geres National Park, and Braganca Natural Park of Portugal.

Although it has been recognised for 20 years that tourism plays an important part in the Portuguese economy, it has only been in the years following the restoration of democracy that there has been any attempt to coordinate the industry nationally. Various governments have indicated that tourism should be a major investment priority, because income from tourism has helped to service the country's external debts at a time of rising oil prices, recession and a fall in emigrants' remittances. It is calculated that the income from tourism covered 18.7 per cent of the deficit of the Portuguese balance of payments in the period 1978–1982 (RPNPTI, 1985).

It was the acceptance of this vital contribution that led to the drawing up, by a then minority government, of a national plan for tourism for the period 1985–1988 (RPNPTI, 1985). It was not initially intended that this should form the basis of legislation, but that the 18 provincial authorities would heed some of the suggestions. Indeed the authors question a minority government's ability to intervene in provincial government decision making. However, following the election of the country's first majority government since the 1974 revolution, in July 1987, the implementation of long term strategic national planning became a more tenable proposition.

In terms of the legislative planning process, therefore, considerable differences exist between England and Portugal. Unlike Britain, where public planning control has been in place for the last 40 years, in Portugal it has only been in the period since the return to democracy in 1974 that a planning framework and legislature has begun to emerge.

Economic diversification and rural tourism development

Both south west England and northern Portugal have long established agricultural regimes but are no longer capable of sustaining viable rural populations. Therefore their governments, along with the European Commission, are actively encouraging diversification of the rural economy into leisure and tourism, for both domestic and overseas tourists.

Analysis of tourism in south west England in the last decade suggests a move away from long stay holidays in serviced accommodation to short stay holidays where self-catering seems to be preferred. There appears to have been a decrease in emphasis on accommodation close to the beach in favour of that in the countryside. These trends suggest a holiday experience which is to some extent weather independent. Available evidence (Cornwall County Council, 1986; Devon County Council, 1985) points to the growth of 'activity' and other 'countryside' holidays and the need for increasing diversity in accommodation and the range of attractions.

As in Britain, domestic tourism in Portugal has traditionally focused upon coastal destinations although, unlike Britain, the renting of part-serviced self-catering units, often fishermen's cottages on the Algarve, or the acquisition of second homes was the normal pattern. Developments in Portugal for the international market have continued this trend of self-catering in the provision of purpose-built villas and apartments. It is only in the Algarve that there has been significant development of hotel accommodation and, interestingly, British visitors account for 50 per cent of the bedspace occupancy in these developments (RPNPTI, 1985).

In considering the development of tourism in the north of the country, the planning authorities take account of the fact that the prevailing climate is far more Atlantic in character than in the Algarve. The essential difference is that whilst the summer months may be as warm, if not warmer, than in the Algarve, strong prevailing onshore winds curtail major coastal tourism developments. As a consequence both rural tourism and 'Turismo Habitação' (tourism in private houses) are suggested as major promotional strategies for tourism development in the area. These are perceived as being the most suitable strategies for enabling tourism to develop in a manner sympathetic to the rich natural and cultural heritage of the area. Additionally, the national plan for tourism calls for continued improvements in access to and through the area.

One of the most powerful arguments in favour of the diversification of the rural economy into the area of leisure and tourism concerns the potential for job creation. In this context 'serviced' accommodation is deemed to have a greater potential for generating employment than the provision of self-catering units. The majority of serviced accommodation provided for tourists in south west England is found in the many coastal resorts and the major towns. In the rural areas serviced accommodation is available in 'country house hotels', inns, farms, guesthouses and private houses. Because of its employment creation potential, the local authorities, working through the planning process, have sought to facilitate an increase in the supply of good quality serviced accommodation in the countryside. For instance, in 1980 Cornwall County Council decided to permit the development of hotels in areas otherwise designated as tourism restraint areas, and Devon County Council has adopted a general policy of encouraging the provision of additional 'country house' hotels in their county (Devon County Council, 1985).

The provision of accommodation has for many years been the major way in which the farming community in Britain has entered into the tourism economy of rural areas. Serviced accommodation in the farmhouse has long been a traditional activity, whilst the provision of self-catering units, often in redundant farm buildings, has enabled the farming community to respond to the increased demand for this type of accommodation. The changes in agriculture over the last few years add further support to the arguments advocated by many authors (for example Hill, 1979; Davies, 1983; Frater, 1983; Bullman, 1985) for farmers to continue to operate, at least in part, within the tourism economy. Those farms involved in tourism gain in terms of receipts of additional income. Benefits also accrue in terms of employment, in the first instance to members of the family and, possibly on a part-time basis, to others in the local community.

In northern Portugal, serviced accommodation has until recently been restricted to relatively few hotels in the larger towns and occasionally at coastal resorts. The inland areas of the north, and throughout Portugal generally, have little serviced accommodation available for tourism, with the one exception of the Pousadas, a chain of high quality state run hotels, emphasising the themes of the history and culture of their location. The restricted nature of this accommodation base is seen as one of the major restraints on the further development of tourism in rural areas. In Portugal, large-scale development in particular is hampered by rudimentary infrastructure. As part of a response to these difficulties, the government in 1978 instigated 'Turismo Habitação', or tourism in private houses. The scheme offers assistance, in the form of low interest loans, to the owners of larger properties, often referred to as 'manor houses', enabling them to renovate and upgrade their homes. In return owners are committed to making some of the rooms available to the tourism industry, at least until such time as the loan is fully repaid. In addition to the obvious advantages of enabling owners to undertake renovation and refurbishment which few, if any, could contemplate privately, the scheme also provides for entry into the tourism economy with its long term potential for supplementing existing income and facilitating continued employment. Part of the appeal of this accommodation, it was argued, would lie in the close contact of guests with their hosts and the local community, and this aspect is very much to the fore in promotions by companies which offer accommodation in these houses.

Another factor which is of significance in understanding the formation of 'Turismo Habitação' relates to political events in post-revolutionary Portugal. Following a substantive move to the left in the period following the 1974 revolution, events in 1976 saw this swing arrested and then reversed, as a series of successive minority governments moved to the centre right. Many of the established land-owning families, some of whom had lived abroad during the mid to late 1970s, felt progressively more at ease. This new-found confidence in democracy was helped by the instigation of 'Turismo Habitação' and the potential this offered for restoration of property, some of which was in a very poor state. A significant concentration of such houses occurs in the north between the River Minho, forming the northern border with Spain and the River Douro, with the greatest concentration in the valley of the River Lima. Consequently the first houses entering into the scheme were located in the Lima valley, with the ancient market town of Ponte de Lima forming a natural administrative focus.

Farm tourism is also being developed in Portugal, having begun in the centre and south of the country. These farm or 'agri-tourism' schemes, however, have taken a number of years to gain momentum. The availability of development funds following Portugal's admittance to full membership of the European Community, has resulted in the provision both of self-catering units associated with working farms and of other accommodation located in the countryside. The latter are referred to in Portugal as 'rural tourism houses' and to some extent resemble the 'gîtes' of France.

The small-scale and scattered distribution of serviced accommodation units in rural areas presents difficulties in terms of individual marketing and promotional activity. This has been recognised for many years by hotel and guesthouse proprietors in Britain, and by rural accommodation providers in some other European countries (Frater, 1983). The successful emergence of farm-based accommodation marketing cooperatives in Britain in the 1980s demonstrates the potential value of such organisations. The organisations were formed for different reasons. The Dartmoor Tourist Association, for example, was initiated at a grass roots level by guesthouse proprietors, developed over two decades and has come to represent tourism generally within the area. The Dorset Farm and Country Holiday Group and The Cream of Cornwall Farm Holiday Group were formed largely as a result of a decline in agriculture, and in part as a result of the encouragement of a variety of government agencies, for example the Ministry of Agriculture and the tourism authorities. Until recently, the groups operating in south west England have received minimal support other than advice from their regional tourist board, which is perceived to respond more to hotel interests than to the small-scale accommodation provider.

The Turihab association in the Alto Minho region of northern Portugal represents established families, entering into the accommodation industry for the first time in response to the governmental initiative of Turismo Habitação, and they were comprehensively supported from the outset by their regional tourist board. One of the major reasons why this group developed under the umbrella of the tourist board is that it was envisaged that the majority of the custom would come from the international market. This is in contrast to the situation in England where the various associations, whilst interested in international tourists, are largely working with the domestic market.

A further characteristic shared by the groups in Cornwall, Dorset and Portugal is the importance of social and kinship ties. In the case of the English groups this most clearly operates through agricultural society. In Portugal the position of many of the members, as the traditional leaders of society, is an example of the importance of kinship ties in that country. As Robinson (1979) states in a discussion of Portugal's land and people: 'The significance of the small size of the elite social class, who is related to whom, who knows whom, are the essential elements in social relationships'.

Not surprisingly these ties are of real significance in business and career development. Such ties appear to be far less significant in the Dartmoor Tourist Association, where the majority of the members are established or aspiring 'professionals' in the accommodation industry and in many cases are relatively recent arrivals in the area.

English and Portuguese hosts' perceptions of rural accommodation

In order to examine and compare hosts' and tourist guests' perceptions of the characteristics of accommodation and its rural location, a survey of 64 hosts and 199 guests was carried out in south west England and of 26 hosts and 76 guests in the Alto Minho region of northern Portugal. Questionnaire returns were obtained from the proprietor hosts and from their tourist guests, and allowed an analysis of those criteria which both groups consider to be important in terms of serviced accommodation facilities and the countryside location. All criteria were assessed by reference to a numerical scale where: 1 = very important; 2 = quite important; 3 = not very important; 4 = of no importance. The analysis was based on responses from members of The Cream of Cornwall Farm Holiday Group, Dartmoor Tourist Association, Dorset Farm and Country Holiday Group and the Turihab group in northern Portugal. These associations provided a mechanism for contacting proprietors which, particularly in northern Portugal, would otherwise have been extremely difficult.

The views of English and Portuguese hosts as to the relative importance of 15 previously selected criteria relating to the accommodation requirements of their guests were obtained. The variables were ranked with respect both to the total sample and, for the English sample, to farm businesses, and the size of both these sample populations permitted the 't' test to be used to determine if there were significant differences between the mean values of each criterion. Such analysis permits the detection of subsets of criteria between whose means there is no significant difference, but which differ significantly from the means of other subsets. The size of the Portuguese sample is too small to allow for further analysis in terms of the determination of statistically significant subgroups. The results are given in Table 8.1.

Table 8.1 English and Portuguese hosts' assessment of accommodation criteria

South west England		Northern Portugal
All hosts	Farm accommodation	All hosts
1. Quality of meals	1. Quality of meals	1. Bathroom facilities
2. Value for money	2. Value for money	2. Privacy
3. Recommended	3. Recommended	3. Character of bedroom
4. Friendly hosts	4. Friendly hosts	4. Traditional building
5. Character of bedroom	5. Character of bedroom	5. Friendly hosts
6. Bathroom facilities	----------------------------	6. Quality of meals
----------------------------	6. Suitable for children	7. Suitable for children
7. Flexible booking	7. Traditional building	8. Flexible booking
8. Traditional building	8. Lounge	9. Telephone
9. Stayed before	9. Bathroom facilities	10. Value for money
10. Lounge	10. Stayed before	11. Old character building
11. Suitable for children	11. Flexible booking	12. Clothes drying facilities
----------------------------	12. Clothes drying facilities	13. Television
12. Television	----------------------------	
13. Privacy	13. Television	
14. Clothes drying facilities	14. Privacy	
15. Telephone	15. Telephone	

Note: Three subsets of criteria are arranged in rank order for the English establishments determined by significant differences of mean values

Determination of the significant differences between mean values of the total sample suggests the presence of three groups of variables, as perceived by proprietors in south west England, in terms of what they are offering to their guests. The first, and therefore the group perceived to be of most importance, are what may be termed key hospitality variables, which relate directly to the individual's personal wellbeing. The second and third subsets comprise less cohesive groups of criteria which refer to more practical hospitality. The combined sample of farm proprietors was the only other group that was sufficiently large (32) to be subjected to further analysis. When tests for significance between the means were performed, very similar groupings emerged to that discerned for the total sample.

There is complete agreement among all English proprietors that the 'quality of the meals' they provide is of paramount importance in attracting guests to stay with them. It is the only variable whose rank order is the same for all three types of proprietor, and is therefore true of all three associations. 'Value for money'

149

was rated the second most significant feature by both farms and guesthouses, but was relegated to fourth in the ranking by hoteliers. This reflects the long tradition of both farm and guesthouse accommodation in Britain of providing low cost, basic but clean accommodation for those from the cities who could not afford the more traditional hotel. Interviews revealed that hoteliers were keen to maintain a price difference, as they perceive that not only are they appealing to a different market but that they are professionals, and they view others in the serviced sector, particularly farm-based operations, with some disdain.

The rank order for the Portuguese sample reflects the underlying philosophy of 'Turismo Habitação' of providing high quality accommodation in houses which reflect the history and culture of their localities. 1. conversation, proprietors would often refer to the importance of 'patrimony', a term used to encompass not only particular architectural styles, materials and decor, but also standards of hospitality. The primacy of bathroom facilities, provision of privacy, friendliness of hosts and meal quality are all incorporated into recent national legislation in Portugal concerning 'Turismo Habitação', and all proprietors had recently been involved in considerable effort both in installing required bathroom facilities and other necessary renovation and decoration. These product-related criteria are, not surprisingly, rated by these recent entrants into the industry as being of greater significance than customer-related criteria such as value for money and booking arrangements.

The apparent disparity revealed by the ranking of 'traditional building' in fourth place and 'old character building' in eleventh is explained by the significance, discussed above, of 'patrimony' which values older houses not simply in terms of their age but also in comparison to 'modern'. This attitude may, in the north of Portugal, reflect an adverse reaction to events of the last 20 years, which have seen an explosion of new house building by returning emigrants who utilise ideas and materials with which they became familiar while working in other parts of Europe, most noticeably France and Germany. These properties, erected with scant, if any, planning control, are widely seen by the established families as being destructive of the area's heritage, culture and 'patrimony'.

A comparison of guests' and hosts' perceptions of rural accommodation in south west England

The guest respondents to the survey comprised family groups (35 per cent), other groups (19 per cent), married couples (44 per cent). The majority of the young families were recorded from Cornwall and Dorset, with 87 per cent of those with children under five staying in farm accommodation. Table 8.2 places the 15 criteria assessed by guests in English rural accommodation in rank order, based upon the calculation of an arithmetic mean of a score on a scale 1–4 as shown above for Table 8.1. The hosts' ranking is included in the final column of Table 8.2 for purposes of comparison.

Table 8.2 Guests' and hosts' assessment of the relative importance of accommodation criteria in south west England: mean scores and rankings (in brackets)

	Cornwall	Dartmoor	Dorset	Hotels	Guesthouses	Farms	All English guests	All hosts
				Guests' assessments				
Quality of meals	1.28 (1)	1.15 (1)	1.32 (1)	1.14 (1)	1.17 (1)	1.32 (2)	1.23 (1)	1.06 (1)
Value for money	1.30 (2)	1.28 (2)	1.33 (2)	1.24 (3)	1.30 (2)	1.30 (1)	1.29 (2)	1.13 (2)
Friendly hosts	1.34 (3)	1.40 (4)	1.51 (3)	1.39 (4)	1.39 (3)	1.45 (3)	1.42 (3)	1.28 (4)
Character of bedroom	1.46 (4)	1.31 (3)	1.60 (4)	1.22 (2)	1.39 (3)	1.54 (4)	1.42 (3)	1.34 (5)
Bathroom facilities	1.85 (5)	1.53 (5)	1.95 (5)	1.48 (5)	1.71 (5)	1.87 (5)	1.73 (5)	1.50 (6)
Traditional building	2.13 (8)	2.25 (7)	2.38 (7)	2.28 (8)	2.15 (7)	2.26 (8)	2.24 (6)	1.56 (8)
Lounge	2.09 (7)	2.43 (9)	2.41 (8)	2.35 (9)	2.51 (10)	2.19 (7)	2.30 (7)	1.72 (10)
Flexible booking	2.64 (9)	2.05 (6)	2.49 (9)	2.04 (6)	2.09 (6)	2.64 (9)	2.36 (8)	1.54 (7)
Suitable for children	1.96 (6)	3.22 (14)	2.00 (6)	3.27 (14)	2.83 (12)	1.97 (6)	2.49 (9)	1.86 (11)
Privacy	2.67 (10)	2.65 (11)	2.67 (10)	2.63 (10)	2.74 (11)	2.64 (9)	2.67 (10)	2.26 (13)
Recommended	3.05 (12)	2.28 (8)	2.98 (11)	2.21 (7)	2.44 (9)	3.08 (12)	2.72 (11)	1.16 (3)
Stayed before	3.07 (13)	2.54 (10)	3.15 (13)	2.83 (11)	2.24 (8)	3.13 (13)	2.87 (12)	1.71 (9)
Clothes-drying facilities	2.85 (11)	3.17 (13)	3.10 (12)	3.09 (13)	3.10 (14)	2.99 (11)	3.04 (13)	2.30 (14)
Telephone	3.15 (14)	2.87 (12)	3.21 (14)	2.84 (12)	2.89 (13)	3.22 (14)	3.04 (13)	2.51 (15)
Television	3.40 (15)	3.34 (15)	3.48 (15)	3.27 (14)	3.44 (15)	3.43 (15)	3.39 (15)	2.22 (12)

   Comparison of the ranking of criteria by guests and hosts demonstrates that in many respects they agree on the order of priorities. There is, for instance, almost complete agreement as to the crucial importance of the quality of the meals, which is the feature that distinguishes serviced accommodation from self-catering. This agreement between guests and hosts also further highlights the dilemma posed to farm-based businesses, where the provision of an evening meal places the host in a position in which very high standards are expected at prices which are possibly 30–40 per cent of the hotel or restaurant equivalent. The uneconomic aspect of meal provision by farm-based operations has been recognised for many years (Hill, 1979). More recent entrants into the sector are less reluctant than established proprietors to charge higher prices with, they detect, no reduction in demand; indeed in those circumstances where the meal is of high quality, demand may well increase. Nevertheless increasing the price of the evening meal is clearly a sensitive topic among farmhouse proprietors, and those who ask higher prices risk the disapproval of established businesses who have come to accept very low returns for this aspect of their operation.

   The major discrepancy which exists between the rankings by guests and hosts relates to the importance attached to visitors either having been 'recommended', or having 'stayed before', which differ by eight (ranked third by hosts and eleventh by guests) and three (ranked ninth by hosts and twelfth by guests) places respectively. Recommendation was rated first, third and fourth by hotel, farm and guesthouse proprietors. However, no single group of guests rated this factor very highly: at seventh, ninth, and twelfth place in hotels, guesthouses and farms respectively. In addition, the results from the survey demonstrate that whilst 62 per cent of guesthouse guests and 37 per cent of hotel guests gave 'stayed before/recommendation' as their means of finding their accommodation, this figure was sharply reduced to 20 per cent for farm visitors.

   These observations suggest a dichotomous perception by tourists with regard to farm-based serviced accommodation as opposed to guesthouse and hotel accommodation. Whereas the latter are evaluated individually, explaining the importance of repeat business and recommendation, farm accommodation appears to have a universality of appeal. In addition to involving the same priorities as other forms of serviced accommodation, farm accommodation is overlain with the perception of its suitability for children and young children in particular. The belief that food is free, or at least very cheap, for farm proprietors may explain the expectation of meals at unrealistically low prices. The other disparity which this comparison reveals relates to the importance assigned to television, which was relegated to last place by guests but which all proprietors rated more highly. This disparity is in part supported by the experience of an hotelier who reluctantly, because of social pressure by other hoteliers, acquired sufficient televisions for each guest room but to date has encountered few customers who will take the necessary step of asking for a set to be taken to their room, preferring instead to spend their time with other guests in the lounge bar.

Similarities and differences between guests' and hosts' perceptions of rural accommodation in northern Portugal

The questionnaires in Portuguese establishments were made available in English and Portuguese. Of all respondents, 92 per cent were international visitors: 62 per cent from the UK, 14 per cent from Germany and the Netherlands, 9 per cent from Scandinavia, and 7 per cent from other countries. This approximates to the general ratio of international visitors to Portugal. The percentage of the respondents who were members of family or other groups was 38 per cent, the majority, 61 per cent, being married couples. Over 60 per cent of respondents were more than 40 years of age. Again visitors were asked to indicate the relative importance of a range of accommodation-related criteria using the predetermined scale. The results, compared with hosts' evaluations, are given in Table 8.3.

Table 8.3 Guests' and hosts' evaluations of accommodation criteria in 'Turihab' houses in northern Portugal: mean scores and rankings (in brackets)

	Criteria	Guests		Hosts	
1.	Character of bedroom	1.41	(1)	1.56	(3)
2.	Traditional building	1.55	(2)	1.57	(4)
3.	Friendly hosts	1.60	(3)	1.60	(5)
4.	Value for money	1.72	(4)	2.43	(10)
5.	Bathroom facilities	1.85	(5)	1.46	(1)
6.	Privacy	2.22	(6)	1.50	(2)
7.	Quality of meals	2.29	(7)	1.65	(6)
8.	Suitable for children	2.80	(8)	1.95	(7)
9.	Recommended	2.82	(9)	N/A	
10.	Telephone	3.33	(10)	2.31	(9)
11.	Stayed before	3.72	(11)	N/A	
12.	Lounge	3.78	(12)	N/A	
13.	Television	3.92	(13)	3.00	(13)

N/A = not applicable

Tests for possible statistically significant differences between the means for the guests' scores (t test) suggest that amongst the top ten criteria there are no clear boundaries to enable the existence of sub-groups to be determined. In contrast, the last three criteria do show a clear prioritisation. The five primary criteria coincide, with one exception, with those assessed as being the most important criteria by the proprietors. Guests were, perhaps not surprisingly, more concerned with assessing their accommodation in terms of possible alternatives, as representing 'value for money'. The comparison of guests' and hosts' rankings underlines the emphasis hosts place upon the fabric and facilities of their houses, an emphasis shared by their guests but to some extent tempered by relative costs and expectations. With regard to the latter it is of note that whilst 'privacy' was

153

important to guests it was not as important as proprietors apparently considered. Since much of the promotion of this accommodation has chosen to emphasise 'contact with the owner', it would presumably deter those for whom privacy was of major concern. The second set of criteria, six to ten, demonstrates greater agreement between hosts and their guests, for instance in relation to the appropriateness of the accommodation for children and the relative importance of a telephone as compared with the unimportance of a television. Neither of the criteria 'stayed before' or 'recommended' were seen to be particularly important by guests, and this may be a further indication that repeat visits are unlikely to represent a major part of bookings over the next few years.

Hosts' and guests' perceptions of accommodation in rural areas: an overview

A comparison of the views of the guests with those of their hosts in south west England finds that they accord in many ways, for instance in giving meal quality and value for money the highest priorities, and clothes-drying facilities and the availability of telephone and television the lowest. A major discrepancy observed relates to the apparent over-emphasis hosts place on the importance of personal recommendation in influencing guests to choose to stay with them. This appears to be of significance in determining the trade of particular hotels and guesthouses, whereas 'farm' accommodation appears to enjoy a more universal image and therefore individual units are less dependent upon specific recommendation. Other authors, such as Hill (1979) record the reliance farm-based operations place upon word-of-mouth recommendation and repeat bookings, for which there was little evidence from this study. This may have been due to the relative under-representation of the 'school holiday' period. However, the present results suggest that farm businesses should be aware of this universality of image. Indeed the comment of one farm proprietor that, 'pole position in the association's brochure was the major determinant of a successful season', would seem to confirm that once a farm holiday is decided upon, little attention is given to which farm. Differences emerge between accommodation types most noticeably with regard to the suitability of the accommodation for children. It is clear that farms are seen to be the most suitable location and hotels the least.

As with visitors to south west England, the views of those visiting northern Portugal, in terms of the relative importance of various accommodation criteria, accorded in many cases with those of their hosts. The most conspicuous difference between the views of Portuguese hosts and their guests and the English hosts and their guests is in terms of the relative importance of the accommodation offering 'value for money'. In this context the work of Moutinho (1982) which investigated the decision-making processes of British visitors to Portugal, is relevant. He demonstrated that 'price' related to geographical position was the key determinant in the pre-vacation decision-making process. This suggests that future price structuring will be of critical importance in the development of these accommodation businesses.

In comparing the two data sets it becomes clear that the greatest measure of agreement between those providing serviced accommodation and their guests is in regard to the importance both parties attach to 'friendly hospitality'. This factor is recognised by proprietors of all the accommodation types included in this study, and was not restricted to private houses or farm-based accommodation. These findings are supported by the extensive work of Thibal (1986) in relation to rural tourism in France, which identified 'hospitality as being of major importance in guests' assessment of the attractions of the rural area'. Further support comes from the work of Pizam *et al.* (1978) who, in their analyses of what Dann (1978) subsequently referred to as the 'pull' factors of Cape Cod, Massachusetts, identified 'hospitality' along with 'scenery and and natural attractions' as major causes of tourist satisfaction with this destination.

It is likely that personalised hospitality is regarded by all the proprietors to be a function of size, in that they perceive that the 'small scale' nature of their operation enhances their ability to become involved with their guests. This emerged in interviews with proprietors in both countries, when it became clear that they were all convinced that the accommodation they offered was in marked contrast to what was perceived to be available in impersonal, unfriendly large hotels. The interviews also confirmed that provision of dinner was a contentious issue. English proprietors generally acknowledged that guests would prefer to have dinner made available, and those who chose not to provide dinner recognised that this altered the type of clientele.

The serviced accommodation currently available in rural areas of northern Portugal is mainly limited to hotel-type accommodation in either the Pousadas or Estalagems, and more recently in private houses operating within the 'Turismo Habitação' scheme. The proprietors of these houses place particular emphasis upon the character of their guests' accommodation in traditional buildings. In particular, both bathroom facilities and privacy for their guests are highly valued, The Portuguese hosts regard the last feature as being of greater importance than do English proprietors.

The underlying philosophy of 'Turismo Habitação' in Portugal is one of welcoming guests into Portuguese homes in order for them to experience the Portuguese way of life. In this context the opportunity to have dinner either with, or provided by the host, may be argued to be a major element. However, most hosts provide only breakfast and guests are obliged to use local restaurants. Dinner is rarely available as few of the hosts/hostesses are suitably trained. Moreover, most houses have a restricted number of staff and do not have the resources to provide meals. Until such time as local labour can be recruited and trained, dinner at these houses is likely to remain an uncommon rather than usual feature. The provision of more meal facilities should be encouraged not only because of the benefits conferred on guests but also for their potential to create jobs. Such benefits have been widely reported with regard, for instance, to the development of farm tourism in England, (Hill, 1979; Frater, 1983, 1986). This situation in northern Portugal is in sharp contrast to that prevailing in the majority of farms, guesthouses and small hotels in England, where the hosts invariably undertake responsibility for providing meals themselves.

This dichotomy between claiming to offer exceptional levels of hospitality, yet not providing the major social meal of the day is highlighted in northern Portugal by the finding of Moutinho that 'good food' was one of the most important attributes that tourists were looking for in visiting Portugal. However

155

hospitable and attractive, accommodation restricted to the provision of bed and breakfast is unlikely to compensate for the failure to provide dinner.   Indeed, it may be the case that the insistence of 'Turismo Habitação' that breakfast be provided detracts from the potential of making available true self-catering accommodation, a type of accommodation which is almost entirely lacking in this region of Portugal and for which there is considerable latent demand.

Hosts' and guests' assessments of rural areas in south west England as locations for tourism

English hosts' and guests' assessments of different aspects of the rural area as a location for tourism were also examined by asking respondents to score 12 equally weighted predetermined criteria on a scale of relative importance. The results of the analysis of the responses of English hosts and guests are given in Table 8.4. As shown in the last column of Table 8.4, the providers of serviced accommodation in rural areas of south west England perceived 'attractive scenery' and 'peaceful and quiet conditions' as paramount. However, looked at on a locational basis, those in Cornwall stand out as rating the 'uncommercialised nature' of the area and 'personal recommendation' as being of greater importance. Indeed there is a sharp contrast between their assessment of the value of 'uncommercialised' with that of members of the Dartmoor association, who place this seventh compared with its overall mean position in third place. This difference in perception may be a reflection of the interrelationship of 'commercialisation' and 'accommodation', Cornish farmers believing that what they offer is in sharp contrast to the commercialised hotel and guesthouse business. Those operating on Dartmoor are less inclined to see the phrase 'uncommercialised' in such a negative way, possibly associating it with the idea of a more sophisticated, but not undesirable, level of service. An interest by guests in 'touring' the area is recognised by all hosts as being of equal importance. However, discrepancies between different groups of proprietors emerged with reference to the recommendations of the area to their guests by friends. This is considered noticeably more important by members of the Cornish farm holiday association than by those of the other associations.

There is a wide measure of agreement among hosts as to the relative importance of the three criteria, 'the avoidance of congestion', 'anticipation of a friendly response from local people' and the importance of guests being 'regular visitors' to the area. Similarly there is general agreement as to the ranking of the least important criteria. There are, however, some variations; for instance those in Cornwall give greater emphasis to their guests' time with them representing something of a 'contrast' to their normal holiday, and members of the Dorset association regard 'interest in the countryside' as being of greater significance than do members of the other groups. There is complete agreement among proprietors that their guests' consideration of 'likely weather conditions' is the least important of all the criteria considered. Although the overall view was that relatively few visitors have any illusions regarding weather, nevertheless,

Table 8.4 Guests' and hosts' assessment of the relative importance for tourism of different aspects of rural areas in south west England: mean scores and rankings (in brackets)

	Guests' assessments							All hosts
	Cornwall	Dartmoor	Dorset	Hotels	Guesthouses	Farms	All guests	
Scenery	1.36 (1)	1.22 (1)	1.37 (1)	1.10 (1)	1.48 (2)	1.33 (1)	1.30 (1)	1.28 (1)
Uncommercialised	1.38 (2)	1.36 (3)	1.63 (3)	1.30 (3)	1.44 (1)	1.48 (2)	1.42 (2)	1.38 (4)
Peace and quiet	1.49 (3)	1.35 (2)	1.60 (2)	1.20 (2)	1.60 (3)	1.51 (3)	1.45 (3)	1.34 (2)
Avoid congestion	1.59 (4)	1.50 (4)	1.91 (5)	1.51 (4)	1.67 (5)	1.66 (4)	1.62 (4)	1.52 (5)
Tour the area	1.93 (5)	1.60 (5)	1.79 (4)	1.58 (5)	1.66 (4)	1.89 (5)	1.75 (5)	1.39 (3)
Countryside location	2.26 (7)	1.96 (6)	2.21 (6)	1.90 (6)	2.02 (6)	2.28 (7)	2.12 (6)	2.08 (10)
Friendly locals	2.20 (6)	2.06 (7)	2.48 (7)	2.08 (7)	2.11 (8)	2.25 (6)	2.17 (7)	1.86 (8)
Regular visitors	2.92 (11)	2.46 (8)	2.77 (9)	2.66 (10)	2.05 (7)	2.98 (11)	2.68 (8)	1.76 (7)
Contrast to normal holiday	2.72 (8)	2.76 (11)	2.57 (8)	2.69 (11)	2.70 (10)	2.71 (8)	2.70 (9)	2.01 (9)
Pursue a chosen activity	2.89 (10)	2.59 (9)	3.18 (12)	2.49 (8)	2.93 (11)	2.94 (9)	2.82 (10)	2.47 (11)
Recommendation	3.05 (12)	2.59 (9)	3.10 (10)	2.64 (9)	2.62 (9)	3.11 (12)	2.87 (11)	1.52 (5)
Weather	2.76 (9)	3.05 (12)	3.10 (10)	2.94 (12)	3.20 (12)	2.85 (10)	2.94 (12)	2.54 (12)

157

particularly among those involved in providing for families, there is a real concern for improvements in the number and quality of all-weather attractions throughout south west England.

The concluding section of the questionnaire was addressed solely to 32 farm accommodation businesses in an attempt to assess their attitudes towards both the attractiveness of a 'farm image' and the access their guests may expect to their farm. Just over half the sample (53 per cent) considered the 'farm image' to be very important, approximately one-third thought it quite important, while the remaining 15 per cent considered it to be of no great importance. All these respondents indicated that their guests would be allowed to walk around the farm. Half of the respondents indicated that they may accompany visitors and in a few cases this would be not simply to explain farming practice, but additionally to point out the high-technology nature of modern farming and its attendant dangers. Interviews with farmers cooperating in the survey yielded the response that guests wanted in the main to 'see' the farm around them, rather than actively to get involved. Children assisting in the feeding of young animals was regarded as very much what visitors appreciated, cleaning out milking parlours very much what they did not.

Guests' assessments of criteria regarded as important in attracting them to countryside locations are also summarised in Table 8.4. As with the assessment of accommodation variables there is agreement with regard to the ranking of many of the criteria. The first five as determined by all guests occur in a slightly different order from the ranking based upon the proprietors' evaluation. As with accommodation, there is a major discrepancy with regard to 'recommendation' of visits. This is ranked fifth by all hosts, but is placed on average in eleventh position by all guests. Although it improves to ninth when rated by those staying in hotels and guesthouses, it is rated the least important of the factors considered by guests at farms and those holidaying in Cornwall. This is of some interest in that Cornish proprietors ranked the area's recommendation second only to its uncommercialised nature. This disparity may, in part, be due to the under-representation of the main season visitor; however it coincides with the findings of the accommodation assessment in suggesting that there may be an established universal image of 'farms' and possibly 'Cornish farms' in particular, and hosts should be aware of the restraints this imposes.

Whilst hosts may be overestimating the importance of an area's 'recommendation', the comparison of rankings suggests they are underestimating their guests' interest in the countryside, a factor hosts placed tenth but guests placed sixth in their order of priorities. Clearly, although all hosts provide information about the area, and in the majority of cases talk to their visitors about the locality, they may not be satisfying their guests' curiosity. Such an interest is not confined to those staying on farms; rather it is true of those choosing to stay in the countryside generally. Nevertheless a 'farm' image is considered to be very important by half the farm businesses, presumably in emphasising the 'rural' imagery.

The nature of what is sought is not readily understood, but in some instances may result in conflict. This is most likely to manifest itself in attempts to involve guests' children in farm activities. The perception among farming businesses is that the majority of guests wish no more than a superficial 'clean, at a safe distance' involvement. This supports the findings of Harrison *et al.*, (1986) in their study of the attitudes towards the countryside of residents of the London suburb of Greenwich, from which they concluded that the urban visitor wishes only to observe the countryside, seeking reassurance rather than involvement, having the freedom to return to the town.

Hosts' and guests' assessments of rural areas in northern Portugal as locations for tourism

Portuguese hosts and guests were asked to assess the relative importance of predetermined features which may play a part in influencing guests in deciding to visit the Alto Minho province of northern Portugal. By ascribing numerical values as indicated above, it was possible to derive mean values and subsequently rank these criteria. The results are summarised in Table 8.5.

As can be seen from Table 8.5, according to Portuguese hosts 'contrast to their normal holiday' ranks highly, along with criteria relating to the widely perceived attributes of country areas namely, 'peace and quiet', 'lack of congestion', 'attractive scenery', 'uncommercialised'. Ranked below these are variables relating to the interest of guests in touring and finding out about the area. Hosts clearly did not consider weather a particularly important factor; neither did they assess 'friendliness of local people' to be of great importance.

Table 8.5 Hosts' and guests' assessment of the relative importance of different criteria influencing the decision to holiday in northern Portugal: mean scores and rankings (in brackets)

	Criteria	Hosts		Guests	
1.	Scenery	1.42	(3)	1.21	(1)
2.	Avoid congestion	1.39	(2)	1.28	(2)
3.	Uncommercialised	1.73	(5)	1.28	(3)
4.	Tour the area	1.76	(6)	1.35	(4)
5.	Peace and quiet	1.12	(1)	1.51	(5)
6.	Find out about countryside	1.85	(7)	1.55	(6)
7.	Friendly locals	2.68	(10)	1.78	(7)
8.	Local food and wine	N/A		1.89	(8)
9.	Weather	2.08	(9)	2.04	(9)
10.	Contrast to 'normal' type of holiday	1.60	(4)	2.10	(10)
11.	Recommendation	1.89	(8)	3.12	(11)
12.	Regular visitors	2.79	(11)	3.51	(12)

N/A = Not applicable

This low ranking of their guests' contact with local people may be a reflection of the social divisions that characterise society in this part of Portugal. All the houses in the Turihab association are owned by the closely knit and interrelated local aristocracy, still accustomed to employing service labour and possibly therefore anticipating that their guests would seek little in the way of contact with the local community. Placing 'regularity of visits' in last place may well result from the fact that many proprietors have been offering accommodation for too short a time to be aware of the level of repeat business.

Tourist guests in northern Portugal were also asked to indicate the relative importance of a range of criteria relating to their choice of the Minho region for their holiday. Table 8.5 above also gives the results of these responses. When the guests' assessment is compared with that of their hosts it becomes apparent that, while there is general agreement with regard to the pre-eminence of the first six criteria, the rank order is noticeably different. For instance, 'peace and quiet', ranked first by hosts, is placed fifth by guests; conversely 'touring the area', ranked fourth by the guests is ranked seventh by hosts. The analysis suggests that guests are seeking an active involvement with the area, and their aspirations are most likely to be met by those hosts who, having obvious and genuine pride in their homes and country, make every effort to advise their visitors. This appears to contrast with the hosts' assessment of a more passive visitor, content simply to be in the locality. This is further borne out in that hosts apparently anticipate that a visit to the Minho will represent something of a change for their guests, whereas the results indicate that for many guests, remoter rural areas typify their normal choice of holiday location. If this interpretation is valid it implies that hosts are receiving discerning guests, well able to make comparisons with other destinations, both in terms of amenities and accommodation.

Hosts' and guests' perceptions of the attractiveness of rural tourism: a comparison

Comparison of the values attached to rural areas as locations for tourism, based upon responses by both hosts and visitors in the two study areas, shows that rural locations are deemed by both hosts and guests to offer attractive scenery, peace and quiet, to be uncommercialised, uncongested and rewarding locations to explore. Significantly, visitors to both south west England and northern Portugal include an interest in 'finding out about the countryside' as an important attraction. This also appears to be recognised by Portuguese hosts but is deemed less important by their English counterparts. This interest in the countryside serves to emphasise the significance of the role played by hosts in introducing their guests to the area. Interestingly, Moutinho (1982) found in his study of vacation tourists visiting Portugal, that whilst price-related variables were the most important factors in influencing pre-vacation decision-making, post-vacation priorities gave much higher emphasis to 'curiosity and relaxation'. This suggests that the desire to 'find out' is a feature associated with British tourists, and is accompanied by the expectation that their enquiries will meet with a sympathetic response by all those they encounter in the locality.

These priorities are similar to those found by Pizam *et al.*, (1978) in their work at Cape Cod, Massachusetts, where they were able to demonstrate that the natural assets of scenery and environmental quality were very highly valued, and that visitors disliked evidence of commercialisation of this location. Pizam's work also demonstrated that when asked to define 'hospitality' in the context of a tourism destination, respondents included not only the hospitality of their particular hosts, but also the friendliness and attitudes of the local population generally. This is clearly a perception shared by the respondents in this study. Thibal (1986) also sees rural tourism as a situation in which both the visitor and host seek enrichment and she goes on to suggest that rural tourism has to be understood as a form of tourism orientated towards human and cultural values.

Results from England suggest that hosts correctly recognise that many of their guests are regular visitors to the area, and it is recognised by both hosts and guests that this is less likely to be the case in Portugal. Nevertheless, in both areas guests did not regard this particular holiday as significantly different from their 'normal' type of holiday. This would suggest that generally such visitors represent a discerning group of clients well able to make comparisons with other rural locations. This point may be particularly relevant to the house owners of northern Portugal, who apparently anticipate a much greater departure from the 'norm' on the part of those who choose to visit them. The results confirm that, for many, the rural area is a destination of general interest, rather than one visited to pursue a specific activity. Even for those choosing Portugal, weather was not regarded as a particularly important factor. In practice several guests indicated that the weather was too hot; it can indeed be warmer in northern Portugal in summer than in the better known Algarve, and less than half of the guests in either area indicated that any decision to revisit the area would be influenced by their experience of the weather on this visit.

Overall, the investigation of visitors' perceptions of the areas in which they spent the holiday suggests that the attractiveness of rural locations as destinations for tourism comprise not only the landscape and other natural amenities, which together represent non-priced attractions, but also the perception on the part of the visitor of a hospitable community among whom it is possible to relax while finding out about the location, perhaps in the words of Harrison *et al.* (1986) to seek reassurance that the 'perceived values of the rural life still pertain'.

The implications of the study

This investigation of guests' and hosts' perceptions of rural tourism, in effect the consumers' and producers' view of the product, reflects the underlying theme of this book. In particular it has illustrated both the coincidence and divergence of perceptions which have implications, not only for further research but at a practical level, for the tourism industry. It parallels Ashworth's discussion in Chapter 7, where he considers the consequences for marketing tourism of the images projected by the industry and those received by potential tourists. It also complements and reinforces Kent's arguments in Chapter 9 concerning the need for the industry to identify and promote the attributes which influence consumers' holiday choice. In some senses the research has suggested the components of perceived opportunity sets analysed by Stabler in Chapter 2.

Although the study's objectives were primarily to gain more knowledge of perceptions for a specific form of tourism, there was an implied hypothesis, namely that there might be a mismatch between the perceptions of consumers and producers. The results suggest that in general this is not so for groups of criteria, even though the rankings of individual items showed some variation; at a more disaggregated level there is thus more variation.

What research and practical questions has the study answered and what further issues has it raised? Clearly it has both confirmed and updated the findings of earlier studies, such as those by Hill (1979) and Moutinho (1982) on the characteristics of those undertaking rural tourism, what attracts them and what they consider are important attributes of both the accommodation and countryside. The project also indicated trends in rural tourism which suggest changes which might occur in other European Community countries, such as France, Germany, Italy and Spain. A few examples suffice to underline the point. For both serviced and self-catering accommodation in rural areas, tourists look for value for money and a personal and informal atmosphere, and they are strongly influenced by previous experience. While these findings have implications for the individual proprietors and any cooperative or trade associations, there are also prescriptions for official (public sector) organisations committed to coordinating and promoting particular forms of tourism in specific areas.

The role of official bodies, especially national, regional and local tourist organisations and local government, is likely to be of fundamental importance in developing farm tourism in particular. For example, the study demonstrated a perception of the universality of farm holidays in that once such a holiday type has been decided on, it did not really matter to the tourist where the holiday was taken. This suggests that promotion is vital if particular areas or locations are to be developed.

The choice of south west England and northern Portugal as survey areas was useful for comparative purposes. The study's focus was mostly on farm tourism, being by definition in rural areas, and the two study areas represent, respectively, a well developed activity in south west England in contrast with an infant industry in Portugal. The comparison is apposite in that both countries wish to diversify their rural economies and create employment in the tourism sector. Given the high proportion of foreign rural tourists in Portugal (92 per cent of which 62 per cent were British in the survey), the English experience might provide some suggestions as to how the Portuguese authorities and industry could develop rural tourism. In turn, Portuguese success in providing value for money and making good use of traditional buildings might indicate how to extend and improve accommodation in the UK.

Further research is required in a number of directions. Though it has been asserted that the findings hold implications for rural tourism elsewhere in Europe, a wide-ranging survey is required to build on the work undertaken by Grolleau (1987) for the European Community. France has a long history of rural tourism through the gîtes, logis and auberge styles of holiday. A study of its experience and marketing of countryside tourism would be of value. The establishment of a study over time, using larger samples to improve statistical reliability, would also be useful. Finally a more comprehensive study would extend the range of accommodation, to include hotels and guesthouses, in rural areas, in order to supplement the information provided by this study.

References

Belo Moreira, M. (1986) *An Outline of Portuguese Agriculture, Facts and Figures about Portuguese Agriculture.* Thirteenth European Congress of Rural Sociology, Braga, Portugal, pp. 1–24.

Bullman, (1985) Farm tourism. In: Davies, E.M. (ed.), *Economic Regeneration – The Role of Local Authorities in Tourism.* INLOGOV, University of Birmingham.

Cornwall County Council (1986) *Discussion Paper on Tourism.* Cornwall County Council, Truro.

Dann, G.M.S. (1978) Tourist satisfaction: a highly complex variable. *Annals of Tourism Research,* 5, 440–441.

Davies, E.T. (1983) *The Role of Farm Tourism in the Less Favoured Areas of England and Wales.* Report 218, Agricultural Economics Unit, University of Exeter.

Devon County Council (1985) *Devon Tourism Review.* Devon County Council, Exeter.

Frater, J. (1983) *Farm Tourism in England and Overseas.* Research Memorandum 93, CURS, University of Birmingham.

Frater, J. (1986) *Farm Tourism.* Internal memorandum, English Tourist Board, London.

Goldey, P. (1981) Agrarian reform in Portugal 1974–1980. *Iberian Studies,* X, 47–58.

Grolleau, H. (1987) *Rural Tourism in the Twelve Member States of the EEC.* Commission for the European Communities, Directorate General for Transport (Tourism Service), Brussels.

Harrison, C., Burges, J. and Lamb, M. (1986) *Popular Values for the Countryside.* Report prepared for the Countryside Commission, Department of Geography, University of London.

Hill, G.A. (1979) *West Herefordshire Farm Tourism Tourism Project.* ADAS for Ministry of Agriculture Fisheries and Food, London.

Hoggart, K. (1988) Not a definition of rural area. *Area,* 20, 35–40.

Moutinho, L. (1982) *An Investigation of Vacation Tourist Behaviour in Portugal.* PhD thesis, University of Sheffield.

O'Flanagan, T.P.O. (1984) Galicia and the Minho. *The Geographical Magazine,* June, 90–94.

Pizam, A., Neumann, V. and Reichal, A. (1978) Dimensions of tourist satisfaction with a destination area. *Annals of Tourism Research,* 5, 314–321.

RPNPTI (1985) *Portuguese National Plan for Tourism : 1985–88.* Secretaria de Estado do Turismo, Lisbon, Portugal.

Robinson R.J.H. (1979) *Contemporary Portugal.* George Allen and Unwin, London.

Thibal, S. (1986) Tendences évolutives de la demande touristique: quelques reflexions sur le tourisme rural. *Revue de Tourisme* No.1, 14–16.

Unwin, T. (1985) Farmer's perceptions of agrarian change in north west Portugal. *Journal of Rural Studies,* 1, 339–357.

Wilkinson, K.P. (1985) Rural community development. *Rural Sociologist,* 5, 119–124.

Williams, S. (1975) Changing patterns of holidaymaking. *Town and Country Planning,* 43, 350–353.

Chapter 9

Understanding Holiday Choices

P. Kent

Introduction

In understanding the future spatial distribution of tourists it is important to remember that aggregate flows of tourists emerge from a huge number of independent decisions made by individual tourists. Possibly the most important of these is 'do I want to go on holiday this year?' A positive response to this prompts a second (arguably more important) question: 'which holiday shall I choose?'. This is the question which lies at the heart of the interaction between the tourism industry and the consumer, as choice represents the moment at which the tourist's tastes and desires are compared against the range of products offered by producers. It is the basic product decision which reflects the distribution and nature of destination infrastructure and attributes and leads to personal spatial behaviour.

This chapter addresses the form and nature of personal holiday choice and seeks to clarify which items are important in such choices. For example, how important is place image in this form of spatial decision making relative to other holiday considerations, such as the standard and type of accommodation, mode of transport and cost? In doing this, a link is forged between the earlier analyses of tourist perceptions and tastes (Chapters 7 and 8), trends in tourist tastes (Chapter 6) and future levels of tourism planning and provision (Chapter 12).

Elements of choice

When holiday choice is examined a number of factors need to be considered. In basic terms, choice represents the comparison of personal needs and desires with a number of products, from which one (that which is perceived to meet these requirements most closely) is selected. Therefore, in noting factors which are important in the choice process of tourists, a distinction must be drawn between elements of demand (i.e. goals which tourists wish to attain during their holiday) and elements of supply (i.e. variety and composition of available holiday products).

The analysis of an individual's holiday needs and desires requires the assessment of the interaction of a number of specific psychological variables (for example, motivations and preferences) and sociological variables (for example, social norms and expectations). Motivation generates the basic positive inclination to undertake a tourist experience. As the initiator of action, motivation has been widely examined by a number of authors (for a review see Ingham, 1986; Dann, 1981). Crompton (1979), for example, suggested that the 'push' factors in holiday choice could be reduced to a number of basic deep-rooted motivations which reflect the socio-psychological condition of the individual. Elements which were identified as being important for holiday choice included 'the enhancement of kinship relationships', 'prestige' and 'exploration and evaluation of self'. Dann (1977) meanwhile recognised 'fantasy' as being an important element of travel demand, suggesting that the desire to escape the monotony of everyday life and the enhancement of self-image are key motivational forces.

However, while motivation initiates action and suggests the approximate direction of satisfactory behaviour, more precise indications for subsequent action emerge from personal preferences. Preferences represent the most favoured options from a range of real or imagined possibilities and evolve from experiences of, and information about, outcomes of previous tourist behaviours over a period of time. Authors have noted a variety of preferences which tourists apply during holiday choice, although there are a number which are frequently cited, such as 'attractive scenery', 'cost', 'a range of facilities' and 'attractions to visit' (Goodrich, 1978; Kale and Weir, 1986; Gyte, 1987, 1988).

The interaction of motivations and preferences generates a series of holiday objectives – goals – which are explicit targets for achievement, as they aim to satisfy prevailing motivations in a preferred manner. Clearly the most satisfactory holiday is one in which all personal goals are attained. However, if any of these goals are not achieved the overall holiday becomes less satisfactory, as neither motivational desires nor personal preferences have been satisfied. This, however, is a function of the precision with which the goals are stated, itself a reflection of the detail in which both motivations and preferences are expressed (Kent, 1990b).

Ingham (1986) notes that preferences, like motivations (and therefore goals), may be either intrinsic (personal preferences) or extrinsic (socially conditioned). The importance of the social context of individuals as tourists has been noted by a number of authors (Furnham, 1981; Colton, 1987; Kent, 1989). Desberats (1983) argues that a valid analysis of human spatial behaviour is only possible when the socio-cultural context of the individual is taken into account. Most of these studies are typified by the use of a Symbolic Interactionist approach, in which it is argued that the attitudes, expectations and behaviour of individuals are developed and reinforced through social interaction with an enclosed in-group. Through interaction, common beliefs, standards and expectations are created which form the basis for future behaviour. As a result individuals are considered to select tourist experiences based on group-defined goals, expectations and standards (Kent, 1989).

The range of products on offer

Choice, however, is also a function of the range of available products from which the selection is to be made. Each holiday experience consists of a number of discrete elements which have to be allowed for in the choice process: a destination, transport to and from the destination, and type of accommodation, nourishment, other factors, such as attractions to visit, places to see and holiday insurance. Two basic forms of holiday experience can be identified according to who provides the services required by the tourist. On the one hand, services may be supplied by commercial organisations in the tourism industry (for example hotels, airlines, travel agents) or, on the other hand, by non-commercial 'outlets' who provide services outside the tourism industry (including friends, family, hitch-hiking).

Foster (1985) notes that commercial tourism requires the purchase of tourism products to make up the entire holiday experience. These products exist in two distinct forms for the tourist selecting a holiday. Tourism products may be discrete items representing a single dimension of the holiday experience (for example an airline seat, hotel room, meal), so that a number of products are required in order for a complete experience to be created. However, tourism products may also include packages of attributes which possess a large number of required holiday components in a single product.

Thus a distinction can be drawn between commercial tourism products which are sold independently and those which are sold as packages. It is important to emphasise this distinction because independent and package commercial tourism products provide fundamentally different holiday experiences. The main difference between such experiences is that independent holidays allow the individual to purchase each aspect of the holiday directly from the producer (or through an intermediary) and allow him or her to determine the composition of the holiday. Package holidays do not allow the individual the freedom to develop the exact holiday experience desired. However, the packages which are on offer do possess most of the necessary components for a holiday at a price less than that incurred if each component were to be purchased individually and independently. Furthermore, through the purchase of certain supplements, a degree of flexibility is permitted by allowing a choice of flights, variations in accommodation standards and catering service. In appealing to price-sensitive segments of the tourist market a variety of packages are developed which evolve through time as their 'manufacturers', the tour operators, compete for market dominance (see Chapters 4 and 5).

Other choice considerations

It must be noted that a further dimension exists to the factors which influence holiday decision-making. In classical economic analysis, choice is seen to represent the matching of demand to supply, which itself is conducted by individuals who aim to maximise their satisfaction in a manner typical of the behaviour of 'economic man'. Such choices are made by individuals who are rational, logical and possess perfect awareness and knowledge of available opportunities. In reality, however, the tourist makes the holiday decision from a position which is not only constrained by temporal and financial limitations but also by incomplete knowledge of the variety of products which exist. Thus tourists make their holiday decisions from positions which are bounded by the limits of attainability and awareness (see Kent, 1990a). The former is clearly a reflection of each individual's social position and economic power in obtaining sufficient funds and holiday time to enable a holiday to be taken. Limitations on awareness, however, can arise from the extent and method of the information searches the tourist may undergo in seeking a suitable holiday. The punctiform nature of such searches can be accentuated further by the manner in which tourism producers and retailers advertise and promote their services. This includes practices as varied as the manner in which brochures are racked and stored in travel agencies, to the accessibility and display of products on computer reservations systems (see Chapter 5).

Based on this position of bounded rationality, and considering that the holiday product is a service which cannot be sampled prior to purchase, choice itself can be considered to be an attempt to make an optimal decision from a sub-optimal position. As a result many previous analyses of the choice process have been limited in scope, for they assume optimality in every dimension, such as in awareness of information, rationality in decision-making and unlimited resources for the search for 'the best holiday' (for example Goodrich, 1978; Scott *et al.*, 1978).

Largely as a result of these inadequacies, alternative, more conceptual approaches to assessing the holiday choice process have been developed. The concept of opportunity sets can be used to describe the range of products available in the market place, or indeed to a given consumer, disaggregated by such definitional criteria as type of accommodation, mode of transport, cost and destination (see Chapter 2). Such criteria have been extended to include the range of holidays of which a tourist is aware and can afford – and which are therefore 'realisable' (Goodall *et al.*, 1988). The choice process itself is then considered to take place in a series of stages during which the range of holidays is reduced from a realisable set to a consideration set, and from there to a smaller choice set and lastly a decision set from which the final selection is made (Stabler, 1988).

In much the same way, Um and Crompton (1990) have conceptualised choice to emerge from an evoked set of holidays which is then further reduced to a smaller decision set from which the final selection is taken. Problems surrounding such an approach, discussed by Kent (1990b), include the inability to make the concept operational and predictive rather than simply descriptive, the absence of identified parameters for the demarcation of one set from another, and no firm empirical evidence that a multi-stage choice process is actually operative in holiday decision-making.

The objectives of the analysis

It is clear from this brief summary that any explanation of holiday choice must take into consideration personal holiday goals, product attributes and personal financial and temporal constraints, and limitations on awareness. What is unclear, however, is the relative strength of each of these variables in evaluating holiday products and in directing choice. More precisely, previous analyses have not addressed the question of the extent to which the perceived attractiveness of a single component influences the desirability of an entire product during the evaluation of available holidays. The question should be addressed, however, because this is the foundation of choice and a key determinant in the selection of appropriate infrastructure for destination tourism development.

The aim of this study is to examine the influence of individual holiday variables in the evaluation of entire experiences. So, for example, the analysis is intended to assess the relative influence which the destination image, type of accommodation, duration and cost have on choice. As different tourist types seek alternative means to fulfil their holiday tastes, and have contrasting infrastructural demands, data were sought to allow comparisons to be made between non-commercial, package and independent tourists.

The way in which these issues were examined was based on a large-scale postal questionnaire survey of the Reading area. The questionnaire was characterised by two distinct types of questions. The first series of questions required each respondent to score the desirability of a large number of distinct holiday attributes. Thus the attractiveness of such attributes as 'three star accommodation', 'direct flights', 'car hire' and 'children's activities' was examined, 65 separate attributes being listed. An indication of preference regarding holiday price was also attained. Price levels, taken from brochures current at the time, were listed for a 'standard holiday' of a specific duration. Several holidays of differing duration were also listed, for example less than four days, four to seven days, eight to ten days, and respondents were asked to score each duration and price combination according to their preferences. Each respondent was told that the total cost of each holiday included basic holiday attributes (i.e. transport to and from the destination, transfers and bed and breakfast accommodation).

The second series of questions required each respondent to score compilations of the attributes listed previously, which were bundled into arbitrary 'products'. On average each 'product' possessed nine separate attributes which included the basic holiday components, such as destination, accommodation and mode of transport, but also such attributes as the availability of cheap car hire and children's facilities (see Table 9.1). Sixteen such 'products' were listed, although two were identical to act as controls to assess the degree of natural variation in scoring.

Other questions which were listed included personal (for example sex, married/single, occupation) and previous holiday performances (for example stay at home, travel abroad to a hotel as part of a package, self-catering accommodation independently arranged, or camping). The preference questions were scored on a seven-point Likert scale for which '1' represented a 'very desirable attribute' and '7' a 'very undesirable attribute'. Performance-related questions were scored on a five-point scale for which '1' represented 'I always select this type of holiday' and '5' 'I never select this type of holiday'.

The preference question format was essential because the results were to be analysed using correlation and regression analyses for which the variations in the scores of the attributes (the independent variables) were to be measured against

Table 9.1 Examples of the 'products' listed in the questionnaire for evaluation by respondents

Destination	Venice	Brighton	Cannes	Salzburg
Accommodation	1* hotel	Camping	3* hotel	Camping
Transport	Ferry/rail	Own	Ferry/coach	Direct Flight
Day of departure	Wednesday	Friday	Sunday	Saturday
Price per person	£500	£200	£400	£250
Duration	14 days	10 days	7 days	8 days
Provision of games facilities	Yes	Yes	None	None
Cheap car hire	No	No	No	No
Children's activities	Yes	None	Yes	Yes
Swimming pool	No	Yes	Yes	Yes
Good nightlife	No	Yes	No	Yes
Excursions	Yes	No	Yes	No

the variation in scores of the product in which these attributes were found (the dependent variables). By using this approach the sign and value of the regression coefficient for each of the independent variables would represent the influence of each attribute in the score of the total product.

Individuals were to be sorted into 'tourist types' according to the type of holiday which they undertook most frequently. Thus those individuals who selected hotel or self-catering packages 'always' or 'mostly' were classified as 'organised tourists', and those who 'always' or 'mostly' select independent arrangements were classified as 'independent tourists'. Those who 'always' or 'mostly' stay at home, visit family or friends, or do not go away at all were grouped as 'non-commercial tourists'. The remaining tourists such as those who go camping or sailing (which could be arranged independently, in a package, or non-commercially) and those who express a tendency towards any single type of holiday were broadly classified as 'others'.

A random stratified sampling frame was defined for the distribution of the questionnaires by the data recorded in the 1981 Census for social class for 10 per cent of the population of each Enumeration District (ED) – the smallest available spatial area for which such data existed. An average social class

170

indicator was calculated for each ED and grouped into strata. A representative random selection of EDs was then made by taking a one fifth sample of EDs in proportion to the number of EDs in each stratum. A 1/50 sample of individuals was then taken from each ED to a total size in proportion to the population of the ED. The final sample size was calculated to be 565, which represented an approximate sampling frame of 1/250.

Results

The study received a total response rate of 35 per cent, which corresponded to that attained during a pilot survey. However, having discarded responses because of missing values and incomplete returns, an effective response rate of 30 per cent was recorded. This sample was tested to ensure representativeness by comparing its average social class score against those of the sample area and was found to be representative at a one per cent level. A further indicator of the suitability of the total sample size is the acceptability of the size of each disaggregated tourist type group. Normal limits of acceptability of sample size for parametric tests are taken to be greater than 30 persons (Short, 1980). In assessing the sample size of these disaggregated groups it was found that the largest group of respondents existed in the 'other' category (47 respondents) which made up 28 per cent of the total number of responses. The smallest group size was found for 'non-commercial' tourists, of which there were only 33 respondents (20 per cent of the total).

Using information on personal characteristics obtained from the questionnaire it was possible to generate a profile for each tourist type. It was found that independent tourists possessed the lowest social class scores for all the groups, but had the highest percentage of families in the sample and the greatest average age. When each of these groups was disaggregated further, the highest social class was found for 'sailing', the highest average age was for 'independently booked hotels' and the greatest proportion of families for any single category was recorded for 'second homes/timeshare', although the sample size of this group was rather small.

The first stage in the analysis of responses was to collate and compare the scores for the individually listed holiday attributes (Table 9.2). Average Likert scores were then calculated. Comparison of the highest and lowest scoring attributes revealed notable differences in preferences between tourist types. For the total sample the most preferred holiday attributes were 'a place with attractive scenery', 'a direct flight', 'a place to rest and relax' and 'half-board facilities'. The least preferred attributes were related to the cost/duration of the holiday and to 'ferry/coach' and 'coach' transport, 'bed only' and 'camping' accommodation. Of the top 15 components, eight directly referred to the nature of the destination. In constrast, only one place attribute – 'the importance to be in a place close to home' – was found in the bottom 15 preferences.

When the highest and lowest scoring preferences were examined for the smaller disaggregated tourist types, it was found that 'non-commercial' tourists had nine place attributes in the highest 15 scores with none in the bottom 15 scores. Similarly 'independent' and 'other' tourists also allocated a large number

Table 9.2   The ranked 15 most and least preferred holiday attributes

Rank		Total sample	Non-commercial	Organised	Independent	Other
Top 15 attributes	1	Scenery	Scenery	Direct flight	Scenery	Scenery
	2	Direct flight	Direct flight	£200 (less than 11 days)	Rest and relaxation	Rest and relaxation
	3	Rest and relaxation	Good food	Half board	Friendly inhabitants	Friendly inhabitants
	4	Half board	Unspoilt scenery	£200 (less than 8 days)	Half board	Half board
	5	Friendly inhabitants	Friendly inhabitants	£250 (less than 11 days)	Unspoilt scenery	Unspoilt scenery
	6	Unspoilt scenery	History	Unspoilt scenery	£200 (less than 11 days)	£200 (11-14 days)
	7	£200 (11-14 days)	Sites of interest	Rest and relaxation	Own transport	Own transport
	8	Food and drink	Rest and relaxation	Good food	£250 (less than 11 days)	£250 (11-14 days)
	9	£250-300 (11-14 days)	Own transport	3 star Hotel	Peaceful	Peaceful
	10	£200-250 (8-10 days)	Peaceful	Friendly inhabitants	History	History
	11	History	Cheap	£250 (less than 8 days)	£200 (less than 8 days)	£200 (8-10 days)
	12	£150-200 (4-7 days)	£200-250 (11-14 days)	£150 (less than 4 days)	Sites of interest	Sites of interest
	13	Sites of interest	£150-200 (4-7 days)	Swimming pool	Self-catering (villa)	Self-catering (villa)
	14	Peaceful	Half board	£300 (less than 11 days)	Saturday	Saturday
	15	£250-300 (8-10 days)	Bed & Breakfast	Unspoilt scenery	Self-catering (Apartment)	Self-catering (Apartment)
Bottom 15 attributes	55	Close to home	Ferry/Coach	£400 (8-10 days)	Children's activities	Children's activities
	56	£300-350 (4-7 days)	£450-500 (11-14 days)	£500 (11-14 days)	£400 (8-10 days)	£400 (8-10 days)
	57	Camping	£300-350 (4-7 days)	£250 (less than 4 days)	Car hire	Car hire
	58	Coach	Coach	Coach	£400 (11-14 days)	£500 (11-14 days)
	59	£500+(11-14 days)	Bed only	Ferry/Coach	Camping	Camping
	60	Ferry/coach	Camping	£450 (8-10 days)	£300 (4-7 days)	£300 (4-7 days)
	61	£250-300 (less than 4 days)	£250-300 (less than 4 days)	£350 (4-7 days)	£450 (8-10 days)	£450 (8-10 days)
	62	£450+ (8-10 days)	£500-550 (11-14 days)	Bed only	£350 (4-7 days)	£350 (4-7 days)
	63	£350+(4-7 days)	£350-400 (4-7 days)	Close to home	Bed only	Bed only
	64	Bed only	£450-500 (8-10 days)	Camping	£250 (less than 4 days)	£250 (less than 4 days)
	65	£500+ (8 days)	£500-550 (8-10 days)	£500 (8-10 days)	£500 (8-10 days)	£500 (8-10 days)
	66	£400+ (4-7 days)	£400-450 (4-7 days)	£300 (less than 4 days)	£400 (4-7 days)	£400 (4-7 days)
	67	£300-350 (up to 4 days)	£300-350 (less than 4 days)	£400 (4-7 days)	£300 (less than 4 days)	£300 (less than 4 days)
	68	£350-400 (up to 4 days)	£350-400 (less than 4 days)	£350 (less than 4 days)	£400 (less than 4 days)	£400 (less than 4 days)
	69	£400+ (up to 4 days)	£400-450 (less than 4 days)	£400 (less than 4 days)	£350 (less than 4 days)	£350 (less than 4 days)

of place attributes in the 15 most preferred attributes. By contrast 'organised' tourists had only four place attributes in their most preferred attributes, which was less than the number (6) relating to the cost/duration of the holiday.

Clearly the final choice of holiday destination reflects the degree to which potential tourists see particular places offering the types of place attributes (for example scenery, relaxation, friendly inhabitants) which they consider to be important and require for a successful holiday. The degree to which place-specific attributes were perceived to exist in the respondents' images of a number of destinations was examined in detail. This was achieved by using a STEPWISE multiple regression technique, which sought to test the strength of the relationship between preference scores given to particular holiday locations listed in the questionnaire (as dependent variables) against the list of preference scores of individual 'place' attributes (independent variables).

Analysis of the regression coefficients for each independent variable revealed the strength and direction of the relationship between the place attribute preference and the place image preference. The results showed considerable variations between images in terms of the relevant attributes to which they were strongly statistically related. For example, the image of Venice had a strong positive regression coefficient with 'a place with a wide variety of sites to visit', Corfu and Florence with 'a place with friendly local inhabitants' and Majorca with 'a place with an interesting history and culture'. Strong negative coefficients were noted for Brighton and Corfu with 'a place where you can be assured of peace and quiet' and Florence and Venice with 'a place with a wide range of recreational activities'.

Some differences were noted between tourist types, and in order to assess the extent of these differences common trends were sought in the attributes most frequently used in the evaluation of images. By doing this it was thought that some indication of 'sensitivity' to particular destination attributes for each tourist type could be noted. Such results would suggest the degree to which each tourist type evaluates destinations by particular variables. Those attributes with significant regression coefficients were compiled from each 'product' and for tourist type. The results showed that non-commercial tourists evaluated place images most frequently with 'a place for rest and relaxation' (25 per cent of all significant regression coefficients), for organised tourists 'a place with an interesting history and culture' (24 per cent) and for independent tourists 'a place which is cheap to holiday in'. Respondents in the 'others' category used 'a place which is unspoilt by tourism' (17 per cent) as the most frequent evaluator of holiday destinations.

In the analysis of the importance of product attributes in the selection of holidays, the relationship between place images and the variables which tourists appear to use in their evaluation are significant. In this research, however, the large number of place attributes listed in the questionnaire preclude a combined analysis using these and non-place attributes, such as the nature of accommodation or transport. The only possible results to emerge from such an examination would be diffuse and of limited significance. Consequently, non-place attributes were examined in conjunction with place images (which had been listed and evaluated in the questionnaire).

The first stage in this analysis was to compare the preference scores for the place images against the scores of the non-place attributes. Having done this it was then possible to identify the most popular holiday attributes from each 'component' group and to develop an idealised product specification (see Table 9.3). Thus for the total sample the destination with the highest overall preference score was Florence, although 'a direct flight' and 'half-board' catering had higher than average scores. There were some variations between the tourist types in terms of attribute differences rather than in the order of the desirability of the components themselves. Most interestingly, there are substantial similarities between non-commercial and 'other' tourists and between 'organised' and 'independent' tourists. The extent of these similarities was limited. For example, non-commercial and organised tourists both preferred three star accommodation, and independent and other tourists preferred self-catering accommodation.

Table 9.3 Attributes with the highest performance scores from each component group for each tourist type

Total	Non-commercial	Organised	Independent	Other
Direct flight	Direct flight	Direct flight	Direct flight	Direct flight
Half board	Half board	Half board	Half board	Half board
Florence	Venice	Florence	Florence	Venice
Saturday	Friday	Saturday	Saturday	Friday
£200/11 days	£200/11 days	£200/11 days	£200/11 days	£200/11 days
3 Star hotel	3 Star hotel	3 Star hotel	Self-catering	Self-catering

In assessing the influence of variables in choice it is important to note that consumer preferences are not necessarily reflected in actual behaviour during holiday choice and product evaluation itself. Therefore, although these product preferences give some indication of the most preferred attributes of any particular component type – and a suggestion of the most preferred holiday which the respondents would seek – the extent to which they are transferred into product evaluation itself must be addressed using a more thorough statistical technique.

At this stage the research sought to use the STEPWISE multiple regression technique to calculate the significance of holiday attributes (the 'independent' variables) against the product scores (the 'dependent' variables). However, the number of missing values compounded over so many questions and responses meant that an insufficient number of responses were recorded to enable a valid and meaningful analysis to take place. However, it was possible to undertake a large series of correlation analyses between individual attribute scores and the product scores in order to assess the strength of the relationship between the two. This process was repeated for each product and for each attribute. The result was a list of correlation coefficients linking the scores of a given attribute against the product score which extend across all products and each attribute found in the composition of the products. In order to rationalise this, mean correlation coefficients were calculated for each component. Thus it could be said, for example, that on average accommodation counts for a given proportion of the total variation in product scores.

The mean correlation coefficients for each component are listed in Table 9.4. This shows that on average destination image has a higher average influence in the evaluation of products than any other product component. Other important components include transport and accommodation. However, the extent of this influence appears to be small; the coefficient of determination reveals that only 15 per cent of the variation in product scores can be attributed to the image scores.

Table 9.4   The number of significant correlations (at 5%) for each product component across all products and for each tourist type

Components	Total	Non-commercial	Organised	Independent	Other
%	%	%	%	%	%
Image	94	12	56	56	69
Accommodation	75	25	19	37	37
Transport	69	6	19	62	19
Cost	44	25	6	12	0
Departure day	6	6	0	6	6
Nightlife	62	0	37	25	12
Games/facilities	22	0	22	33	22
Children's Activities	36	0	9	27	0
Excursions	16	16	0	50	16
Car hire	16	0	0	16	0
Swimming pool	9	9	0	36	0

This may be due in part to the scoring system used in the research and analysis of the questionnaires, and also to the large number of responses used to calculate the factors. Furthermore, as other coefficients of determination for other components are even lower it suggests that choice may reflect the interaction of a number of attributes working in conjunction rather than independently. However, when the correlation coefficients between image and product scores were examined for each product, it was found that only three of the 16 were not significant at the five per cent level. This suggests that although the causal power of image in holiday choice appears to be relatively limited, it is the most important of all the factors examined and has a significant influence on choice. Of the other variables considered in the choice process, accommodation and transport had relatively strong and significant correlation coefficients, although there were fewer significant relationships when each product/image pair were examined than for place image.

The importance of these, and other variables, was found to vary substantially between tourist types. For example, 'independent' tourists, were found to have a stronger average correlation coefficient with 'transport' and 'accommodation' than with image, while 'organised' tourists had a strong mean coefficient with accommodation. 'Other' and 'non-commercial' tourists tended to demonstrate strong relationships between place image scores and product preference scores.

Although the use of mean correlation coefficients can only be seen as an indicator of the influence of certain product components in holiday choice, it would appear that place images are the most important considerations in the selection and evaluation of products. This varies between tourist types. Possible reasons for these variations may be suggested. However, it should be noted that the importance of place images and other product attributes varied substantially between the product range. For example, for one product the total sample may consider the place image to be the most important consideration in choice, while in another the mode of transport dominates. Clearly, the importance of image is also a function of the actual destination which is being 'pictured'. Similarly, the desirability of 'mode of transport' is a reflection of the specific mode given in the product's attributes.

This suggests that while components can be calculated as having a general level of importance in choice (as noted above) the actual importance of a component in the selection of any single holiday is a function of the attribute found in the product. In exploring this further, those products in which place images had relatively small correlation coefficients with product scores were examined in more detail. It was found that in these products, attributes with very low preference scores (i.e. 'camping' and 'ferry/coach' transport) had correlation coefficients which were significantly higher than those found for place images. In other words, attributes such as 'ferry/coach' transport, while having lower preference scores than 'direct flight', 'own transport' and 'rail', and also lower scores than the other attributes in the product of which they were a part, had a more significant role in product evaluation than these other more attractive attributes.

It therefore appears that when respondents evaluated each product, the potential benefits of an attractive location, for example, were obscured by the exceptional unattractiveness of other particular attributes. The products were thus scored as being unattractive, and hence stronger correlation coefficients were generated with the unattractive attributes than with the more attractive place images. The same trends were observed for each tourist type, although the trends within some products were complicated by low (and insignificant) overall coefficients, especially for non-commercial tourists. However, 'independent' tourists had high correlations for less attractive attributes such as 'direct flights', compared with their more preferred attribute 'own transport', and 'organised' tourists perceived 'ferry/coach' travel to be less attractive than 'direct flight', yet consistently gave the former higher correlation coefficients.

Therefore although images are important determinants in choice in general terms, their correlation coefficients with product scores may be affected by the desirability or undesirability of other product components. As a result the final influence of a particular image in holiday choice is a reflection of the attractiveness or unattractiveness of the other product attributes.

Discussion

This research raised two general questions relating to the holiday choice process. Firstly, what variables influence the importance of particular attributes in the holiday choice process and, secondly, what further insights into the choice process are gained? On a superficial level the reason for the variations in holiday demands, and therefore in the importance of certain attributes in holiday choice, can be ascribed to variations in holiday preferences and goals between holidaymakers. Thus those products which possess attributes suitable to the needs of particular tourists will be scored more favourably than those with unsuitable attributes.

More specifically, however, general trends in taste and preferences can be ascribed to three major factors: position in the family life cycle, social position and special needs. Of these factors, the influence of the family life cycle was the most obvious. Analysis of the age structure of each tourist type revealed that while 'organised' and 'non-commercial' tourists dominated early life, 'independent' tourism became more important later in the cycle, peaking between the ages of 34 and 41 years. It appears that 'independent' tourists have priorities and preferences which emerge from their position as family-oriented individuals. Thus 'organised' holidays may be rejected because of the extra worry and effort required in travelling abroad and the lack of flexibility imposed by 'packages'. These tourists show a greater sensitivity to the mode of transport offered by particular products during choice, rather than other attributes such as 'image'. By contrast, younger and single 'organised' and 'non-commercial' tourists are limited in their choice of holiday by cost, as this age-group is possibly beginning full-time employment and is financially constrained.

A further influence in the attractiveness of attributes in holiday choice is the social status of the tourists. In broad terms, using the UK Registrar General's occupational categorisation, it was found that the 'other' tourists were predominantly from the highest social classes, with independent tourism being mainly the middle classes and 'organised' tourism being particularly strong in the lower classes. Non-commercial tourism tended to increase down the class structure. This pattern reflects the general level of costs associated with each type of tourism. Sailing, for example, requires a larger immediate capital expenditure and recurring costs than an organised holiday or visiting family and friends. In this way the patterns of choice reflect the general levels of economic power associated with each class type. However, these patterns are highly generalised because of the broadness of the class categorisation, the response rate, the influence of other factors (such as the family life cycle) and problems with cross-tabulation. Despite this the influence of social status and economic power is strong in holiday choice, as other studies have revealed the influence of social groups in the direction of leisure decision-making (for example Colton, 1987) and spatial location and decision-making (for example Jones and Eyles, 1977).

Special needs *per se* were not sought during the analysis, although each tourist's preferences represent a certain combination of 'special' needs to be fulfilled during the holiday experience. Taken to an extreme, blind people, or those with special dietary needs, would assess destinations according to the provision of facilities which would fulfil their requirements. Products without these facilities would be immediately discarded. On a more general level, the desire to visit a particular environment or place would mean that products which do not possess the required location would be rejected. In this way, in being less constrained to a particular form of accommodation, more 'footloose' tourist types, such as those who like camping or sailing (in the 'other' category), demonstrated greater sensitivity to changes in destination across products than other tourists.

In addition to indications concerning the influence of special needs, the family life cycle and social position in the development of holiday preferences and choice, the research also provides an insight into the complex nature of choice itself. In particular, it suggests a process where product evaluation is evolved over a series of stages. The concept of choice developing over a series of stages has been suggested by such authors as Um and Crompton (1990) and Kent (1990c). The idea here is that a holiday is finally selected from a small range of possibilities, which itself has been selected through a series of filters from the total market range of opportunities of which the tourist is aware. It is suggested that the filters which are applied to the holiday opportunities in order to identify the most suitable are based on the search for certain product attributes which fulfil holiday preferences. Those products which possess desirable features are then assessed for other preferred attributes in a continuous process, which is ended only when a product is found not to possess a certain attribute (and is therefore omitted from any other evaluation) or when no competing products remain (in which case a final selection can be made).

The results from the study appear to support this concept. In the evaluation of products it was found that those attributes which were relatively undesirable had high correlation coefficients. For example, the total effective sample had more significant correlation coefficients with undesirable forms of transport, such as 'ferry/coach' and 'ferry', than with more preferred modes such as 'direct flights'. Analysis of individual products revealed that many highly preferred components scored smaller correlation coefficients than less preferred components.

These results imply that during evaluation those preferred attributes were sought, and if located, evaluation continued on to the search for other preferred attributes. When an undesirable attribute is met, the final preference score attributed to the entire product reflects this undesirability. Thus, when correlation coefficients are examined, the scores reveal that highly preferred attributes have relatively low product coefficients (because they permitted evaluation to continue to a later stage), and less preferred attributes have stronger coefficients because they did not permit evaluation to continue any further and therefore directed final product evaluations.

This analysis itself raises a number of issues. First, it suggests that place images were perceived to be the least preferred product components because they scored significant correlation coefficients more frequently than any other single component. Yet in the analysis above this was taken to be a sign of strength and influence in choice. In response to this doubt, the strength of individual image–product correlation coefficients was compared against the preference scores of each image. It was found that, in general terms, the size of the image–product correlation increased with the perceived unattractiveness of the image. In addition the highest mean preference score for any of the images was 2.1 (on a scale of 1 = highest to 7 = lowest). This would suggest that individuals evaluated the images as being attractive, yet not as attractive as others which could have been listed. Thus a general level of dissatisfaction could have caused product preferences to be scored similarly to image scores.

A second possible explanation is that the respondents reacted to the listed place image (which always headed the list of product attributes) and then scored the product without a detailed examination of the remainder of the product. This is a strong possibility. In suggesting this, however, it should be noted that the order in which the attributes were listed reflected the order in which they are generally advertised by such tourism organisations as travel agencies. Thus if this explanation of the scores is true, it is itself a reflection of the advertising and marketing procedures of the primary sales mechanisms.

A second issue which this analysis does not resolve is the order in which preferences are applied in evaluation. In previous research it was suggested that the most important attributes to the success of a holiday are the first to be sought during product evaluation (Kent, 1990b). Logically, the order of the search is irrelevant because a product will contain a particular combination of attributes no matter in which order they are sought. However, as many individuals aim to minimise time and effort wasted on sorting undesirable and inappropriate holidays, some form of prioritisation of needs is required. This facilitates evaluation by focusing searches on preferred attributes which have significant influences on the holiday experience. In this way, the information search process can be directed more productively.

Thus the importance of attributes, and the order in which they are sought in the evaluation process, is significant because it can direct the tourist to certain types of holiday information. For example, a tourist who considers location to be the most important consideration in the holiday experience will direct subsequent searches to learn more about potential destinations through destination guides, travel guides and maps. Tourists more concerned with accommodation may seek further information through lists of hotels, bed and breakfast accommodation, and so on. Although both forms of information may be used by a single individual, in many cases the information search will be selective.

The effect is that, due to selective advertising and promotional procedures by tourism organisations, the range of opportunities advertised in one source of information is unlikely to be the same as that found in another. As a result individuals may be presented with a different range of options from which to choose, and this will influence the final choice of holiday. Thus due to selective information collection on the part of the consumer, and selective advertising and promotion on the part of the producer, different combinations of holiday products will be discovered by individuals with differing holiday priorities. In this way, the first attributes to be sought in choice are important because they can significantly influence the range of products from which choice is finally made.

Some indication of the relative importance of components and attributes in holiday choice was provided by the research. It was apparent that image demonstrated a stronger influence over the evaluation of products than any other product component. Although this could be due to the fact that some of the images listed in the products were perceived to be relatively unpopular (as noted above), it is also an indication that they were frequently considered during evaluation. In other words, the frequency with which the correlation coefficients were significant suggests the frequency with which they were referred to in the evaluation of the products. Thus although their perceived attractiveness may have been limited in the opinion of the consumers, the significance of images in choice is revealed by the extent to which they were used in evaluation.

In this way it would appear that place images are the single most important components in the holiday choice process. Similarly, other important product components were type of accommodation and mode of transport. For the total effective sample it also emerged that a good nightlife and cost were also important considerations. There were some apparent differences between tourist types; for example, 'non-commercial' tourists found the type of accommodation and cost to be the most important factors, whereas 'organised' tourists found the place image and nightlife to be more important. Independent tourists considered the mode of transport to be most important in choice, with place image and excursions also having importance. 'Other' tourists were found to consider place image to be by far the most important product component. These findings have implications for both the understanding of tourist choice and patterns of decision-making, and for associated future infrastructure development.

Conclusion

This chapter set out to provide an insight into the relative importance of particular variables in holiday choice. Although the coefficients of determination are relatively low, the results from the survey do reveal a definite significant trend in the selection process of holidaymakers. In general terms, it is apparent that personal preferences, motivations and goals direct the tourist in selecting, firstly, a suitable holiday location (as suggested by the importance of place images) and then a suitable standard of accommodation, style of transport and cost. Thus even when each particular product attributed is examined it is clear that the holiday choice process is guided by a personal reaction to specific product features. In this way a product which may be acceptable in every other respect may be rejected because one particular attribute does not fulfil a certain goal. Clearly, the rejection of a product on the basis of a single attribute is a function of the relative attractiveness of the variable itself, and the role that it is expected to play in the total tourist experience. For example, whether a product is rejected because it has no swimming pool is a reflection of the significance which the tourist ascribed to that feature for a successful holiday. A significant role would mean that a new product would have to be sought, while an insignificant role would mean that the product would be sufficiently satisfactory.

Although there were variations between tourist types, the survey results, showing that a suitable holiday destination is more important than any other consideration during choice, have a number of important implications and provoke a number of comments. First, having regard to the importance of place images, no indication has been given about their scale. It is highly unlikely that a holidaymaker will not refine the choice of resort during choice. However, the scale of images is a function of the awareness which tourists have of the world. Initially, tourists specify general areas of interest – relating to their spatial awareness – which may then be differentiated further as more information is uncovered during the search process. Alternatively, tourists may define wide spatial areas as being 'the same' and, having satisfied their spatial preferences and goals, search for a hotel and other suitable product features in that area. Clearly, in order to promote an area successfully, tourist boards must be fully aware of the image which the tourist holds of their area and the distinctiveness this image possesses over other neighbouring areas.

Second, the importance of image in choice has been suggested to vary with such factors as special need requirements and the stage in the family life cycle. As a result of these pressures other components, such as accommodation, assume a greater role in choice. The importance of market segmentation in developing tourist facilities need not be repeated here. However, from these results it is evident that products which stress inappropriate attributes to certain segments will not be successful.

Thirdly, much has been written about methods of market segmentation and its significance in both place and product promotion and infrastructural development. The results from the survey suggest that improvements in destination environmental quality, accommodation stock, access and value for money are required to encourage tourists. The priorities which should be attached to these should reflect such characteristics as existing levels of accommodation and access, and future expectations of demographic trends and market segments to be targeted. Consideration should also be given to the facilities and standards offered by competing destinations/products. This does not necessarily imply the advocation of fierce competition between producers, but allows for a place/product to acquire a level of specialisation through which a comparative or absolute advantage may be exercised.

Acknowledgements

This chapter is based on research undertaken in the Department of Geography, University of Reading, funded by the Economic and Social Research Council.

References

Colton, C.W. (1987) Leisure, recreation, tourism: a symbolic interactionist view. *Annals of Tourism Research*, 14, 345–360.

Crompton, J.L. (1979) Motivations for pleasure vacation. *Annals of Tourism Research*, 6(4), 408–424.

Dann, G.M.S. (1977) Anomie, ego-enhancement and tourism. *Annals of Tourism Research*, 4(4), 184–194.

Dann, G.M.S. (1981) Tourist motivations: an appraisal. *Annals of Tourism Research*, 8, 187–219.

Desberats, J. (1983) Spatial choice and constraints on behaviour. *Annals of the Association of American Geographers*, 13(3), 340–357.

Foster, D. (1985) *Travel and Tourism Management*. Macmillan, Basingstoke.

Furnham, A. (1981) Personality and activity preference. *British Journal of Social Psychology*, 20(1), 57–68.

Goodall, B., Radburn, M.R. and Stabler, M.J. (1988) Market Opportunity Sets for Tourism. *Geographical Papers* (Tourism Series) No.1. Department of Geography, University of Reading.

Goodrich, J.N. (1978) The relationship between preferences for and perceptions of vacation destinations: application of a choice model. *Journal of Travel Research*, 16(2), 8–13.

Gyte, D.M. (1987) Tourist Cognition of Destinations: An Exploitation of Techniques of Measurement and Representation of Images of Tunisia. *Trent Working Papers in Geography*, Trent Polytechnic, Nottingham.

Gyte, D.M. (1988) Repertory Grid Analysis of Images of Destinations: British Tourists in Mallorca. *Trent Working Papers in Geography*, Trent Polytechnic, Nottingham.

Ingham, R. (1986) Psychological contributions to the study of leisure – part one. *Leisure Studies*, 5, 255–279.

Jones, E. and Eyles, J. (1977) *An Introduction of Social Geography*. Oxford University Press, Oxford.

Kale, S.H. and Weir, K.M. (1986) Marketing Third World countries to the western traveller: The case of India. *Journal of Travel Research*, 25 (Fall) 2–7.

Kent, P.J. (1989) The desire to conform?: another role of image in the destination choice of potential holidaymakers. In: Botterill, D. (ed.), *Leisure Participation and Experience: Models and Case Studies*. Leisure Studies Association, Brighton 39(6) pp.18–35.

Kent, P.J. (1990a) People, places and priorities: the application of the opportunity set concept to holiday choice. In: Ashworth, G.J. and Goodall, B. (eds), *Marketing Tourism Places*. Routledge, London, pp. 41–61.

Kent, P.J. (1990b) *The Role of Place Image in the Holiday Choice Process of Potential Tourists*. Unpublished PhD Thesis, Department of Geography, University of Reading.

Scott, D.R., Schewe, C.D. and Fredrick, D.G. (1978) A multibrand, multiattribute model of tourist state choice. *Journal of Travel Research*, 17, 23–29.

Short, J. (1980) *Urban Data Sources*. Butterworths, London.

Stabler, M.J. (1988) The image of destination regions: theoretical and empirical aspects. In: Goodall, B. and Ashworth, G.J. (eds), *Marketing in the Tourism Industry: The Promotion of Destination Regions*. Croom Helm, Beckenham, pp.133–161.

Um, S. and Crompton, J.L. (1990) Attitude determinants in tourism destination choice. *Annals of Tourism Research*, 17(3), 432–448.

Chapter 10

The Tourism Industry and Foreign Exchange Leakages in a Developing Country: The Distribution of Earnings from Safari and Beach Tourism in Kenya

M.Thea Sinclair

Introduction

Tourism's importance as a source of foreign currency has attracted the attention of increasing numbers of developing countries, which are faced with inelastic demand for their primary products and high levels of protection against their exports of manufactured goods. Many developing countries are considered to have a comparative advantage in tourism, owing to their attractive climatic, cultural and scenic resources. However, destination areas only supply part of the tourism product, in particular accommodation, infrastructure and other destination-specific characteristics. Foreign ownership or control of such assets, as well as of the airlines used to transport tourists, can be considerable. Moreover, payments for holiday expenditure are often made to travel agents and tour operators in tourist origin countries so that only a percentage reaches the destination. Further reductions in the potential revenue of the destination occur in the form of payments for imports consumed by tourists in the destination area and remittances of profits, interest and dividends to foreign owners of tourism businesses. A major issue related to tourism in developing countries is therefore the distribution of the revenue obtained from tourism between firms and individuals in destination and origin countries.

Some research has been undertaken on the import content of tourist expenditure, which varies between small and large countries and according to the degree of complementarity between the tourism, agricultural and manufacturing sectors of the destination economy. However, the distributional consequences of foreign intermediaries' participation in the tourism industry have received little attention. This chapter will therefore focus on the foreign currency leakages and retention which are associated with expenditure on different types of package holidays, which are an increasingly important form of tourism in developing countries. Original data will be provided for Kenya, which is a major developing country destination for tourists.

The chapter will follow the sequence of analysis in this book by considering, first, the supply side of tourism in Kenya. The demand for tourism, its origins and spatial features will then be discussed. The trends over time in total and per capita foreign currency earnings from tourism will provide the context for an examination of safari and beach package holidays in Kenya, marketed by large UK tour operators. The prices of different types of package holidays will be examined and the constituent prices of food and accommodation, ground and air transportation will be estimated. The distribution of the revenue from each type of package holiday between firms in Kenya and foreign tourism intermediaries will then be calculated. The policy implications and dilemmas for developing countries will be considered in the final two sections.

The tourism industry in Kenya

Developing countries are renowned for their climatic and beach tourism resources, which are particularly popular during the winter months in the northern hemisphere. However, a variety of resources, in addition to those of 'sun, sand and sea', are key components of a range of tourism products supplied by developing countries, for example wildlife, culture, heritage and city tourism. Kenya is an interesting case as it is one of the world's major long haul tourist destinations, supplying safari, beach and city tourism. Package holidays in Kenya are marketed both by local tour operators and travel agents and, increasingly, by foreign intermediaries throughout the world.

The hotel sector in Kenya is one of the best endowed in Africa, supplying almost 30,000 bed-spaces, of which 77 per cent were in hotels and lodges of three, four or five (highest) star category in 1989, as indicated in Table 10.1. A further 500 bed-spaces are available in the tented camps which, along with lodges, provide accommodation for tourists on safari. Tourist accommodation is highly concentrated by 'product' and geographic area, as is shown by the last two columns in Table 10.1 and by Figure 10.1. In 1988 coastal areas contained 47.6 per cent of all (non-camp site) bed-spaces, most of which were in the Mombasa area, the south coast, Kilifi, Malindi and Lamu to the north. The supply of coastal tourism has increased in absolute and relative terms, as is indicated by comparison of the shares of bed-spaces in different areas in 1980 and 1988, shown in Figure 10.1. The city of Nairobi's share of bed-spaces decreased over time, to 26.4 per cent in 1988, while the shares of lodges in national (game) parks and reserves, and of other areas remained approximately constant. The majority of bed-spaces in wildlife areas are supplied in a small number of national parks and reserves; the Masai Mara, for example, contained 16 per cent of lodge bed-spaces and 74 per cent of those in camp sites.

The distribution of restaurants, tour operators, vehicle hire enterprises and curio shops in Kenya is also spatially concentrated, as is shown in Table 10.2. Restaurants, tour operators and vehicle hire companies are highly concentrated in Nairobi, followed by coastal areas. The Kenyatta International Conference

Table 10.1 The supply of hotels, lodges and tented camps by area, 1989

Area	5 Star No. of estab.	Beds	4 Star No. of estab.	Beds	3 Star No. of estab.	Beds	2 Star No. of estab.	Beds	1 Star No. of estab.	Beds	Total No. of estab.	Beds
Nairobi	6	2751	2	310	7	1814	10	814	17	899	42	6588
Mombasa Island	0	0	0	0	4	510	1	38	1	50	6	598
Mombasa North Coast	4	1361	3	950	9	2254	2	394	1	130	19	5089
Mombasa South Coast	4	1119	5	1576	4	982	3	592	3	150	19	4419
Malindi, Lamu and Kilifi	0	0	2	560	12	2015	7	540	4	266	25	3381
National parks and reserves	3	466	12	1415	13	1227	8	551	5	172	41	3831
Other	0	0	0	0	5	517	12	833	15	649	32	1999
Total	17	5697	24	4811	54	9319	43	3762	46	2316	184	25905
Tented camps	0	0	0	0	0	0	6	338	3	162	9	500
Total	17	5697	24	4811	54	9319	49	4100	49	2478	193	26405

Source: The Hotels and Restaurants (Classification of Hotels and Restaurants) Regulations, 1988, *Kenya Gazette*, 1989.

Centre, a 32-storey complex which is capable of seating 25,000, is also located in the capital. The majority of curio shops are located in coastal areas, where tourists have most free time for shopping, followed by Nairobi, where most holiday tourists stay briefly, after arriving and before departing.

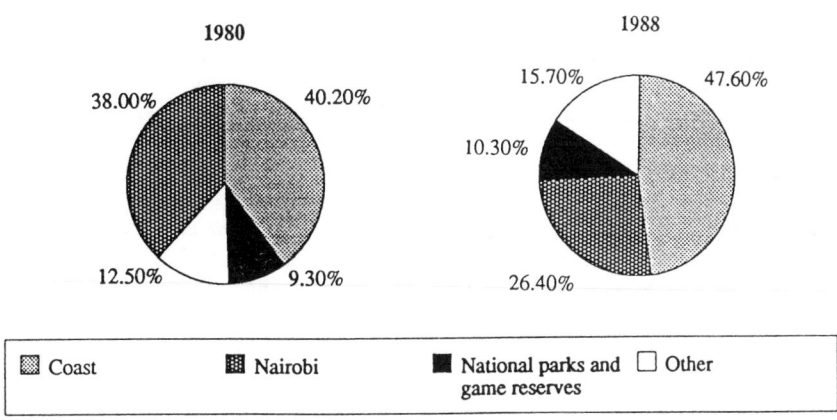

Source: *Economic Survey*, Central Bureau of Statistics, 1981 and 1989

Figure 10.1 Bed supply by area

Table 10.2 Percentage of tourism enterprises in different areas

	Nairobi	Coastal areas	Other areas	Total
Restaurants	58	26	16	100
Tour operators and vehicle hire	66	28	6	100
Curio shops	35	58	7	100

Source: Ministry of Tourism and Wildlife, Tourist Industry Licensing Office

Kenyan tour operators sell tourism services to domestic and some foreign tourists. Some tour operators, UTC (United Touring Company) being the most important example, also undertake a coordination role for foreign tour operators, providing transportation for tourists throughout their stay. A few Kenyan tour operators and hotel chains, including the tour operator Abercrombie and Kent and the state hotel chain and tour operator African Tours and Hotels, engage in marketing abroad. African Tours and Hotels has the objective of investing in and promoting relatively undeveloped rural areas, and has a policy of purchasing from local suppliers whenever possible.

The large quantity and high quality of accommodation in Kenya results, in part, from the Kenyan government's positive stance towards direct foreign investment. Inward investment has been welcomed, even in the 1980s context of official encouragement of greater local ownership ('Kenyanisation'). By 1988 there was foreign direct investment in approximately 78 per cent of major hotels in coastal areas, 67 per cent of hotels in Nairobi and 66 per cent of lodges in national parks and reserves, the percentages of coastal and city hotels and wildlife lodges which were entirely foreign-owned being 16 per cent, 17 per cent and 11 per cent respectively (Sinclair, 1990).

Some French, German, Swiss and UK tour operators have equity holdings in hotels, as do such airlines as British Airways, as was shown in Chapter 4, Table 4.1, by Bote and Sinclair. However, for the reasons given in Chapter 4, vertical integration involving ownership of Kenyan hotels by foreign tourism intermediaries has been a less prevalent method of ensuring the availability of accommodation than contractual relationships (Sinclair *et al.*, forthcoming). Some horizontal integration with multinational hotel chains, for example Inter-Continental, has occurred. There has also been considerable investment by multinational conglomerates, including Lonhro and the Aga Khan's company. Most hoteliers, tour operators and travel agents participate in their respective trade associations, the Kenya Association of Hotelkeepers and Caterers, Kenya Association of Tour Operators and Kenya Association of Travel Agents. These associations act as private sector pressure groups, engaging in such activities as lobbying the government to maintain and improve the quality of tourism infrastructure, for example roads and water availability.

The demand for tourism in Kenya

The total demand for tourism in Kenya, measured in terms of departures by residents of foreign countries (Central Bureau of Statistics, 1976–1989), was fairly stable between 1973 and 1982, ranging between a minimum of 333,300 departures in 1978 and a maximum of 424,200 in 1976. The number of departures decreased in 1983 but experienced a very high mean annual growth rate of 18 per cent over ensuing years, attaining a figure of 676,900 departures in 1988. Demand by residents of other African nations has always been important, and Sako (1990) noted the potential for further developing intra-African tourism. During the years 1973–1976, Africans, followed by Europeans and Americans, constituted the main component of demand, as is shown in Figure 10.2.

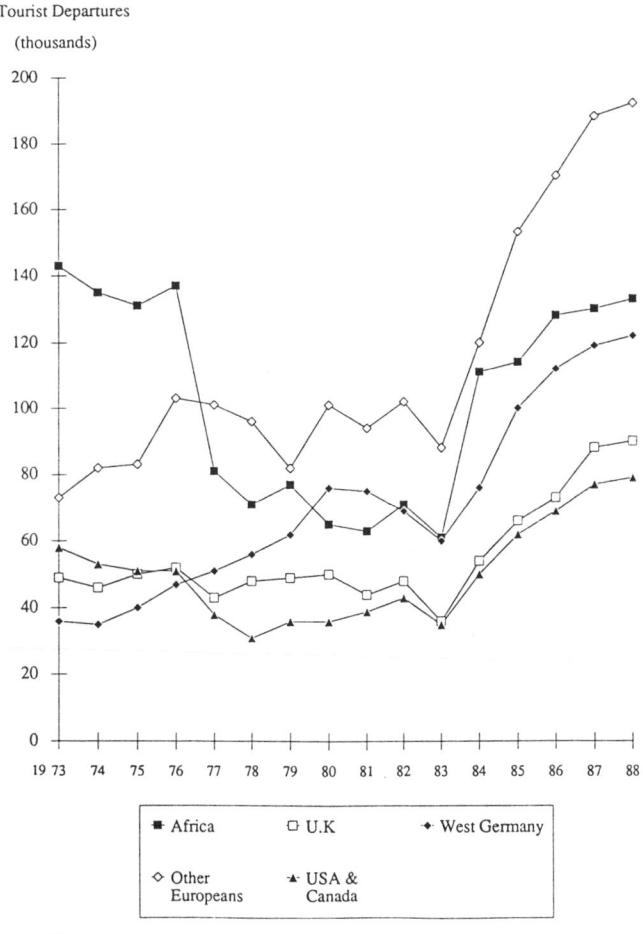

Source: *Economic Survey*, Central Bureau of Statistics, 1974–1989

Figure 10.2 The demand for tourism by origin

189

Between 1976 and 1983 there was an increase in demand by Europeans and a drop in demand by Africans, mainly owing to the closure of the Kenya–Tanzania border between 1977 and 1983. After 1983 there was a large increase in demand by all nationalities, with the Germans consolidating their place as the most important origin country. In 1988, 59 per cent of departing tourists were from West Germany, the UK, Switzerland, Italy and France, 20 per cent were Africans and 12 per cent were residents of the USA and Canada. Of all those staying in Kenya in 1988, 88 per cent were classified as on holiday and 12 per cent on business.

The demand for different tourism products has changed in line with changes in supply. The distributions of bed-nights by area in 1973 and 1988, shown in Figure 10.3, demonstrate a considerable increase in the relative importance of the demand for tourism in coastal areas and a relative decline in city tourism in Nairobi, the main change having occurred by 1980 (Sinclair, 1990). African, American and UK demand, measured by the numbers of bed-nights, was of most importance in Nairobi in 1988. In coastal areas the largest source of demand was West Germany, the share of demand by tourists from other European countries being greater than in Nairobi, and tourism from Africa and the UK being of lower relative importance. American, German and UK tourists constituted the largest sources of demand in lodges in national parks and game reserves. The level of demand in the remaining areas of the country was low, and mainly of African origin.

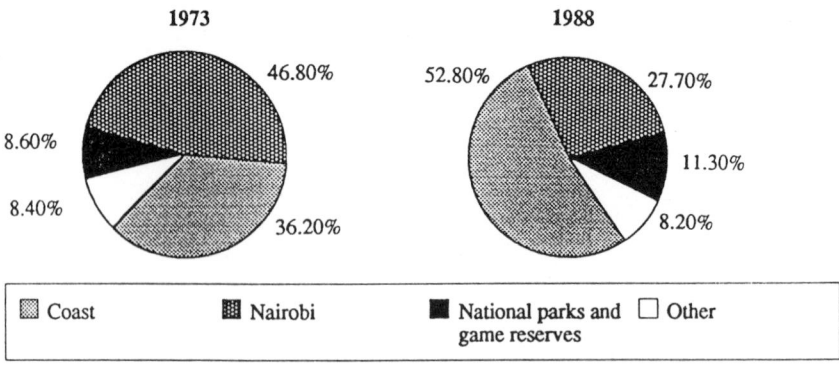

Source: *Economic Survey,* Central Bureau of Statistics, 1974 and 1989

Figure 10.3 Bed-nights by area

Although holiday tourism exceeds business tourism in terms of the numbers of tourists involved, business tourism generally has the advantages of a higher level of expenditure per tourist and a lower level of seasonality than holiday tourism. The comparative seasonality of holiday and business tourism is shown in Figures 10.4 and 10.5, though having different scales owing to the smaller numbers of business tourists, demonstrate the smaller quarterly variations in demand for business tourism (measured by tourist departures) in the years 1973, 1980 and 1988.

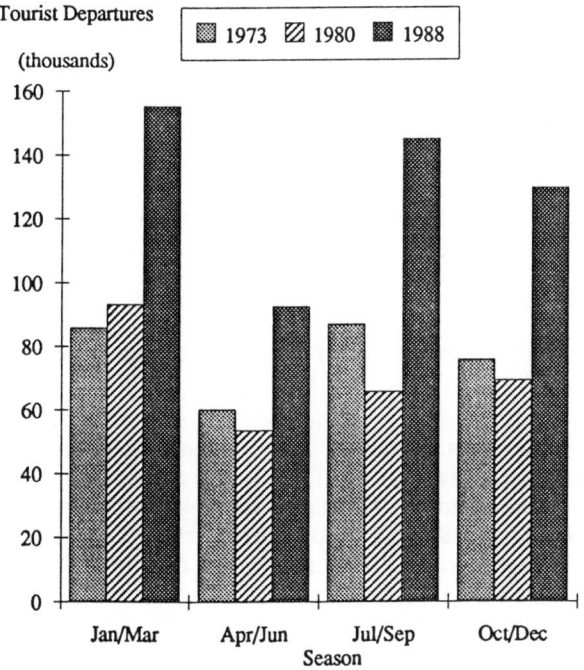

Source: *Economic Survey,* Central Bureau of Statistics, 1976, 1982, 1989

Figure 10.4 The seasonality of holiday tourism

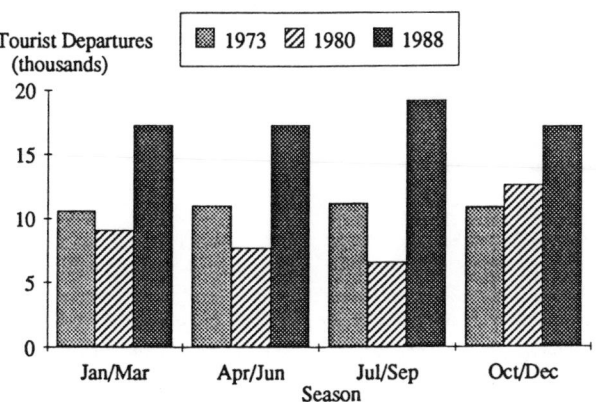

Source: *Economic Survey,* Central Bureau of Statistics, 1976, 1982, 1989

Figure 10.5 The seasonality of business tourism

191

In the case of holiday tourism, demand is considerably lower in the second quarter owing to the heavy rains which occur in April and May. On an international scale, the degree of seasonality of Kenyan tourism demand is lower than that of Mediterranean countries with established tourism industries, for example Spain (Clewer *et al.*, 1990). Kenya's policy of promoting domestic tourism could decrease seasonality, as could increased conference tourism in the Kenyatta International Conference Centre, which has been very under-utilised in past years (Sinclair, 1990). The promotion of complementary business and holiday tourism would have the advantage of increasing the level of earnings per tourist.

Total and per capita foreign currency earnings from tourism

Many developing countries wish to increase their foreign currency earnings in order to pay for expenditure on imports and finance debt repayments. Tourism can make a large contribution to the balance of payments. In 1988 Kenya's travel receipts, (commonly used as a proxy for tourism earnings) constituted 20 per cent of total export earnings and 14 per cent of the total import bill, as is shown in Table 10.3. Comparable figures for other developing and intermediate income countries with established tourism sectors are given in Table 10.3. On a worldwide basis, tourism receipts were 9.6 per cent of the value of export earnings for all developing countries in 1988, compared with a figure of 7 per cent for industrialised market economies (World Tourism Organization, 1990).

Table 10.3 Travel receipts and merchandise exports as percentages of total exports and total imports, 1988

Developing and intermediate income countries	Travel receipts as a percentage of total exports	Merchandise exports as a percentage of total exports	Travel receipts as a percentage of total imports	Merchandise exports as a percentage of total imports
Cyprus	36	28	35	27
Fiji	21	56	20	56
Greece	21	52	15	37
India	9	75	5	49
Jamaica	30	48	24	38
Kenya	20	52	14	37
Malta	25	49	23	45
Mauritius	11	73	11	73
Mexico	12	64	11	58
Morocco	20	67	13	45
Singapore	6	73	6	74
Thailand	12	74	11	70
Tunisia	22	62	19	53
Turkey	13	66	12	64

Source: Author's own calculations, based on International Monetary Fund *Balance of Payments Statistics Yearbook*, 1988, 1989.

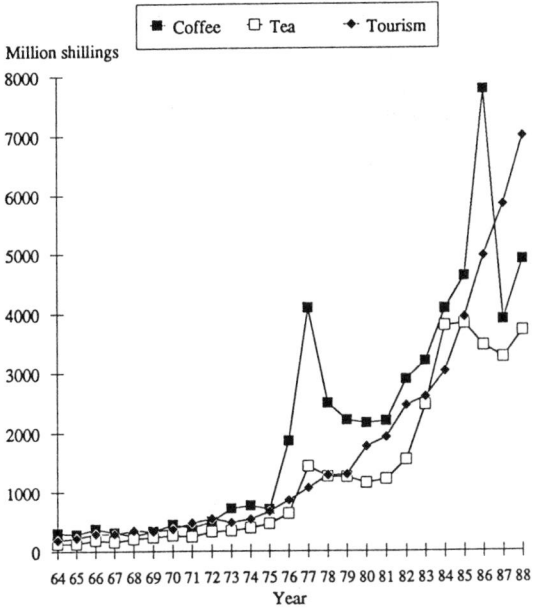

Source: *Economic Report*, Central Bank of Kenya, 1974–1989

Figure 10.6 Export earnings from tourism, coffee and tea (millions of Kenyan shillings, current prices)

Receipts from tourism have become the largest source of earnings in Kenya, exceeding receipts from coffee and tea, traditionally the country's main sources of export earnings. The growth over time in earnings from tourism, coffee and tea, based on current prices and denominated in Kenyan shillings, is shown in Figure 10.6, which appears to indicate high growth in tourism earnings during the 1980s. However, the choice of units with which tourism's contribution to the economy is measured is important, as alternative units, for example the unit of currency, the use of real or current prices or of total or per capita earnings, can provide very different views of its contribution. The relevance of this point can be shown by converting the current shilling values of tourism earnings over time into pounds sterling, and deflating the hard currency values by Kenya's upper income price index in order to obtain the real sterling values of tourism earnings over time (1985 prices). The resulting values are depicted in Figure 10.7.

Figure 10.7 clearly demonstrates the tendency for real sterling tourism earnings during the 1980s to be equal to or lower than their 1970s levels. This is mainly due to the depreciation of the Kenyan shilling which occurred over the period. The calculation of the real dollar value of tourism earnings shows a similar trend (Sinclair, 1990). Foreign tour operators, in particular, have benefited from the depreciation of the shilling since, until 1990, it was common practice to negotiate accommodation prices in terms of shillings.

193

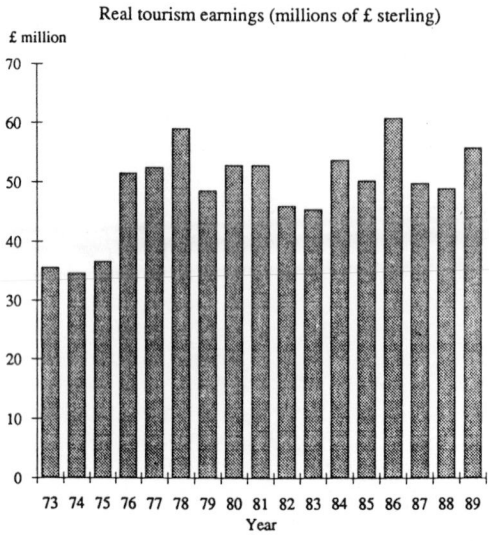

Source: *Economic Report*, Central Bank of Kenya, 1974–1989

Figure 10.7 Real tourism earnings (millions of £ sterling)

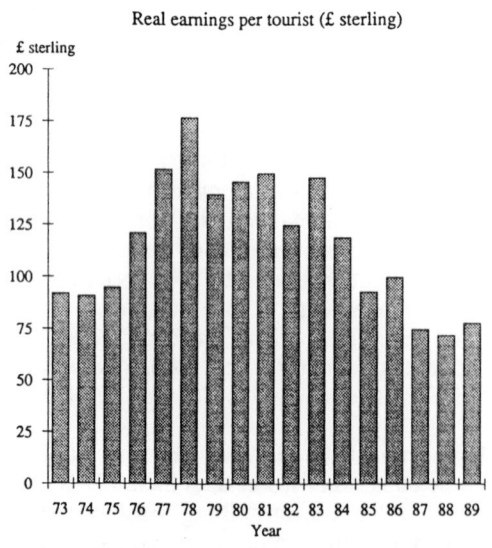

Source: *Economic Report*, Central Bank of Kenya, 1974–1989
Economic Survey, Central Bureau of Statistics, 1976–1989

Figure 10.8 Real earnings per tourist (£ sterling)

A further disturbing trend in Kenyan tourism receipts is shown in Figure 10.8, which demonstrates a considerable fall in the level of foreign currency receipts per tourist. The downward trend in per capita receipts coincides with the high growth of package holidays in Kenya, which increased as foreign tour operators evaded Kenyan restrictions on charter flights to the country and the Civil Aviation Board of Kenya subsequently increased its licence concessions for charter flights (Sinclair *et al.*, forthcoming). The decrease in per capita receipts is a generally unrecognised consequence of the increase in numbers of package holiday tourists; no policy objectives concerning the value of earnings per tourist staying in the country have accompanied Kenya's stated aim of receiving one million tourists per annum.

Foreign exchange earnings and leakages from safari and beach tourism

It is probable that the growth of tourism in Kenya and many other developing countries will continue to result, in large part, from the increasing demand for package holidays which are organised by foreign tour operators and pre-paid in the tourists' countries of origin. It is therefore important to examine the percentage of the tourists' expenditure on package holidays which is received by the destination developing country, and the percentage which remains overseas as tour operators', travel agents' and foreign airlines' costs and profits. The percentage remaining abroad has sometimes been termed the foreign exchange 'leakage' from tourist expenditure, although the term is also used to define the percentage of tourists' expenditure within the destination country which is lost in the form of payments for imported inputs, or to refer to the evasion of foreign currency controls.

In order to estimate the percentage of tourists' spending which is received by Kenya and the 'leakage' percentage which goes to foreign tour operators, travel agents and airlines, data for 235 package holidays in Kenya, obtained from brochures supplied by major tour operators, available in travel agencies in the UK, were analysed. The tour operators' holidays considered were Airtours, British Airways' Sovereign, British Airways' Speedbird, Hayes and Jarvis, the (now defunct) International Leisure Group's Select holidays, Jetset, Kuoni Worldwide, Thomas Cook and Thomson Holidays Worldwide. The types of holiday products marketed by these tour operators are beach, safari, city, city and beach, and safari and beach. Safari and beach holidays are the usual 14-day holiday combination; city holidays and safari-only holidays are, as yet, unusual.

The brochure prices of seven- and 14-night holidays were examined for the months of April, July and December 1990. The mean prices of different types of package holidays are given in Table 10.4. The prices should be interpreted with care because of variations in the numbers of holidays supplied by the different tour operators and variations in the characteristics of the holidays, including differing categories of hotel or lodge accommodation and different destinations (Clewer *et al.*, forthcoming; Sinclair *et al.*, 1990). Nevertheless, Table 10.4 provides a broad indication of the variations in holiday prices between tour operators, and shows considerable differences between the prices of the same types of holiday.

Table 10.4 Mean prices for different types of package holidays, 1990 (£ sterling)

Tour operators	7 nights			14 nights		
	April	July	Dec	April	July	Dec
Beach						
Kuoni	559	610	581	650	744	705
Thomson	508	571	571	659	738	738
BA Speedbird	527	634	629	-	-	-
BA Sovereign	621	664	607	812	899	869
ILG Select	746	778	763	859	1046	1010
Jetset	618	847	815	-	-	-
Thomas Cook	659	831	1002	791	1053	1359
Air Tours	-	-	-	-	614	-
Hayes & Jarvis	446	546	551	-	-	-
Safari						
Kuoni	852	1006	1006	-	-	-
BA Speedbird	-	-	-	-	-	-
Jetset	1355	1541	1350	-	-	-
Hayes & Jarvis	530	630	640	-	-	-
Safari & Beach						
Kuoni	.	.	.	966	1071	1057
Thomson	612	674	674	806	912	912
BA Speedbird	-	-	-	928	1191	1222
Jetset	-	-	-	1648	1901	1663
Thomas Cook	-	-	-	1478	1288	1576
Air Tours	-	-	-	-	798	-
Hayes & Jarvis	532	632	636	703	885	934
Town & Beach						
Kuoni	-	-	-	897	972	933
ILG Select	-	-	-	819	1033	1177

Source: Author's own calculations based on tour operators' brochures

Table 10.5 gives the mean prices of different holiday products, 'weighted' by the number of different types of holiday offered in each tour operator's brochure, which acts as a proxy for the operator's share of the Kenyan holiday market. The percentage differences in the mean 'weighted' prices for different holiday products are included in Table 10.6, which shows the higher prices charged for safari or safari and beach holidays relative to beach, or city and beach holidays. (Such price differences clearly exceed the amounts required to compensate for the provision of full board in the lodge accommodation used for safaris, in comparison with the half board provided in beach hotels). The only exception is the comparison for seven-night safari and beach holidays relative to beach holidays, for which the numbers of holidays supplied are low and the price differences negligible. Safari or safari and beach holidays are between 28 per cent and 44 per cent more expensive than beach-only holidays, and between

Table 10.5 Mean holiday prices, 1990 (£ sterling)

| Holiday type | Mean holiday prices | | | | | |
| | 7 nights | | | 14 nights | | |
	April	July	Dec	April	July	Dec
Beach	562	654	640	755	791	886
Safari	733	917	891	-	-	-
Safari & beach	540	636	640	970	1137	1180
Town & beach	-	-	-	834	960	975

Source: Author's own calculations

Table 10.6 Percentage differences in mean holiday prices, 1990

| | 7 nights | | | 14 nights | | |
	April	July	Dec	April	July	Dec
Safari/beach	30	40	39	-	-	-
Safari/safari & beach*	36	44	39	-	-	-
Safari & beach/beach	-4	-3	0	28	44	33
Safari & beach/ Town & beach	-	-	-	16	18	21
Town & beach/beach	-	-	-	10	21	10

*   7-night safari and beach holidays are unusual and are only offered by Hayes and Jarvis and Thomson
Source: Author's own calculations

16 and 21 per cent more expensive than city and beach holidays. Fourteen-night city and beach holidays are also more expensive than beach-only holidays, in spite of the fact that package holiday accommodation in cities is supplied on a bed and breakfast basis.

The 'weighted' holiday prices were then disaggregated into the amounts received by hoteliers in Kenya, by suppliers of local ground transportation, national parks and game reserves, airlines and foreign tour operators. The amounts pertaining to foreign tour operators include commission paid to foreign travel agents who sell the holidays. Estimates were made of all of the preceding amounts except foreign tour operators' receipts, which were treated as the residual. In order to estimate the amount relating to the provision of accommodation and food (initially including tour operators' profits), it was first necessary to subtract the mean price of a seven-night holiday from the price of a 14-night holiday of the same type (beach or safari), the data being obtained from tour operators' brochures. This procedure permitted the deduction of the airline's receipts, as well as of seven nights' accommodation, food, ground transportation and fees. The amount charged by local suppliers for the provision of seven days' ground transport, (and national park and reserve entrance fees in the case of safari holidays), was then subtracted from the previously calculated values, to provide the mean price of seven nights' accommodation and food.

The price of accommodation and food for a 14-night safari and beach holiday was calculated by summing the seven-night prices for beach and safari accommodation and food, while the 14-night beach holiday accommodation and food price was simply obtained by doubling the seven-night price. The amounts of the total prices charged by tour operators for accommodation and food, which are received by Kenyan hoteliers were then estimated. The estimates were made by calculating the differences between a sample of the prices which tour operators charge for an additional night's accommodation and food, obtained from tour operators' brochures, with the revenue received by hoteliers, provided by interviews with hoteliers in Kenya. It was found that considerable percentages (often between 30 and 50 per cent) of the total prices charged for accommodation and food were retained by tour operators to cover their overseas costs and profits. Estimates for city, city and beach and seven-night beach and safari holidays were not made, owing to the small numbers of these types of holiday product supplied. The cost of air transport was estimated using data provided by national airlines.

The estimated percentages of the total prices paid by tourists for different types of package holiday which are received by Kenyan and overseas enterprises are included in Table 10.7. Table 10.7 includes estimates for both the case when the tourist travels with a foreign airline and the case when the tourist travels with Kenya Airways. Recalculation of the percentages using 'unweighted' data, which did not take account of the differing numbers of holiday types supplied by the different tour operators, provided figures of similar orders of magnitude. The percentages relate only to the initial expenditure on the package holiday purchased in the tourist's country of origin; additional expenditure on food, drinks, souvenirs and entertainments which the tourist incurs while in Kenya is almost entirely a net gain to the country. Although, as in any empirical study, the calculated results are subject to a margin of error, a variety of implications and conclusions can, nevertheless, be drawn from them.

Tourism earnings distribution: the role of air transport

The outstanding feature of Table 10.7 is the high percentage of the total expenditure on a package holiday which is retained overseas if the tourist travels to and from Kenya with a foreign airline, as is the case for most tourists. With respect to beach-only holidays, the total foreign exchange 'leakage' attributed to the overseas tour operator and airline ranges between 62 per cent and 78 per cent for the 14-night holidays which are most common. The leakage from Kenya is significantly lower in the case of safari or safari and beach holidays, since the Civil Aviation Board of Kenya requires the tourist who wishes to travel by air between Nairobi (the usual point of departure for and arrival from safaris) and Mombasa or Malindi (the arrival and departure airports for beach holidays) to use the state airline. However, the leakage still ranges between 34 and 45 per

Table 10.7 Estimates of Kenyan and foreign percentage shares of tourists' expenditure on package holidays

Tour operators	7 nights			14 nights		
	April	July	Dec	April	July	Dec
Beach						
Accommodation and food	24	13	26	36	21	37
Park & reserve fees & ground transport	1	1	1	1	1	1
Kenya share excluding air transport	25	14	27	37	22	38
Overseas tour operator & airline share	75	86	73	63	78	62
Kenya share including air transport	78	82	74	77	78	88
Overseas tour operator	22	18	26	23	22	12
Safari						
Accommodation and food	17	16	23	-	-	-
Park and reserve fees, & ground transport	32	26	26	-	-	-
Kenya share excluding air transport	49	42	49	-	-	-
Overseas tour operator & airline share	51	58	51	-	-	-
Kenya share including air transport	90	87	96	-	-	-
Overseas tour operator	10	13	4	-	-	-
Safari and Beach						
Accommodation and food	-	..	-	27	20	31
Park and reserve fees, & ground transport	-	-	-	24	21	20
Domestic air transport	-	-	-	15	14	14
Kenya share excluding international air transport	-	-	-	66	55	65
Overseas tour operator & airline share	-	-	-	34	45	35
Kenya share including all air transport	-	-	-	82	80	88
Overseas tour operator	-	-	-	18	20	12

Source: Author's own calculations

cent, so that for every £1,000 spent on a 14-night safari and beach holiday, Kenya receives between £550 and £660 if the tourist travels to and from Kenya with an overseas carrier. The greater expenditure on ground transport and national park and reserve entry fees are an important cause of the higher Kenya share for holidays including a safari component, and the mean expenditure on such holidays is considerably higher than that on beach holidays.

The leakage estimates provided by this study can be contrasted with Green's (1979) assumption that the total leakage from tourists' expenditure on holidays in Kenya was of the order of 30 to 40 per cent. This study has shown that the leakage varies considerably between different types of holidays and, even without taking account of the first round import content of expenditure, is far greater than Green's estimates when the tourist travels with a foreign airline. Only holidays incorporating a safari component have a leakage approximating to or lower than Green's estimate. The considerably higher leakage figures for beach holidays are similar to those provided by the ESCAP study (1978), cited by Britton (1982), which estimated a leakage from developing countries of between 75 and 78 per cent for the case in which both the airline and hotel were owned by non-nationals, and between 55 and 60 per cent for the case of a foreign airline but locally owned hotel. Farver's (1984) estimate for the Gambia of a 77 per cent leakage from 'charter operations' is in line with the higher estimates provided in this chapter. Even in the case of an intermediate income country such as Spain, the leakage percentage is as high as 58 per cent when tourists travel in a foreign airline (Instituto de Estudios Turísticos/Consultores Turísticos, 1987).

The leakage percentages for Kenya are considerably lower if Kenya Airways provides the international air transport, decreasing to between 12 and 33 per cent for a 14-night beach holiday, and between 12 and 20 per cent for a 14-night beach and safari holiday sold to a UK resident. The percentages of holiday expenditure which Kenya receives are highly sensitive to the prices of aircraft seats which Kenya Airways negotiates with foreign tour operators. The considerable increases in the percentages of the total holiday prices which Kenya receives if its national carrier provides the international air transport for UK residents may, in part, reflect good negotiating skills and past excess demand for air transportation between the UK and Kenya.

If Kenya Airways could increase its share of the traffic between Kenya and the tourist origin countries, the percentage of tourist expenditure received by Kenya would rise considerably, although the net gain would be lower than the gross increase in receipts because of the high import content of airline expenditure, not taken into account in the preceding calculations. The first round import content of the airline's foreign exchange revenue was estimated to be of the order of 40 per cent in 1979 (Economist Intelligence Unit, 1979), although the percentage, excluding loan repayments, is likely to be lower in 1990, as more of the previously imported inputs are now produced locally. A reasonable estimate of the past and 1990 first round import content of Kenyan tour operators' revenue is 17 per cent (EIU, 1979), and the first round import content of ground transport (including park and reserve entry fees) was approximately 10 per cent in 1990, since some vehicles are now assembled within Kenya.

Interviews with hoteliers in Kenya showed that the first round leakages from expenditure on food are minimal, and that the import content of expenditure on drinks was of the order of 35 per cent in 1990. Although many of the items used in hotels were previously imported, all the equipment and furniture in hotels in 1990 was produced locally, with the exception of such specialist items as air-conditioning units, bakery equipment, telephone wiring and computers. Thus by 1990 the import content of the tourism industry in Kenya was even lower than the overall estimate of 18 per cent provided by Mitchell (1968), the Economist Intelligence Unit's (1979) estimates of 16 per cent for hotels, lodges and camps, 7 per cent for restaurants and 17 per cent for local tour operators, and Bachmann's (1988) estimates of 10 per cent for food and 50 per cent for beverages consumed by tourists in Malindi. The import content estimates for Kenya are favourable in comparison with those for various other developing country tourist destinations, for example the 62 per cent import content for food and 69 per cent import content for beverage and cigarette consumption by tourists in Jamaica (Cazes, 1972), the 56 per cent and 45 per cent import content for food and beverage consumption in Fiji (Varley, 1978) and the overall import content for tourism in the Gambia of 55 per cent (Farver, 1984). Kenya benefits from the fact that the agricultural and manufacturing sectors of the economy can provide many of the inputs required by its tourism industry.

Conclusions and implications

Package holidays in developing countries are supplied and marketed mainly by firms from industrialised countries. Marketing by travel agents and tour operators can bring about considerable and rapid changes in the demand for and supply of different types of holidays. Foreign intermediaries can benefit developing countries by increasing the demand for tourism and the total foreign currency receipts of the destination. However, a decrease in earnings per tourist can accompany the increase in demand, as occurred in the case of Kenya. Tourist destinations may be able to offset a fall in per capita earnings and increase their total revenue from tourism by developing and promoting under-utilised wildlife areas, in the context of an appropriate pricing policy for wildlife and other natural resources (Pearce *et al.*, 1989). Developing countries can thus take advantage of the growth in demand for tourism in natural areas, as noted by Redmond in Chapter 6.

The key role which the use by tourists of the national airline and local ground transport plays in increasing the developing country's share of tourism receipts raises issues of transport policy and the quality of service. Tour operators use ground transport provided by locally based firms of which they may have total or partial ownership, depending upon the destination country's policy towards foreign investment. Even in the absence of ownership, control may be exercised by tour operators by means of integration in the form of the contractual arrangements which they negotiate with local firms, as was shown by Bote and Sinclair in Chapter 4. Although it is difficult to monitor contractual arrangements, knowledge of the prevailing terms of contracts is a necessary basis for policy making to increase the destination country's returns from tourist expenditure.

Tour operators tend to use airlines from industrialised countries for a variety of reasons, including the greater availability of seats, routes and flights, some tourists' preference for a well known airline name and the superior quality of service provided by some large airlines. Developing countries are faced with the problem of whether to build up an airline fleet, in the context of protection from increased competition, on the part of industrialised countries, in such forms as preferential allocation of landing and take-off slots to their own national carriers. Inefficiency and corruption occur in some state-owned airlines so that public resources are used sub-optimally. Most developing countries do not possess the latest computer hardware or have access to innovations in information technology of the type discussed by Bennett and Radburn in Chapter 3. Kenya Airways, for example, had not completed the computerisation of its passenger numbers, revenue and expenditure data in 1990. Airlines from developing countries have, however, co-operated to establish their own computerised reservation systems, with the objective of competing more strongly with airlines from industrialised countries.

Developing countries often aim to increase the revenue of their national carrier via a policy of protection. In Kenya, for example, foreign charter airlines are not permitted to provide internal flights for tourists. However, attempts to increase Kenya Airways' revenue by limiting charter airlines' flights to and from the country resulted in the evasion of restrictions. A high degree of protection can also lead to retaliation by overseas countries. Many developing countries are therefore faced with the problem of whether to continue to use their scarce national resources to subsidise a loss-making national carrier.

Two proposals which have been put forward as possible solutions are those of privatisation and an increase in foreign participation in the public sector. Participants in international lending institutions, including the International Monetary Fund and World Bank, have argued that these measures would have the advantage of increasing developing countries' earnings from key sectors and eliminating the need for costly subsidies. Developing countries are understandably reluctant to see majority ownership of their 'flagship' airline pass into foreign hands; however some increase in private, possibly foreign participation, for example in the form of a joint venture, might be advantageous. The net social benefit of such measures will, of course, depend in part upon the distribution and use of the revenue earned. The appropriate balance between public and private provision, local and foreign ownership, protection and competition varies between different regions (for example, Africa and South-East Asia) and countries within regions, according to the specific circumstances of the country and region in question. The issue of the appropriate balance between state intervention and the market, and local and foreign participation in the tourism industry, is an important and relatively unexplored aspect of tourism, requiring further research.

A further issue of fundamental importance is that of the long term sustainability of tourism development. The range of package holidays which are supplied in developing countries is, as yet, fairly limited and is often accompanied by geographic concentration. There may also be concentration of demand by product and by tourist origin. Problems of sustainability of development can occur because of excess demand and supply in particular areas, bringing about deterioration of environmental resources. Problems can also result from an unequal distribution of the returns from tourism which, as shown by Veronica Long in Chapter 11, can result in alienation and hostility on the part of the host population. Investigation of pricing, taxation and expenditure policies which are appropriate for sustaining natural environments and for switching more of the benefits from tourism development towards the local population, is necessary if tourism development is to be viable over the long term.

In attempting to establish a tourism industry, developing countries are faced with a variety of difficulties and dilemmas. Moreover, some of the problems which are commonly viewed as specific to developing countries derive from the actions of individuals, firms and governments in industrialised countries. Such problems are not amenable to easy or quick resolution. Developing countries are subject to widely differing economic, social and political circumstances and have different goals and priorities. The policies which are both feasible and acceptable as possible means of increasing developing countries' returns from tourism development are therefore likely to vary considerably detween different countries and groups of countries. Although no universal set of policy prescriptions is appropriate for all countries, the need to take account of different forms of intervention by foreign participants, during the process of policy formation, is common to all tourist destinations.

Acknowledgements

This chapter draws on research which was supported by the World Bank. I would like to thank the many Kenyan people whose insights and help were so important. Particular thanks are also due to Ann Clewer, David Clewer and Betty Sinclair for all the assistance they provided. The views expressed are the sole responsibility of the author.

References

Bachmann, P. (1988) *Tourism in Kenya: Basic Need for Whom?* Peter Lang, Berne.
Britton, S.G. (1982) The political economy of tourism in the third world. *Annals of Tourism Research*, 9, 331–358.
Cazes, G. (1972) Le rôle du tourisme dans la croissance économique: réflexions à partir de trois examples antillais. *The Tourist Review*, 27, 93–99 and 144–148.
Central Bank of Kenya (1974–1990) *Economic Report*. Central Bank of Kenya, Nairobi.
Central Bureau of Statistics (1976–1989) *Economic Survey*. Ministry of Planning and National Development, Nairobi.
Clewer, A., Pack, A. and Sinclair, M.T. (1990) Forecasting models for tourism demand in city dominated and coastal areas. *Papers of the Regional Science Association*, 6, 31–42.

Clewer, A., Pack, A. and Sinclair, M.T. (forthcoming) Price competitiveness and inclusive tour holidays in European cities. In: Johnson, P. and Thomas, B. (eds), *Choice and Demand in Tourism*. Mansell, London.

Economist Intelligence Unit (1979) *Study of Pricing Policy for Tourism*. Economist Intelligence Unit/Ministry of Tourism and Wildlife Kenya, London.

Economic and Social Commission for Asia and the Pacific (ESCAP) (1978) The formulation of basic concepts and guidelines for preparation of tourism sub-regional master plans in the ESCAP region. *Transport and Communications Bulletin*, 52, 33–40.

Farver, J.A.M. (1984) Tourism and employment in The Gambia. *Annals of Tourism Research*, 11, 249–265.

Green, R.H. (1979) Towards planning tourism in African countries. In: de Kadt, E. (ed.), *Tourism — Passport to Development?* Oxford University Press, Oxford, pp. 79–100.

Instituto de Estudios Turísticos/Consultores Turísticos, S.A. (1987) El gasto turístico. Análisis del escandallo de los Paquetes Turísticos. Distribución por tipologías y nacionalidades. *Estudios Turísticos*, No. 93, 3–26.

Mitchell, F. (1968) *The Costs and Benefits of Tourism in Kenya*. Institute for Development Studies, University College, Nairobi.

Pearce, D., Markandya, A. and Barbier, E.B. (1989) *Blueprint for a Green Economy*. Earthscan Publications, London.

Sako, F. (1990) Tourism in Africa: an expanding industry. *The Courier*, No.122, 69–72.

Sinclair, M.T. (1990) *Tourism Development in Kenya*. World Bank, Washington DC.

Sinclair, M.T., Alizadeh, P. and Atieno Adero Onunga, E. (forthcoming) The structure of international tourism and tourism development in Kenya. In: Harrison, D. (ed.), *International Tourism and the Less Developed Countries*. Belhaven, London.

Sinclair, M.T., Clewer, A. and Pack, A. (1990) Hedonic prices and the marketing of package holidays: the case of tourism resorts in Malaga. In: Ashworth, G. and Goodall, B. (eds), *Marketing Tourism Places*. Routledge, London, pp. 85–103.

Varley, R.C.G. (1978) *Tourism in Fiji: Some Economic and Social Problems*. Occasional Papers in Economics, No. 12, University of Wales Press, Bangor.

World Tourism Organization (1990) Tourism activity in the 1980s and 1990s. Facts and figures. *The Courier*, No. 122, 52–55.

Chapter 11

Government – Industry – Community Interaction in Tourism Development in Mexico

Veronica H. Long

Introduction

Tourism development is often seen as a relatively quick and simple solution to the problems of economically underdeveloped regions, as the use of the natural attributes of an area for tourism can provide a quick economic return. The reasons for developing tourism are many but the impacts that accompany such development need examination. This chapter begins with a general review of social impacts discussed in tourism literature, followed by an introduction to tourism development in Mexico. The body of the chapter concentrates on a government-stimulated resort development called 'Las Bahias de Huatulco', involving the creation of a multinational tourism complex along 22 miles of the Pacific coastline. The main concern of the chapter is to examine the interaction of the developers and the local community upon whom the resort development was imposed.

The effects of tourism on local communities

Positive impacts

The positive impacts of tourism development include an increase in economic opportunities and an increase in the standard of living for the local community (Hudman, 1978; Leathers and Misiolek, 1986; Crandall, 1987). Increased employment opportunities enable young people to remain in the community instead of leaving to look for work (Pizam and Milman, 1986; Smith 1988). Women obtain an independent source of income as they find work outside the home in resort employment (de Kadt, 1979; Samy, 1980; Dogan, 1989). The economy becomes more diversified, thus being less susceptible to possible downturns of a single industry (Runyan and Wu, 1979). In addition to economic benefits, there are several positive social impacts that accompany tourism development. The attention to local culture can stimulate ethnic pride and preserve cultural heritage (MacCannell, 1984; Deitch, 1989; Dogan, 1989). Local arts and crafts may also be preserved as a result of tourist interest (Crandall, 1987; Greenwood, 1989; Swain, 1989). The social interaction between tourists and local community members can serve to increase cross-cultural understanding and promote world peace (Perez, 1973; D'Amore, 1988).

Negative impacts

Often, traditional occupations are replaced by jobs in the resort (Crandall, 1987; Smith, 1988). The transformation of a society based on traditional forms of employment to one with employment based on a resort can place the local culture in a volatile position as the local economy often becomes dependent on tourism (Mathieson and Wall, 1982; Crandall, 1987; Wilkinson, 1989). This makes economic survival very sensitive to the tourism industry. Socio-cultural impacts can be devastating to a local community. With the influx of tourists, young people are exposed to the often uninhibited leisure behaviour of outsiders (Smith, 1988). Repeated performance of ceremonial rituals for tourists, or the mass production of icons and crafts, may cause the loss of their traditional significance (Graburn, 1977; de Kadt, 1979). Preister (1989) suggests that a community may lose its original identity due to a large and rapid increase in outsiders.

Disadvantaged areas, more dependent on the benefits of tourism, are relatively vulnerable to tourism development impacts. Development of structures without proper infrastructure may result in pollution, which can drive tourists away and ruin the local economy (Mathieson and Wall, 1982; Murphy, 1985). Originally friendly locals may reach their thresholds of tolerance and become rude and threatening to tourists (Knox, 1982; Getz, 1983; Preister, 1989). While the benefit of increased employment opportunities may be substantial, the loss of community lifestyle and traditional culture may be overwhelming. Unchecked negative impacts can result in intense social problems and in the subsequent loss of tourism resources (Turner and Ash, 1975; Preister, 1989).

Modern tourism development planning stresses the need to mitigate the negative impacts on the community (Hudman, 1978; Murphy, 1985). Various techniques are suggested to ensure that the community benefits as much as possible without suffering from overwhelming negative impacts. Developers are paying increasing attention to the needs of the local community in the hope of creating tourism that benefits the community as well as bringing in profits for themselves (Mathieson and Wall, 1982; Preister, 1989).

Tourism in Mexico

Mexico, a developing country, aims to glean the benefits of tourism development, particularly from North American tourist inflows. Tourists come seeking warm beaches and low-priced recreation. Tourism development provides Mexico with an industry that takes advantage of its natural attributes, the beaches along the Pacific and Caribbean Coasts, bringing in foreign investment and foreign consumption of goods and services.

Mexico received tourist inflows for many decades but until the early 1970s it was predominantly the 'explorer' type of tourist, who ventured out to remote beaches and historical sites. In the 1970s, the government realised the potential benefits for development and foreign trade and began actively investing in and promoting tourism development (Truett and Truett, 1982). The Mexican government decided to use its tourism industry as a development tool for economically disadvantaged areas. It therefore brought modernization to some of its remote underdeveloped regions and increased its range of destination areas (Evans, 1976). The number of visitors to Mexico doubled in the period 1970–1980 (Gibbons and Fish, 1984). By 1988, the tourism industry was Mexico's second highest source of external revenue next to oil, and Mexico ranked tenth in the world in tourist revenues (Shacochis, 1989). Tourism helps Mexico address its balance of payments deficits. The demand for tourism in Mexico is relatively stable (Gibbons and Fish, 1984) and 600,000 jobs were created in the tourism sector in the 1980s (Shacochis, 1989). Apart from small family farming operations, tourism is Mexico's main source of employment. However problems occurred in the form of illegal foreign investment in resort land, unrestricted business operations, and underdeveloped infrastructure (Evans, 1976).

Government participation in tourism development

In 1970, the Mexican government formalised its commitment to tourism development with the formation of the National Trust for Development of Tourism (Fondo Nacional de Fomento al Turismo or FONATUR). FONATUR is responsible for all developmental aspects of the national tourism development projects, handling land acquisition and expropriation. It also handles marketing and courts foreign investors, as well as coordinating infrastructure and community relations. FONATUR is thus the catalyst and coordinator of new development by the tourism industry.

The Mexican government acknowledges the importance of planning. Acapulco is a Pacific Coast resort area that typifies the results of a lack of planning. There, unplanned tourism development has resulted in a polluted bay and a large squatters' settlement (Bosselman, 1978; Shacochis, 1989). The pitfalls of poor planning were recognized by FONATUR and it has implemented developmental projects which include strategies for social impact mitigation (Reynoso y Valle and de Regt, 1976).

The involvement of FONATUR in mitigating the negative social impacts of the tourism projects is fairly substantial in the beginning phases of the project (Reynoso y Valle and de Regt, 1976). It has a team that works directly with the community during the development. When the development site has sufficient infrastructure, FONATUR coordinates established state and federal agencies for the delivery of social services. The presence of the Community Development Team is dictated by the philosophy of the federal government in office. At the Ixtapa-Zihuatanejo site, a change in political leaders resulted in the removal of the Community Development Team. In time, problems arose between developers and community members and a community development team had to be reinstated to mediate between the two groups.

To date, FONATUR has initiated five tourism development projects: Cancun, Ixtapa-Zihuatanejo, Loreto, Cabo San Lucas, and Las Bahias de Huatulco. The Huatulco project, being the most recent, benefited from the experience that FONATUR gained at the previous development sites. One such example is the Cancun development, where no provisions were made for low income housing, resulting in the growth of an unsightly shanty town (Bosselman, 1978). The need for low income housing was addressed at Huatulco by FONATUR through the coordination of credit programmes, involvement in employee housing, and housing for those whose properties were expropriated for tourism development purposes.

The success of the mitigation efforts is unclear. The literature on the social impacts of FONATUR developments in Cancun, and Ixtapa-Zihuatanejo gives conflicting reports of the success of social mitigation at those sites (Reynoso y Valle and de Regt, 1976; Lee, 1977; Bosselman, 1978; Howard, 1982). This chapter provides a detailed examination of the social impact mitigation techniques used at the Las Bahias de Huatulco development and the affected community's response to them. An analysis of the project at an early stage of the development is presented. During this stage, the impacts from tourism, *per se*, were yet to occur. Instead there were severe impacts from the industry development process and the anticipation of tourism.

Las Bahias de Huatulco

The Huatulco tourism development site is a desert beach on the Pacific coast of Oaxaca (Figure 11.1), cut off from the interior of Mexico by a mountain range. The 'Bahias de Huatulco' project is a 23,200 hectare resort development extending 35 kilometres along the coast and encompassing nine secluded bays. This research focused on the principal bay of Santa Cruz (Figure 11.2). There, FONATUR was creating an immense multinational tourism complex, superimposed on a small underdeveloped community. It projected a resident population of 300,000 by the year 2018, supporting two million tourists per year.

Before the tourism development was initiated, the population of Santa Cruz Bay was 735 (250 households). The average household consisted of traditional nuclear families of five people (Vasquez, 1986). The land in the area was communal and residents expanded their homes and gardens as they needed. Community members worked portions of the communal land to support their families. The unemployment rate in Santa Cruz was 56 per cent and the community lived at a subsistence level. The principal occupation was agriculture, with fishing the second most common. The general level of education of the original population was low. Among the heads of households, illiteracy was 49 per cent. As there was no high school, children of the Santa Cruz community had either to travel by a public bus to the nearby town of Pochutla or live in the capital city of Oaxaca, an eight-hour bus ride away. Only three per cent of the population finished high school while 16 per cent completed grade school (ICIC, 1988; Gonzalez, 1985).

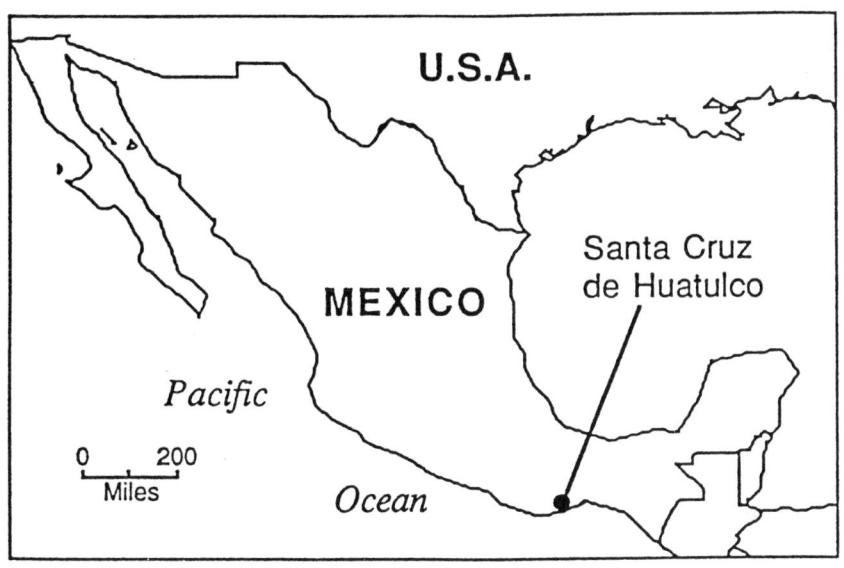

Figure 11.1 Location of Las Bahias de Huatulco, Oaxaca, Mexico

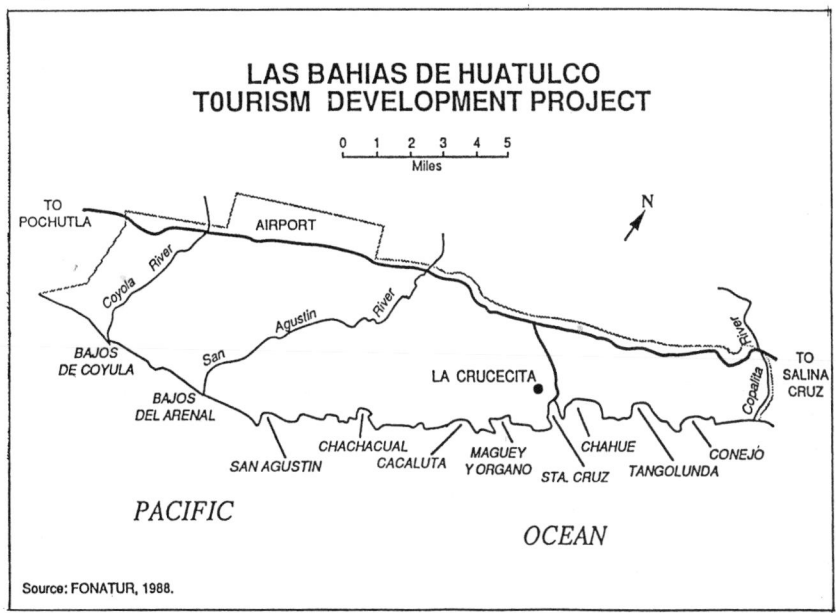

Figure 11.2 Las Bahias de Huatulco, Oaxaca: tourism development project

Developmental impacts

With the advent of the development in 1984, the slow pace of community life in
Santa Cruz Bay changed drastically. The community population grew from 735
to 9300 in just a few years. The demographics of the population changed and the
homes and places of business of community members were expropriated, the area
becoming a huge construction site. Following a series of negotiations over a
period of two years (1984–1986), the community of Santa Cruz was relocated to
a new site, over a hill, and a kilometre inland from Santa Cruz Bay. The
relocation site, La Crucecita, was a bustling town, developed by FONATUR.

Although impacts created by the physical presence of masses of tourists
were as yet incipient, local residents anticipated many of the problems. Local
infrastructure was in some aspects deficient and stores could not maintain
adequate supplies and groceries for the burgeoning populace. Public
transportation was inadequate; buses had sporadic schedules and taxis were
usually full. Residents complained that a visit to the public health clinic took an
entire day, as there were insufficient facilities and staff for the demand. Medical
services in the area had improved according to most of the respondents, but many
were still dissatisfied with the services available. Many said they sought out
private doctors in the town of Pochutla, an hour's bus ride away.

Another anticipated impact of the resort development was the loss of their
beaches. Already lost were the beaches of the Club Med resort. Non-guests were
not allowed to enter any part of the Club Med facility. The indigenous people of
Santa Cruz felt that as soon as the resort was in operation, they would no
longer be able to use the beaches. They had been moved off their beach front
properties to observe resort construction as well as luxury homes coming in for
the leisured wealthy. They saw Santa Cruz Bay as the future playground for
foreigners. The beach restaurants were relocated just off the beach. In spite of
having been informed by FONATUR to the contrary, restaurant owners felt that
hotels and luxury restaurants would be constructed in front of their relocated
restaurants. They felt that they could not trust FONATUR and would be blocked
from the important beach traffic.

Socio-cultural impacts

Socio-cultural impacts on the original Santa Cruz community were quite
forceful. New social classes that did not previously exist in the Santa Cruz
community came into the area . The newcomers to the development site were of
three groups: rich vacationers buying second homes and establishing businesses;
middle class business people buying primary homes or renting homes and either
starting businesses or working for someone else; and low-income workers
renting shacks or staying in the homes of others. These people were mainly
Mexican, but included a few North Americans. The original population was a
mere 20 per cent of the community by 1988. The original residents of Santa
Cruz were suddenly faced with social stratification. The in-migrants did not blend
into the existing community, but instead changed its structure, and the original
community disappeared under the massive in-migration of a new society. The

incoming upper and middle class community members openly referred to the indigenous people of Santa Cruz as ugly and stupid. Some of the indigenous people of Santa Cruz referred to themselves as, or teased one another about, being 'ugly Indians'.

The contrast between the various economic and social classes was stark. The original residents of Santa Cruz did not have cars and had to walk the kilometre over the hill separating Santa Cruz and La Crucecita to visit people, go to work, seek out services or go to the stores that were divided between the two communities. As they walked over the steep hill, cars and trucks raced by, forcing the pedestrians into the drainage ditch along the side of the road. The locals' use of roads did not appear to have been considered in road design, as no sidewalks were installed.

Socio-economic impacts

The socio-economic impacts of the development were related to employment and inflation. The rapid development was accompanied by rapid inflation and also resulted in a great deal of occupational change. The economic impact of these forces was substantial. The occupations of many original residents of Santa Cruz shifted. Of the original Santa Cruz inhabitants, 26 per cent had changed occupations, and nearly one-quarter of these attributed their shift to the loss of their land by expropriation. In the beginning phases of the project, construction jobs were available to the local people and offered a great deal of employment, but the arrival of a flood of trained workers from other regions in Mexico soon dominated the labour market. Workers from the immediate project area comprised 27 per cent of the construction labour force (FONATUR, 1987). Many local people did not seek out construction jobs because they were not accustomed to the type of work offered, did not have enough skills, or did not feel the jobs paid enough. Table 11.1 provides a comparison of the occupations in April 1985 and December 1987.

Table 11.1 Occupations of Santa Cruz community members

April 1985		December 1987	
Agriculture	354	Agriculture	200
Fishing	101	Fishing	100
Business	46	Business	180
Construction	18	Construction	8020
Other	36	Services	800
Total	555	Total	9300

Source: La Brecha, FONATUR, 1988

Families felt compelled to seek multiple sources of employment, as one income was not sufficient in the inflationary environment of the development. Many families that moved to La Crucecita had opened small businesses such as grocery stores or restaurants in their homes. In general, these businesses would not have a place in the future sophisticated community of La Crucecita. These businesses were desperate attempts to have some economic involvement in the community.

The potential opportunities offered by the creation of the resort were vast, but their significance was not often grasped by local residents. People in Mexico have a tendency to distrust promises and plans made by the government, as so often they are not carried through. The in-migrants attracted to the development were entrepreneurs from big cities, and understood the types of business in demand in the development site. When the project was first announced there were opportunities for small-scale business investment, but many local leaders doubted its viability or success, thus missing those opportunities. Only about ten original residents had any substantial economic standing.

High inflation paralleled the rapid developments. The value of the peso dropped severely, while the value and sales of resort sites increased. Newcomers, migrating into the community could afford to pay higher prices for scarce goods than could the local residents. Land prices were high and construction materials were expensive. With such a high level of in-migration, commodities were scarce and local inflation soared even higher than the rampant inflation experienced in the rest of Mexico. Tables 11.2 and 11.3 provide comparisons of prices of construction materials and food respectively in 1986 and 1987. The original Santa Cruz residents suffered from the combination of restricted cash income and rising prices.

Table 11.2   Comparison of construction material prices 1986–1987

Product	Price in pesos 1986	Price in pesos 1987	Per cent increase
Cement (ton)	43,000	125,000	190
Lime (ton)	29,000	82,000	183
Wall partition (1000)	35,000	100,000	186
Shingles (1000)	60,000	250,000	317
Rod iron (3/8 ton)	248,000	880,000	255
Wire (ton)	375,000	1,300,000	247
Wire screen (ton)	325,000	990,000	205

Source: Adapted from: Fondo Nacional de Fomento al Turismo. (1986a) *Brecha*, 4:11-12; Fondo Nacional de Fomento al Turismo (1986b) *Brecha*, 5:7

Table 11.3   Comparison of food prices 1986–1987

Product	Price in pesos 1986	Price in pesos 1987	Per cent increase
Oil (litre)	358	780	118
Sugar (kg)	91	160	76
Black beans (kg)	265	308	16
Pasta (200 gs)	65	155	138
Onions (kg)	127	250	97
Lettuce	50	350	600
Tomatoes (kg)	160	300	87
Potatoes (kg)	90	250	178
Carrots (kg)	160	200	25
Beef (kg)	1,750	2,400	37
Pork (kg)	1,350	1,600	18
Chicken (kg)	700	1,400	100

Source: Adapted from: Fondo Nacional de Fomento al Turismo. (1986a) *Brecha*, 4: 11-12; Fondo Nacional de Fomento al Turismo. (1986b) *Brecha*, 5:7

From Santa Cruz to La Crucecita

The change from Santa Cruz to La Crucecita was reflected in various ways. The original residents no longer lived in the little touristic village of Santa Cruz which was becoming the resort core. Instead, in La Crucecita, they lived in the 'direct support zone' (Smith, 1980), a subsidiary residential community for the staff and employees that supports the main 'core' of the resort. Because La Crucecita had no tourism resources, tourists seldom ventured there. La Crucecita provided goods and services for the local populace and received indirect economic benefits from the resort development.

The shift from Santa Cruz beachside homes to the inland La Crucecita affected the family interaction of fishermen. Formerly, when families lived alongside the beach, men and boats came to shore periodically during the day. Children sometimes joined their fathers or older brothers on a tour boat ride or fishing activity, or waved to them as they came and went from the beachfront restaurants run by their mothers. Fishermen now left home in the early morning for the new 'commute' to Santa Cruz and did not return until late evening.

As a consequence of relocation, former beach front families now lived on hot, dusty, urban streets. La Crucecita has straight streets with automobile traffic, whereas Santa Cruz had a few dirt roads and very little vehicular traffic. The lots received through indemnification were too small to permit gardens and restrictions prevented the raising of chickens and pigs. There were no sidewalks and children played in the streets. Native Santa Cruz residents were put next door to businesses, people with whom they may have felt uncomfortable, or across the street from noisy cantinas.

213

The new, identical, white cement houses aligned in straight rows in La Crucecita were radically different from those made from various local materials constructed by local people in Santa Cruz. The new houses came equipped with electricity, water and sewerage systems, gas ranges in their kitchens and washing tubs just outside the back doors. The former homes in Santa Cruz had not had sewage and there had been many health problems due to the unsanitary conditions.

In spite of all its planning, La Crucecita lacked sufficient housing or products to support the influx of in-migrants. The native people who had been moved from Santa Cruz often could not afford furniture for their new houses (at the inflated prices), when a supply was available. Residents commonly slept on the cement floors on straw mats or in hammocks. Due to the overall housing shortage, many relocated families constructed wooden shacks at the rear of their new homes where they could live and rented out the main house to the many engineers, architects, and businessmen who desperately sought housing. In so doing, families reverted to the same living conditions they had left in Santa Cruz.

Social impact mitigation by FONATUR

The FONATUR organisation was in full operation on the development site, coordinating the construction, marketing the resort to potential investors, and 'mitigating the impacts' on the local population by the techniques shown in Table 11.4. It had constructed office buildings, possessed a fleet of cars, trucks and buses, and had a medical staff. The Community Development Team occupied an on-site office and supervised the expropriation of land from the residents of Santa Cruz, community relations, training programmes and the coordination of social services.

Social mitigation by FONATUR generally involved training and education programmes in conjunction with the indemnification of local residents for the loss of community property. In an effort to involve local people in the resort project, FONATUR initiated classes to train local inhabitants for employment in construction, hotel/restaurant and secretarial positions as well as cooperative formation. FONATUR also undertook a public communication campaign involving assemblies and newsletters (for the literate). A team of social workers canvassed the community to help residents on an individual basis with adjustments to the development impacts. FONATUR assumed initial responsibility for these efforts until various state and federal agencies also began to provide social services. The indemnification process was the activity that occupied most of the Community Development Team. Residents of Santa Cruz Bay were classified into three different categories, depending upon how long they had lived in the area. Community members received lots and houses in La Crucecita. A property evaluation was undertaken and they were subsequently paid for the materials used in their homes and other structures in Santa Cruz Bay. This process was fraught with misunderstandings and disagreements, thus requiring a great deal of sensitive handling by the Community Development Team.

Table 11.4   Social mitigation techniques used by FONATUR

- Training programmes for employment were coordinated.

- Medical and health services facilities were built and agencies brought in.

- Information and communication was conducted through newsletters and tours.

- Public assemblies were held, both general and with special interest groups.

- Funds and training for cooperatives were coordinated.

- Indemnification, involving compensation for physical property in the form of money and land, was coordinated.

- La Crucecita, a new town, was built.

- New schools were constructed and staffed.

- Recreation programmes were initiated.

- Infrastructure was provided, including a water system, electrical system, sewerage system, airport, streets, telephone lines.

- Police services were provided, facilities built and agencies brought in.

Community response to mitigation

Santa Cruz residents were divided in their views regarding the development project and efforts at mitigating the accompanying impacts. Some recognised the economic opportunities that would materially improve their lives. They formed new cooperatives, obtained financing, and made plans for tourism-related businesses. Many adults recognised the development process as very difficult for themselves, but of ultimate benefit for their children. Others rejected changes to their ways of life, and were pessimistic about the effects of relocating their homes and businesses.

In spite of the mitigation efforts of FONATUR, many community residents were unhappy with what was happening to them and fought the expropriation of their land. They felt they were not being paid enough for the structures and improvements on their properties. Residents received payments in pesos of amounts worth between $32 and $5,600 (in US dollars) for their homes and structures in Santa Cruz in 1986. By 1988, due to the devaluation of the peso, their money was worth $9 and $1,590 respectively. The land their structures were on in Santa Cruz was being sold to resort developers for between $3,000 and $10,000 per square metre.

Some Santa Cruz residents said that they were not going to move. Some said they would move when they received more money. Another group wanted to preserve the village of Santa Cruz as an example of an authentic fishing village; they wanted to develop a type of tourism that they would be able to control. These Santa Cruz residents, with the help of sympathetic lawyers, filed an injunction with the Supreme Court which was denied. Many Santa Cruz residents felt they were being treated unfairly and held periodic 'juntas' to discuss strategies for dealing with FONATUR. Like the 'poor and uneducated' Evans (1976) described in Puerto Vallarta, many of the community members did not understand the project. As a consequence they blamed the governmental developmental agency for anything wrong in the community.

The responses to a community survey administered to a random sample of original residents indicated a general dissatisfaction with FONATUR's mitigation efforts. The communication with FONATUR through initial meetings was perceived quite differently among respondents. People said the meetings occurred after their land had been expropriated. Most people had very negative feelings about FONATUR; slightly over half of the survey respondents stated that FONATUR had deceived them, and 61 per cent thought that FONATUR had treated the native Santa Cruz residents badly. The indemnification process had not proved to be satisfactory; most of the respondents were dissatisfied with the land and houses received, and 98 per cent were dissatisfied with the amount of money received. Only half of the respondents had used the sports facilities provided by FONATUR. Attendance at community dances had dropped after they had been moved to La Crucecita; residents mentioned that the drunken brawls at the dances made them too unsafe.

The original Santa Cruz residents had more negative comments about La Crucecita than about Santa Cruz. When asked if they liked La Crucecita as a town, many said they did. However, the majority said they would have preferred to continue to live in Santa Cruz. Less than half of the respondents said that there had been an improvement in the electrical system, water system and schools. When asked what they liked about Santa Cruz, most said they liked being near the ocean. When discussing the negative aspects of La Crucecita, residents mentioned the lack of fresh air, the many drunken people, crime and the lack of safety.

Exclusion of locals from a changing tourism industry

Tourism development is not new to the bay of Santa Cruz. 'Tourism' was not perceived as negative; most community members said they liked having tourists in their community. Locals had previously welcomed beach tourists who had come to Santa Cruz Bay for the day. They had provided restaurants on the beach, boat rides to nearby bays, and small souvenirs. The income from these enterprises, although small, had been a welcome addition of cash to an otherwise subsistence fishing/farming economy. The presence of other Mexicans as tourists had been a source of social contact with a larger world, and therefore added interest to their lives.

Now relocated in La Crucecita, most of the residents would have little direct contact with tourists. They had already noticed a shift in the types of tourists coming to the area and commented that they were more wealthy and came from abroad. Those who were going to have contact with these 'new' tourists were worried about learning how to serve them. Some of the residents mentioned that they disliked the lack of tourists in their new community of La Crucecita. As experienced professionals were to operate the new tourist facilities, the control of and participation in the tourism industry was lost to most Santa Cruz natives.

Mitigation efforts tried to involve the local residents directly in resort employment; they included training for the entire community and attendance was high. However, many people said the courses were too short to learn anything substantial. The most popular course would have been English conversation; old women at fruit stands, middle-aged restaurant owners, young fishermen-turned-tourboat guides, and parents sought English instruction for themselves and their children. Most studied diligently with outdated books and cassette tapes. Some walked along the beaches hoping to practise speaking with tourists. They were desperate to learn English, for a working knowledge would give them a better chance of economic survival with a resort job (Cohen and Cooper, 1986).

At the time of the study in 1988, the Sheraton Hotel had just begun to accept employment applications. Qualification for front desk applicants included 100 per cent English fluency: maids needed to be 80 per cent fluent. The vast majority of the community members in Santa Cruz would not qualify, even minimally, due to lack of language capabilities. FONATUR did not offer English conversation instruction, which therefore restricted employment only to educated outsiders.

Discussion

The reaction of local residents to the impact mitigation programme undertaken by FONATUR was unclear. In some ways it would seem that FONATUR was unsympathetic to local needs, thereby causing a negative response by the Santa Cruz Bay residents. But one must look more closely at some of the characteristics of Mexican society to understand the situation. As in Hollinshead's (1988) study of Euro-Australians and Aboriginal Australians, the society of Mexico is split among distinct classes. Hollinshead mentioned the tourism industry developers' view of Aboriginal society as 'backward and meagre'. He mentioned the lack of cultural understanding between the tourism industry personnel and the indigenous population. A similar situation exists in Mexico.

The large-scale Mexican resort was designed and the social impact mitigation plans were made by tourism industry professionals far away from the actual resort site. A tourism development plan and a set social mitigation plan were superimposed upon a small, low socio-economic, indigenous community. The lack of empathy is exemplified by the failure to provide sidewalks for a population that does not own cars, and the lack of English classes for a community that is being encouraged to participate in a resort that will serve North Americans. This lack of empathy on the part of FONATUR is probably a reflection of its place in and associated perspective on Mexican society. As a result of their place in society, it is expected that poor indigenous populations will adapt to the exogenous forces that run their lives.

However, several authors suggest that adaptation to tourism impacts by the local population is possible (Cheng, 1980; Getz, 1983; Dogan, 1989). In his study of socio-cultural impacts of tourism, Dogan suggested that the ability of people affected by tourism development to cope with the impacts depends on the characteristics of the host society and the level of tourism development. Dogan thus implies that a particular type of development may be, in fact, a form of mitigation. The appropriate type of development would take account of the needs, objectives and adjustment processes which are specific to local communities from the earliest stages of planning for tourism development. It would be a type of development that is appropriate to the way in which residents cope with impacts. This implies that there are certain types of development to which residents will adjust with considerably less need for impact mitigation, and challenges the premise that social impacts must be mitigated in order to achieve the positive goals of tourism development. Therefore, care must be taken with the prescription of tourism development projects and associated mitigation techniques to include the needs and adjustment process of the host community.

Conclusions

Most of the 735 original community members of Santa Cruz Bay will not be involved in the abundant financial opportunities generated by the Las Bahias de Huatulco development – they do not know how to be. The local people benefited from an improved standard of living but their lifestyles were completely changed by the development. The people of La Crucecita will receive education, they will be healthier, live longer lives, and they will have access to modern communication and transportation networks. They had to sacrifice their homegrown vegetable and fruit gardens, be forced into a faster-paced lifestyle for economic survival, and adjust to a community with crime and drug abuse.

This chapter depicts a volatile situation where a community was under the strain of intense development impacts. The community response to FONATUR's formula of social mitigation techniques was mixed. Some Santa Cruz residents fought expropriation and others settled into a new life in La Crucecita. The relative success of the social mitigation techniques can only be known in the future when the initial shock of development has passed and the original Santa Cruz Bay community members are, or are not, settled into their new lifestyles.

Epilogue

This chapter examined a stage of development four years into the project. A site visit two years later showed further 'adjustment' by locals to their new lives in La Crucecita. By 1990, many of the original Santa Cruz residents were in some way integrated into the tourism development. The existence of five luxury hotels on the bays of Santa Cruz and Tangolunda, provided enough facilities for limited tourism in the area. Four small hotels had appeared in La Crucecita to supply less expensive lodging for the tourists exploring the new resort.

Local residents were concerned with establishing a foothold in the new, expanding resort. Their time and energy was devoted to their various entrepreneurial activities. Many young Santa Cruz natives were working in tourism-related jobs such as hiring out snorkelling equipment, running a beach restaurant, or working in tourism boat operations. Many were constructing new homes when previously they would have lived longer with their parents. In general, the standard of living for local people was higher. Most had nicer houses and were in positions to consider business opportunities.

In contrast to those residents cooperating with FONATUR and fitting smoothly into the development, a group of non-conformists persisted in Santa Cruz. Their seemingly poverty-stricken shacks stood next to three-storey hotel buildings, banks and a discotheque. This core group of original residents still opposed the development and claimed they were not being treated justly by FONATUR. They were demanding increased opportunities for business in the Santa Cruz area.

FONATUR had undergone internal changes as the 1988 elections brought new politicians into office. There had been three different project directors in two years. The Community Development Team had been changed. Most of the social services had been passed on to social service agencies. Negotiations with the community had slowed as those still residing in Santa Cruz Bay remained steadfast in their demands.

In late 1989, the municipal president who still lived in Santa Cruz, was murdered. This caused a great deal of tension for both FONATUR and the community. No murderer was found, and relations between FONATUR and Santa Cruz Bay residents deteriorated. Many community members said that FONATUR had killed him. The FONATUR director at Santa Cruz at the time of the murder had his car stoned, and began to wear a bullet-proof vest. He left his post soon afterwards. FONATUR said the murder was probably the result of conflicts between original Santa Cruz Bay residents and newcomers. The result of this situation was a cessation of any action on the part of either the community or FONATUR. While developers, new landowners and construction companies waited, FONATUR waited for tension to subside, while the community waited to see what FONATUR was going to do. As more and more time passed, the community members still in Santa Cruz Bay were increasingly establishing themselves as a part of the tourism industry. One group set up a complex of wooden stands selling craft items in the main plaza of Santa Cruz.

Some of those residents still in Santa Cruz said that FONATUR was going to begin to use force to move them from their homes in Santa Cruz. The new director of FONATUR's community relations department said he would devote the next year to negotiating with the remaining residents in Santa Cruz Bay. He said his negotiations would be based solely on a cost–benefit analysis, giving the community members as much as was possible without incurring too high a cost. At this point, a good working relationship between the community and FONATUR may have made the situation more tolerable. The social impacts of tourism development must not be underestimated. Failure to consider the social impacts will not only prejudice the interests and welfare of the local community; governments and developers who seek an efficient development project but who fail to consider the social aspects of the development risk wasting valuable time and resources.

Acknowledgements

The author wishes to acknowledge the assistance of Dr. Valene Smith and Dr. Ronald Hodgson. Research for this chapter was supported in part by the Organization of American States (OAS) and forms part of a Master of Arts Thesis, Department of Recreation and Parks Administration, California State University, Chico.

References

Bosselman, F. (1978) *In the Wake of the Tourist: Managing Special Places in Eight Countries.* The Conservation Foundation, Washington, DC.

Cheng, J. (1980) Tourism: How much is too much: Lessons for Canmore from Banff. *Canadian Geographer*, 24, 72–80.

Cohen, E. and Cooper, R. (1986) Language and tourism. *Annals of Tourism Research*, 13, 533–563.

Crandall, L. (1987) The social impacts of tourism on developing regions and its measurement. In: Ritchie, J. R. Brent and Goeldner, C.R. (eds), *Travel, Tourism and Hospitality Research.* John Wiley & Sons, New York.

D'Amore, L. J. (1988) Tourism – A vital force for peace. *Annals of Tourism Research*, 15, 269–270.

Deitch, L. (1989) The impact of tourism on the arts and crafts of the Indians of the Southwestern United States. In: Smith, V.L. (ed.), *Hosts and Guests: The Anthropology of Tourism.* 2nd edn. University of Pennsylvania Press, pp. 223–236.

de Kadt, E. (1979) *Tourism – Passport to Development?* Oxford University Press, Washington DC.

Dogan, H. (1989) Forms of adjustment: Sociocultural impacts of tourism. *Annals of Tourism Research* 16, 216–236.

Evans, N. (1976) The dynamics of tourism development in Puerto Vallarta. In: de Kadt, E. (ed.), *Tourism – Passport to Development?* Oxford University Press, Washington DC., pp. 305–320.

FONATUR (1986a) *Brecha*, 4.

FONATUR (1986b) *Brecha*, 5.

FONATUR (1987) *El Huatulqueno*, 43.

FONATUR (1988) Avances, *Brecha*, 8.

Getz, D. (1983) Capacity to absorb tourism. *Annals of Tourism Research*, 10, 239–263.

Gibbons, J. and Fish, M. (1984) Changes in the composition of Mexico's international tourists, 1970–1980. *Journal of Travel Research*, 22, 6–13.

Gonzalez, S. (1985) *Detección de necesidades de capacitación y educación en Bahias de Huatulco, Oaxaca.* ICIC, FONATUR, INEA, Mexico, DF.

Graburn, N. (1977) *Ethnic and Tourist Arts.* University of California Press, Berkeley.

Greenwood, D. (1989) Culture by the pound: An anthropological perspective on tourism as cultural commoditization. In: Smith, V.L. (ed.), *Hosts and Guests: The Anthropology of Tourism.* 2nd edn. University of Pennsylvania Press, pp. 171–186.

Hollinshead, K. (1988, October) *First Blush of the Long-time: A Commentary of Care for the Unveiling of Australia's Dark Dreaming.* Paper presented at First Global Conference, Tourism: A vital force for peace, Vancouver, Canada.

Howard, C. (1982) Cancun: a scientifically designed resort area. In: van Harssel, J. (ed.), *Tourism: An Exploration.* National Publishers of the Black Hills, Elmsford, New York.

Hudman, L. (1978) Tourist impacts: The need for regional planning. *Annals of Tourism Research* 10, 112–125.

Instituto de Capacitación de la Industria de la Construcción (ICIC) (1988, April) *Detección de necesidades de capacitación y educación en Bahias de Huatulco, Oaxaca.* Informe, Mexico, DF.

Knox, J. (1982). Resident–visitor interaction: a review of the literature and general policy alternatives. In: Rajotte, F.(ed.), *The Impact of Tourism Development in the Pacific.* Environmental and Resource Studies Program, Trent University, Peterborough, Ontario, pp. 76–101.

Leathers, C. and Misiolek, W. (1986) Cost–benefit analysis in planning for tourism development: The special problem of socio-cultural costs. *Tourism Recreation Research* 11, 85–90.

Lee, R. (1977) *The Tourist Industry in Yucatan: A Case Study in the Interaction Between Class Structure and Economic Development.* Doctoral Dissertation, University of California, Irvine.

MacCannell, D. (1984). Reconstructed ethnicity: tourism and cultural identity in Third World communities. *Annals of Tourism Research* 11, 375–391.

Mathieson, A. and Wall, G. (1982) *Tourism: Economic, Physical and Social Impacts.* Longman, New York.

Murphy, P. (1985) *Tourism: A Community Approach.* Methuen, New York.

Perez, L. (1973) Aspects of underdevelopment: tourism in the West Indies. *Science and Society* 37, 473–480.

Pizam, A. and Milman, A. (1986) The social impacts of tourism. *Tourism Recreation Research*, 11, 29–33.

Preister, K. (1989) The theory and management of tourism impacts. *Tourism Recreation Research* 14, 15–22.

Reynoso y Valle, A. and de Regt. J. (1976) Growing pains: planned tourism development in Ixtapa-Zihuatanejo. In: de Kadt, E. (ed.), *Tourism – Passport to Development?* Oxford University Press, Washington, DC, pp. 111–134.

221

Runyan, D. and Wu, C. (1979) Assessing tourism's more complex consequences. *Annals of Tourism Research* 6, 448–463.

Samy, J. (1980) Crumbs from the table? The workers' share in tourism. In: Rajotte, F. and Crocombe, R. (eds), *Pacific Tourism: As Islanders See It*. The Institute of Pacific Studies of the University of the South Pacific, Fiji.

Shacochis, B. (1989) In deepest gringolandia. Mexico: The Third World as a tourist theme park. *Harper's Magazine*, July, 42–50.

Smith, V.L. (1980) Anthropology and tourism: A science–industry evaluation. *Annals of Tourism Research* 7, 13–33.

Smith, V.L. (1988) *Geographical implications of 'drifter' tourism: Boracay, Philippines*. Paper presented to the symposium on tourism, International Geographical Union, Christchurch, New Zealand.

Smith, V.L. (ed) (1989) *Hosts and Guests: The Anthropology of Tourism*. 2nd edn. University of Pennsylvania Press, Philadelphia, Pennsylvania.

Swain, M. (1989) Developing ethnic tourism in Yunnan, China: Shilin Sani. *Tourism Recreation Research* 14, 33–40.

Truett, L.J. and Truett, D.B. (1982) Public policy and the growth of the Mexican tourism industry, 1970–1979. *Journal of Travel Research* 20, 11–19.

Turner, L. and Ash, J. (1975) *The Golden Hordes: International Tourism and the Pleasure Periphery*. Constable, London.

Vasquez, R. (1986) *Diagnóstico de salud*. Instituto Mexicano del Seguro Social, Delegación Estatal en Oaxaca, Santa Cruz Huatulco, Oaxaca, Mexico.

Wilkinson, P. (1989) Strategies for tourism in island microstates. *Annals of Tourism Research* 16, 153–177.

Chapter 12

Challenge and Change in East European Tourism: A Yugoslav Example

Douglas G. Pearce

Introduction

This chapter maintains the theme of the role of public agencies and their interrelationship with the tourism industry considered in Chapters 10 and 11. In examining Yugoslavia, some insight can be gained into key factors likely to be of importance in eastern European countries in their efforts to develop domestic and foreign tourism.

Tourism in Yugoslavia has developed significantly since the economic reforms of 1965, the country ranking as one of the medium-sized destinations in Europe. The number of foreign tourists increased from 2.6 million in 1965 to 8.4 million in 1985. Registered foreign exchange from tourism throughout this period grew from US $81.1 million to just over US $1 billion. The 1985 statistics represent just under 4 per cent and 2 per cent respectively of Europe's tourist arrivals and foreign exchange earnings from tourism. There has also been a marked expansion of the internal market, with domestic tourists accounting for 54 per cent of the 111 million bed-nights recorded in Yugoslavia in 1986.

Aspects of this development are explored at a local level. In particular a number of issues raised in the national Tourism Development Strategy (Barjaktarovic, 1988) with regard to Split on the Dalmatian coast are addressed. Emphasis is given to aspects of the development and organisation of tourism there, and to the way in which the tourism industry in Split is responding to recent changes and challenges. While some of these issues elsewhere have been touched on by other writers (Griffin, 1988), much of the English language literature on tourism in Yugoslavia has been written from a national and regional perspective and deals with broad patterns of demand and impact based largely on published statistical data (Pepeonik, 1984; Sallnow, 1985; Allcock, 1986; Gosar, 1989a and 1989b). A local case study such as this provides greater opportunity for examining, elucidating and illustrating the processes and problems involved. In addition to local and regional statistics, the study is based on fieldwork and in-depth discussions with officials and tourism personnel, carried out while preparing a report on the tourism potential of Split for an international agency. In its lesser reliance on tourism and the more diversified structure of its tourist industry, Split is to some extent atypical of tourist destinations along the Adriatic coast, but many of the other characteristics of tourism there are central to the issues raised in the national tourism plan. A review of the major elements of the plan is followed by a discussion of the characteristics of tourism in Split. These are then put in a regional and national context. The constraints and challenges facing Split are then analysed and conclusions are drawn which relate back to the national plan.

A tourism development strategy for Yugoslavia

As the Tourism Development Strategy of 1987 indicates (Barjaktarovic, 1988) the development of the tourism industry in Yugoslavia since 1965 has been rather erratic, both in the provision of accommodation and other facilities and in the growth rates of tourist arrivals. The dynamism experienced during the 1966–1970 plan period and the early 1970s has not been sustained. The strategy stated that there were marked oscillations in individual plan periods, depending primarily on incentives for its development, its organisation, and trends in the international tourist market. The view was expressed that while tourism had contributed significantly to the socio–economic development of the country, this contribution could have been much greater if tourism had been better organised and the sector had been supported by adequate long-term policies. The new plan aims to provide this support and direction, suggesting that under the current circumstances of a pronounced need for structurally adjusting the Yugoslav economy with a view to expanding exports, tourism should assume the role of an efficient export channel, as is the case in the competing tourist countries.

The goals of the new tourism plan are to:

- use the resource potentials and tourist demand to generate a strong and large export market;
- increase the foreign exchange inflow;
- develop domestic tourism;
- contribute to increased employment;
- distribute production forces more evenly.

The achievement of these goals calls for a programme to modernise and develop the country's tourist facilities and infrastructure. An effort is to be made to reduce the long-established concentration on coastal tourism along the Adriatic by targeting new forms of tourism and its development in other localities: transit tourism, nautical tourism, hunting, spas and health tourism, tourism in mountain areas, along the Danube and in big towns. Two-thirds of the projected 40,000 beds per annum to be built through to the year 2000 are to be in the 'complementary' category, that is, in private accommodation and contemporary motor camps. Moreover, the plan explicitly recognises the role of small-scale tourist businesses, suggesting that they will attract a part of the funds generated by Yugoslav citizens in the country and abroad. However, it also notes that the activities of the private sector should be considered as complementary with the tourist supply of the social sector.

Private savings are projected to provide 5 per cent of the funds needed through to the year 2000, with 20 per cent coming from the tourist industry itself, 25 per cent from other sectors of the economy and 5 per cent from the Fund for Underdeveloped Regions. The remaining 45 per cent would come from external sources (joint ventures, long-term leasing and foreign credits) and credit from domestic banks. This emphasis on external funding, particularly new forms of joint ventures, represents a significant change in policy and reflects recent proposals to open up the national economy in general.

Obtaining adequate funding is vital if the plan's objectives are to be met. Other essential conditions identified in the plan are to:

* improve the organisation and operation of the industry, particularly with regard to marketing;
* establish better links long-term with other sectors of the economy: transport, energy, construction, agriculture;
* develop long-term policy measures supportive of tourism in areas such as export incentives, fiscal policy, foreign economic relations.

Tourism in Split

Located in central Dalmatia, Split, situated on the peninsula between Kastela Bay and the Splitski Kanal, is today the largest urban industrial centre along the Adriatic coast of Yugoslavia (Figure 12.1). Growing up initially within, then outside the walls of the vast palace built by the Emperor Diocletian around 300 AD, Split has experienced rapid population growth in the years following the second World War. From just over 50,000 in 1948, the greater Split urban area today has a combined population approaching a quarter of a million inhabitants. Following administrative changes in 1986, the area is now comprised of three separate municipalities: the major urban centre of Split (with its constituent communes such as the island of Solta, Stobrec and those along the Podstrana Riviera), and the two new municipalities of Kastela Bay (30,000) and Solin (19,000). In keeping with the local convention, the term GZO Split will be used with statistics referring to the combined area.

Much of the population growth has been due to the post-war industrial expansion in the Kastela Bay–Solin area (shipbuilding, cement, plastics). The emphasis on industrial development, both through the diversion of resources to the industrial sector and through the substantial environmental degradation which has occurred in Kastela Bay, has meant that tourism in Split has not developed to the extent it might. Split has neither the well-established tradition of historical tourism, which Dubrovnik has effectively fostered, nor the mass coastal tourism of Makarska which has had few other development options. However, Split's regional importance is much greater than its share of total bed-nights might indicate. The city is a key node for regional communications. Through Split airport (located in Kastela), tourists arriving by air are

225

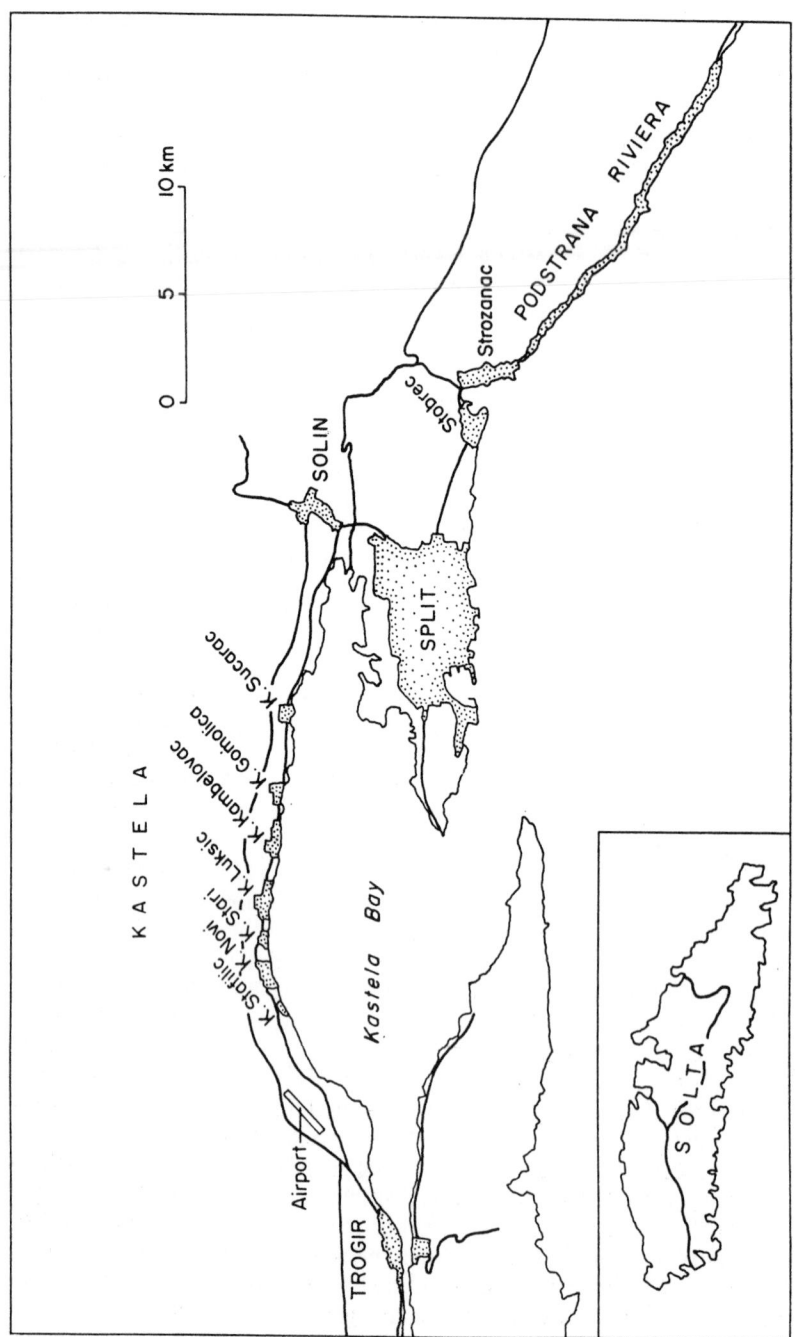

Figure 12.1 Split: location and place names

redistributed along the coast, for example to Trogir and Makarska, and to the islands of middle Dalmatia. The port of Split also serves a similar function, both for local transfers and, increasingly, international ferry services to Italy, Greece and other parts of the Mediterranean. Union Dalmacija, which has hotels and other operations on the islands and at Trogir, as well as in Split, has its headquarters in the city along with other tourist companies, travel agencies and many businesses servicing the tourism industry. Splitska Banka provides banking services from Zadar to Makarska.

As a tourist destination in its own right, the Split area is much more diversified than the other centres along the Dalmatian coast. Apart from being a vibrant Mediterranean port city, Split has a rich cultural and architectural heritage and an attractive physical setting. These cultural and physical elements provide the backdrop for a variety of different forms of tourism. The 'historic quarter' of the city consists of Diocletian's Palace, the medieval core and the surrounding zone which lay within the Venetian walls. The interest and attractiveness of this quarter is increased by its setting alongside the port of Split, by the activity of the open-air market to the east of the palace, the presence of several important museums and the organisation of various cultural and artistic activities. Split is also the centre of a broader region of historical interest which includes the Roman ruins at Salona (Solin), the seven small medieval castles of Kastela and Trogir with its cathedral. With the exception of the latter, there has been little restoration of these buildings, and they are not yet significantly developed as far as historical tourism goes.

Split has a favourable Mediterranean climate but is not blessed either with pure clear waters or extensive beaches, and attracts only limited numbers of visitors seeking a sunlust holiday, notably at the Hotels Split and Lav and along the Podstrana Riviera. In the inter-war period Kastela was one of the leading resorts along the Adriatic but industrial development has seriously damaged this tradition and much of the area today is given over to social tourism (for example workers' hostels) and to private accommodation of a lower quality. Split has participated in the recent move to develop nautical tourism with the 400-berth marina opened in 1985 being a major addition to several other older and smaller pleasure ports nearby. Plans have also been prepared for marinas at Kastela and Stobrec. Split also has a strong sporting tradition and is well equipped with a wide range of quality facilities, many of which were built expressly for the Mediterranean Games in 1979 and were used in 1990 to host the European Games. Congresses and fairs have been identified by the tourist office as a potential growth area, but strong competition can be expected from cities such as Zagreb which have a more established tradition in these areas.

The greater Split area had a dozen hotels in 1988 with a total capacity of 3500 beds. While hotel capacity represented only 14 per cent of all beds (24,000), hotels accounted for 44 per cent of total bed-nights. Conversely beds in the private sector made up 38 per cent of total capacity but only 15 per cent of bed-nights. Other accommodation is provided by apartments, camping grounds, union resthouses and children's hostels. All the hotels in Split at that date, with the exception of the military's Hotel Zagreb, were owned and operated by one local self-management enterprise: Union Dalmacija. Union Dalmacija also runs tourist apartments and camping grounds, together with other tourist accommodation in Trogir and on Lastovo. The enterprise also operates most of the non-private restaurants in Split and its travel agency subsidiary, Dalmacijaturist, is the main one in the city, running its own buses and ships. The enterprise also has 20 duty free shops. The value of its total fixed assets in 1988 was US$200 million. Altogether, approximately 4000 people are employed.

This geographical grouping of related activities in one enterprise in the form of an Organization of Associated Labour is typical of decentralised socialist commercial organisation in Yugoslavia (Singleton and Carter, 1982). In some respects the structure of the enterprise is comparable to a vertically integrated tourism company along Western lines, although more geographically localised. However, the monopoly on hotels, tourist apartments and camping grounds in one area, in this case Split, does raise questions about the effects of a lack of local competition in the accommodation sector in terms of marketing, service and so on.

After a period of 15 years which saw little change in hotel capacity, Split now seems poised on the threshold of a new phase of expansion. Two new small hotels were opened in 1989, one a luxury hotel converted from the former presidential summer residence, the second a 50-room hotel built jointly by the water polo club in association with an import/export business. The Hotel Split was extended in time for the European Games, and feasibility studies have been completed for two new hotels. One of these is for a first class hotel, with management to be provided by an international chain in order to bring in managerial, marketing and technological input and expertise. This could provide a useful stimulus to the existing hotel sector. Joint venture partners are being sought to provide investment capital. Provision is also being made for seven small hotels in the forthcoming physical plan for the central city, but how these are to be financed and managed has yet to be determined.

The recently completed physical plan for Solta also makes provision for the construction of over 10,000 beds in hotels and other forms of accommodation for the island in the period up to the year 2015. Current capacity is only about 1000 beds, mainly in apartments. The projected total represents estimates of physical capacity based on site conditions, population and infrastructure rather than on market demand. No demand studies were undertaken. The physical plan appears to have been prepared in part to prevent the proliferation of illegal weekend residences, with appropriate sites being zoned for tourist accommodation, rather than for private dwellings. The one project that appears likely to go ahead in the short term is that for Sesula, where an Italian partner has been brought in and detailed planning is going ahead for an initial programme involving investment of US$60 million in a 500-bed hotel and apartment complex, a marina and associated infrastructure.

In contrast to the stable hotel situation, in recent years there appears to have been a steady increase in private accommodation, a trend which is expected to continue in the immediate future. Private accommodation in Split is mainly located along the Podstrana Riviera and at Stobrec, although a number of rooms are also let within the city itself. The main clusters in Kastela are around Kastel Luksic, Kastel Stari and Kastel Stafilic, which lie to the west, away from the industrial zone and closer to the airport and hotel and apartment complexes (Figure 12.1).

Much of the investment appears to have come initially from returning guest-workers, particularly Yugo-Germans, who see Split as an attractive place in which to settle. A number of these have not only financial capital but also small business or tourism industry experience acquired abroad. Sale of land to these individuals also provided capital for the existing landowners to expand their properties or to undertake new construction. In the past, private owners could let no more than 14 beds, but a recent change to the law has extended this to 50 beds. Private accommodation is of varying standard, but can be of a very high quality, with full facilities for all rooms. There appears to be a general trend to upgrade existing rooms as well as build new ones.

The increase in the scale of private accommodation permitted may have important marketing implications. At present most demand comes from individuals and small parties, some from passing traffic and some generated from personal contacts in Germany or other markets. A large share of the demand also comes from domestic holidaymakers. All bookings, even those generated personally, have to pass through the local Turistik Buro. Since the late 1980s there has been some tour operator interest in packaging this form of accommodation in other parts of Dalmatia such as Hvar, Brac and Primosten. Increasing the number of rooms available and clustering these at particular localities will assist the development of this trend, though perhaps at some loss of individuality which may, at present, appeal to some tourists. The main effect of tour operator involvement may be to extend the season beyond the current average of around 60 days, but of course owners will see some proportion of guest expenditure retained by the tour operators.

Development of private rooms has in many places, particularly in Podstrana, been accompanied by the emergence of privately owned bars, restaurants, amenity provision along the foreshore and a general improvement in the communities concerned. Such development can certainly provide an attractive alternative to large riviera hotels and is apparently meeting a demand from both the foreign and domestic markets. It appears to be largely a self-generating process and one not heavily dependent on external involvement, except through the individual remittance of money from abroad. It is, however, dependent on adequate infrastructure, for example water supply, sewage and roads. In some places questions have arisen over the construction of 'illegal' rooms.

The regional and national context

Figures 12.2 and 12.3 present data which enables tourism in Split and Kastela to be set in a broader regional and national context. Total bed-nights in GZO Split increased from 1,469,479 in 1978 to 1,653,955 a decade later (Fig. 12.2), when 333,832 arrivals were recorded. Figure 12.2 also depicts an erratic pattern of growth at all three levels in the period since 1978, but especially in Dalmatia and Split where decreases occurred in five different years. Split experienced successive decreases in 1987 and 1988. In 1988, domestic bed-nights in Split, as in Dalmatia as a whole, reached their lowest level since 1978. Some growth in foreign bed-nights has occurred in recent years but this now appears to have stabilized.

Overall, the evolution of demand in Split closely follows that of the region and country as a whole. As a consequence, little change has been recorded in its market share for all bed-nights. Over the decade 1978–1988, GZO Split registered just under 2 per cent of all tourist bed-nights in Yugoslavia and from 6 per cent to 7 per cent of all tourist bed-nights in Dalmatia. Within the region, Split is clearly outdistanced by Dubrovnik (20.2 per cent of bed-nights), Makarska (19.2 per cent) and other centres further north, notably Sibenik (11.5 per cent) and Zadar (11.4 per cent). Split also records fewer bed-nights than the nearby islands of Hvar, Korcula and Brac (Figure 12.3).

With the exception of Makarska, all these resorts also have a much larger share of foreign bed-nights (in excess of 60 per cent) than Split (44 per cent). GZO Split, however, attracts a wider range of foreign tourists than the region as a whole. The three leading markets accounted for 58.3 per cent of Dalmatia's foreign bed-nights in 1988 but just under 50 per cent of Split's. In particular, Split is less dependent on the German traffic which nevertheless remains its single largest foreign market (27 per cent of bed-nights). The mean length of stay in all the larger resorts, particularly the islands, is also greater than for Split (4.2 days). In GZO Split, significant differences in length of stay occur from nationality to nationality, ranging from over a week in the case of the Germans, British and Czechoslovaks to just over a day for the Americans.

Tourism demand throughout Dalmatia is concentrated in the peak summer months of July and August. The four months from June to September accounted for 83.5 per cent of all bed-nights in Dalmatia in 1988 and 94.1 per cent of foreign bed-nights. Demand in GZO Split is less concentrated but three–quarters of all bed-nights are recorded from June to September. Domestic demand is more evenly spread throughout the year but a significant shoulder season in foreign bed-nights also exists (May/June and September/October). Within GZO Split there has been some slight lengthening of the main season in the decade 1978–1987. The average length of season for Split hotels (measured by dividing bed-nights by bed capacity) varies greatly by type of hotel, but in the period 1984–1988 only exceeded 200 nights per year in Split's two B grade hotels and in the smaller lower quality city hotels.

Many of the differences between Split and other parts of Dalmatia reflect the city's urban and regional functions and its diversified attractions. Whereas other parts of Dalmatia, especially the islands and various rivieras, are dominated by 'sun, sand, sea' holidays, Split generates a broader mix of visitors. Some riviera tourism exists but the city also attracts business travellers, those in transit to other places, visitors on sightseeing tours, conference delegates and so on. Such urban tourism is characterised by shorter lengths of stay, a broader seasonal distribution of demand, a larger domestic component and the more diversified foreign demand.

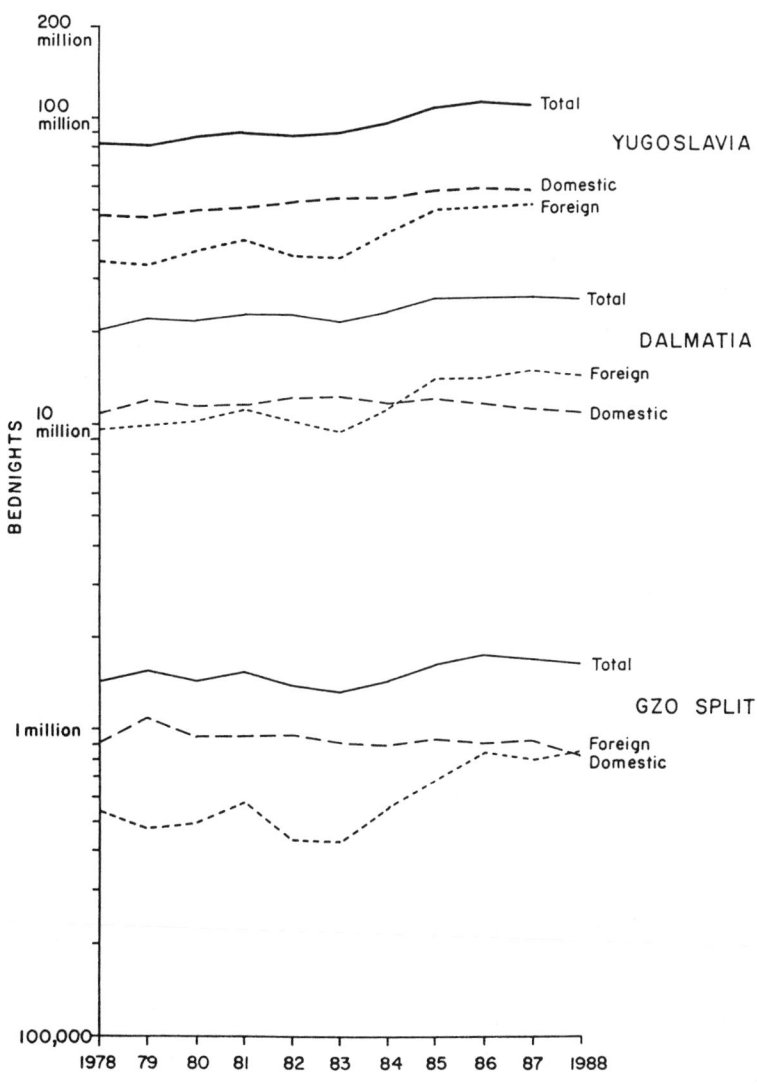

Figure 12.2 Evolution of tourism in Yugoslavia, Dalmatia and Split (1978–1988)

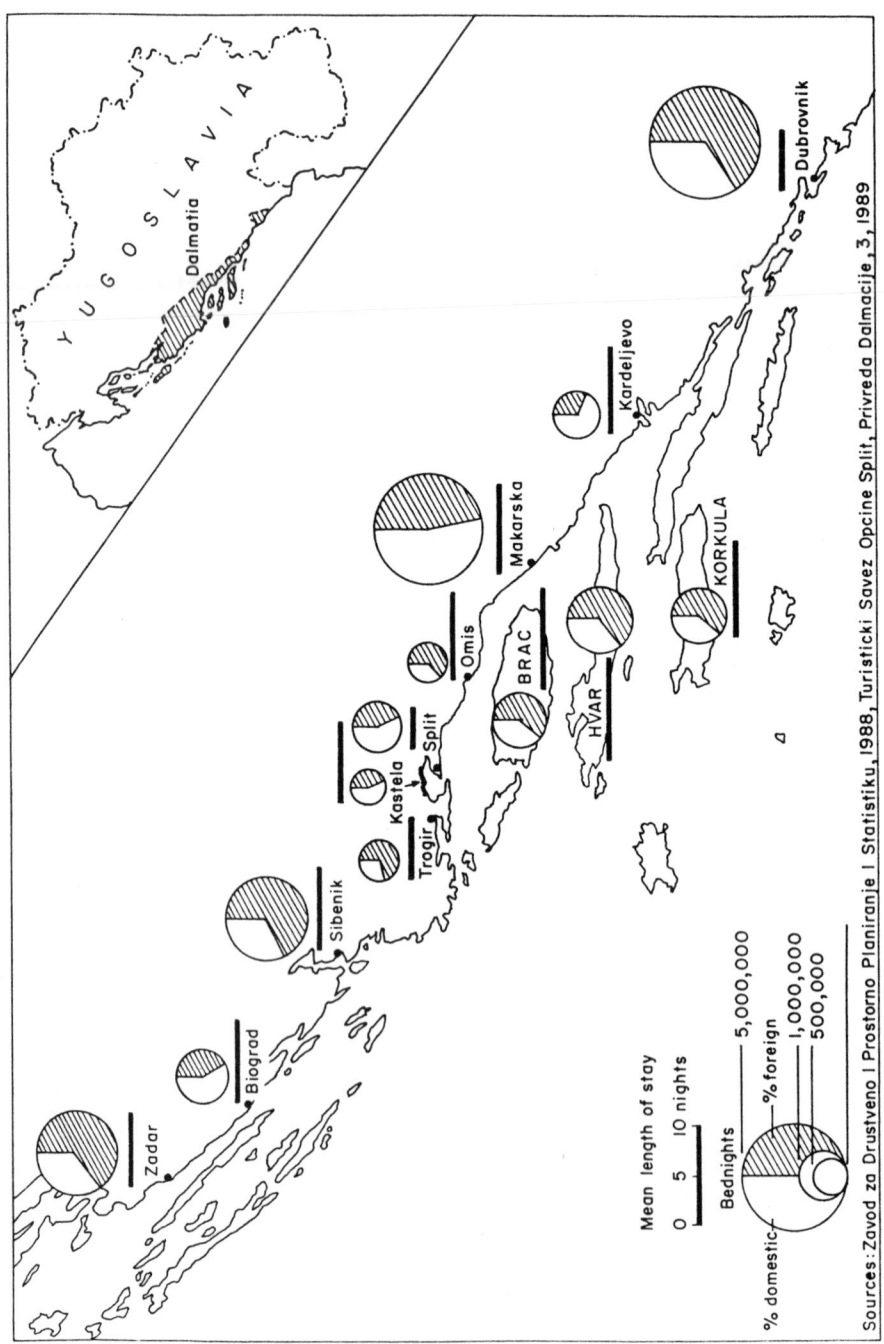

Figure 12.3 Distribution of foreign and domestic tourism bed-nights along the Dalmatian Coast

At the same time, the parallels in the generally sluggish and erratic performance of tourism at all three levels of spatial scale – local, regional and national – suggests a variety of general factors depressing demand or limiting development. The decrease in domestic demand in recent years reflects economic conditions throughout the country. The recent stabilisation in foreign bed-nights may result from increasing prices due to inflation (offset in part by continuing devaluation of the dinar), competition from other Mediterranean destinations, and a foreign image adversely influenced by some political instability and, in 1988 and 1989, by reports of pollution in the north Adriatic. These factors would especially depress the demand for 'sun, sand, sea' tourism, a sector in which Split is already not particularly competitive when compared to other coastal destinations in Dalmatia.

Constraints and challenges

Many of the factors cited above are clearly beyond the influence of those in the tourism industry or other sectors of the community in Split. Others are more local in nature, although these too may reflect more general conditions in Yugoslavia noted in the national plan:

- capacity;
- financial investment capital;
- foreign exchange;
- access and transport;
- presentation, promotion and marketing;
- socio-political context and tourism planning;
- environment.

Capacity
One argument is that lack of growth in tourist numbers reflects a lack of capacity in Split and that more hotels are needed. There may be some truth in this, particularly in the upper end of the market, though current occupancy rates for existing hotels such as the Marjan are not particularly reassuring. Certainly in the field of nautical tourism, increased marina capacity has quickly been taken up. While this may in part be due to deferred demand for boating and sailing on the Adriatic, the success of the new Split marina also no doubt reflects the dynamic and more aggressive nature of the marina's developer, the Adriatic Club Yugoslavia (ACY). This club has expanded rapidly, developing in the space of six years a chain of 20 marinas which now account for 70 per cent of marina capacity along the Adriatic Coast of Yugoslavia. The new marina at Split is one of several jointly operated by ACY and the Italian company Grassetto, a partnership which has not only provided investment capital but also assisted the development of marketing outlets abroad.

Financial investment capital
Lack of local investment capital is generally seen as the main factor limiting the expansion of tourism. Much hope is being placed on the new law which opens

up the possibility for greater foreign investment. Everyone with a project in mind is looking for a joint venture partner abroad. The Croatian Chamber of Commerce has prepared a special publication for foreign investors, outlining 125 potential tourism projects in Croatia, including several of the hotel projects in Split.

As this is a recent and continuing development – questions such as keeping dollar accounts rather than dinar accounts have yet to be resolved – it is difficult to assess what the effects of these new conditions will be and how much interest there is from foreign investors. Some Italian investment has already been noted in the area of nautical tourism, but for other projects the local parties are less than explicit on who their foreign partners might be. Foreign investors are no doubt wary of current high rates of inflation and other general factors such as prevailing political conditions.

It is hoped that foreign partners will provide not only capital but also be a source of managerial, marketing and technological expertise which would benefit the local tourism industry both directly and indirectly through the competition new ventures would provide. Locally, however, there is little discussion of the economic costs of foreign investment or of social consequences of introducing large externally funded projects such as marinas into small communities. In answer to the suggestion that building a large marina in his small community might have some adverse social effects, the community leader in Stobrec simply replied that given the lack of other economic opportunities and a desire not to be swallowed up by the expansion of the city, the greater risk was to do nothing.

Different types of tourism development draw on different sources of foreign capital. While developers of large projects such as the proposed hotels and marinas are looking to large overseas partners or investors, the development of private accommodation has been stimulated by the 'bringing home' of guest-workers' savings, particularly from Germany. There would appear to be few costs associated with this second process; indeed tourism provides a means of reinvestment in the Yugoslav economy and as such might be encouraged. Whether tourism is necessarily the most profitable sector for migrant savings from a national or regional perspective is not, however, known. Migrant investment appears to be essentially on an individual basis in owner-operator businesses such as pensions, bars and restaurants. Yugoslav law at present discourages large private enterprises. Bringing together guest-worker capital on a larger scale through the development of share companies might be an alternative source of financing for hotel and marina projects if Yugoslav law and Dalmatian character allowed.

Foreign exchange

At present different forms of tourism generate different possibilities for creating local or regional sources of foreign currency which might be reinvested in tourism. Foreign currency exchanged at banks and exchange offices accrues to the national reserves while overseas earnings remitted abroad, notably from tour operators, goes into the accounts of the bank concerned, for example, the Splitska Bank, and is available for reinvestment locally. From this perspective, package tourists are more beneficial than individual tourists. Analysis of the net economic costs and benefits of different forms of tourism in the Split area awaits further research.

Access and transport

The further expansion of tourism in Split and elsewhere along the Adriatic coast will also depend in part on questions of access and transport infrastructure. So far Split airport, which is served by scheduled and non-scheduled flights from 50 international airports as well as by domestic connections, appears to have coped with demand and there is confidence that it will be able to cater for future growth. Proposals to improve and extend the Adriatic Highway would provide a boost to all tourism sectors, particularly to private accommodation, making the coastline more accessible for overland travellers from such markets as Germany and Austria. While of direct benefit to Split, any such proposals will depend on region-wide and national decisions. The most immediate access issue in Split itself is that of the multi-mode transport interchange in the eastern part of the port. The Split railway terminal is located here, buses discharge and take on passengers, cars and other vehicles pass through the port on ferry services to the islands (Fig. 12.3) and increasingly on ferries to other parts of the Adriatic, such as Venice, Ancona, Pescara and Bari in Italy, and the Mediterranean, for example Greece. The total volume of traffic passing through the area is estimated to be around eight million passengers annually (although this may include some double counting) and increasing, for example with the introduction of larger ships on the Italian run. Plans have existed for some time for a large, multi-level interchange complex but the multi-mode nature of the project presents a number of difficulties, both organisational and practical. Given the range of different owners and users (for example the port authority, the railways, coach operators) it will not be easy to coordinate the financing of the project. Likewise, its phased development will present problems of how inconveniencing some users can be avoided while construction of the different aspects of the project goes ahead.

Presentation, promotion and marketing

More and better presentation, promotion and marketing are also critical to the expansion of tourism in Split. The lack of effort and emphasis in these areas appears to stem not only from financial constraints but also the structure of the tourism industry and the socialist economy of Yugoslavia, which have not effectively fostered a very competitive environment. While plans have been prepared over the years, these have involved essentially physical planning with very little attention being paid to the market, as was noted in the case of Solta. Likewise in Stobrec, a physical plan is being prepared which will make provision for a marina, including the zoning of the present camping ground for dry-land servicing facilities. Other studies including marketing ones may then be undertaken. Whether demand exists for a marina, and if so what sort, is not yet known. Physical planning is essential but the time has come for more attention to the market if projects are to succeed and Split is to derive full advantage from its tourism potential. This is especially the case in terms of historical and cultural tourism.

235

Split's historical resources have been well protected by successive city plans which have preserved the character of the city centre and provided a physical context for future tourist development. Of particular importance here is the traffic plan which has removed most vehicular circulation from the historic centre and also led recently to the pedestrianisation of the area between this centre and the port. A very detailed physical plan for the historic centre of the city will also play a dominant role in guiding the future development of this key area. Detailed historical and archaeological research appears to have been complemented by sociological studies on the structure of the resident population and economic studies on the structure of existing businesses, although demand-oriented research such as that undertaken in the historic centre of Porec (Vukonic and Tkalac, 1984) is still awaited. It is now a question of presenting, interpreting and marketing Split's historical resources more effectively.

For example, the city's museums, appear not to be fully utilised. The Archaeological Museum, housing exhibits from Salona, had only 15,000 visitors in 1988, less than 4 per cent of all visitors to Split. It is not difficult to see why numbers are so few: the entrance gate is kept locked and the only signs displayed there are in Croatian and French. The new museum of Croatian Archaeological Monuments is spacious and the exhibits are generally well presented, but there are virtually no explanations in anything other than Croatian so that foreigners would not derive full benefit from their visit.

Much of the interest of Diocletian's Palace lies in its heritage as a 'living palace', because it has been continuously inhabited for the last 17 centuries. The existence of residential, commercial, administrative and other functions presents both advantages and conflicts. Such activities bring life to the palace but at the same time they disguise what the palace is. To the uninitiated it is not clear where the palace begins and ends, and what actually constitutes the palace away from the Peristyle. That is to say, it is not clearly identifiable and does not have a distinctive image. The transition to the medieval quarter is not always apparent and the Venetian zone is probably not well appreciated by those without a guide or guidebook. For the experienced traveller, such conditions provide a sense of discovery but many visitors, one suspects, are unaware of all that the historic quarter has to offer and go away without a full appreciation of it. Many visitors appear to have been previously unfamiliar with Diocletian's Palace and were in Split only because it had been included on their Yugoslav itinerary. Split would certainly not appear to have the image and recognition that Dubrovnik has, a factor that is not always appreciated by some in Split who take the historical significance of the palace for granted.

The need for promotion and marketing can be illustrated by the example of the palace. An important first step in improving this situation would undoubtedly be the development of a visitors' centre. An attractive and informative visitors' centre in Diocletian's Palace could be the focal point for furthering the development of historical tourism in Split. Better presentation and interpretation would lead to a greater appreciation of what Split has to offer and enhance word-of-mouth advertising to future visitors. At the same time, more marketing and promotion will be needed to enhance the image of the palace, and thus of Split. Development of a visitors' centre needs to be seen in this broader context – it could be a pilot project showing how historical and architectural research and restoration can be combined with interpretation, presentation and promotion.

Socio-political context and tourism planning

Similar developments are also needed in other sectors of the tourism industry with a broader approach to tourism planning in Split being adopted. As with the national strategy outlined earlier, such planning would need to articulate goals and objectives for tourism in the wider context of socio-economic development, outline areas of tourism potential, market conditions, infrastructural requirements and so on. A tourism plan could provide a framework for drawing together the increasingly wide range of types of tourism emerging in the Split area, and coordinating the activities of the different enterprises and institutions which are involved in their development. Such a plan would also be valuable in providing guidance and direction for small communities, such as Stobrec, wanting to become more involved in tourism. Planning for tourism in the Split area might be accomplished more effectively at a scale greater than that of the individual resort or locality.

What is less apparent is how this might be achieved. While physical planning is required by law, no such requirement exists in Split, nor indeed in most countries, for marketing and promotion to be undertaken. Nor is there at present much of an institutional framework to support such activities and a more comprehensive approach to tourism planning. The existing tourist office, Turisticki Savez Opcine Split, would need to be significantly strengthened and given more resources if it were to fulfil this task effectively. A case might also be made for a more regional approach to tourism planning.

These ideas received a mixed reaction when raised with different groups. There was general recognition that more needed to be done in the areas of marketing and promotion and an appreciation in some quarters that this might best be done jointly. In other areas, such as Makarska, the view was expressed that they could best handle these matters themselves in conjunction with tour operators; they expressed no enthusiasm or support for a broader regional approach. In general in Dalmatia, and perhaps elsewhere in Yugoslavia, there appears to be a strong tradition of and desire for local control and a lack of confidence in any centralised or regional planning. There may also be a feeling that only the local community can help itself, for example, Stobrec in Split. It is particularly noteworthy that no one referred to the National Tourism Strategy discussed earlier. Given these conditions it is unlikely that any regional, or other, tourism plan originating externally would succeed. What is required now as a first step in a process which might ultimately lead to the preparation of such a plan, or at least the development of more explicit policies on tourism, is a general increase in public and political awareness of tourism in the Split area, and informed discussion and debate over the direction tourism there might take in the future. As noted throughout, the area is not lacking in opportunities or initiatives in the field of tourism – what is absent is much of a sense of direction or coordination. Existing energies need to be harnessed together more effectively, particularly at a time when the economy appears to be opening up and the process of tourist development is starting to undergo some changes.

Environment

There can be no doubt that tourism in Kastela Bay and around parts of Split has been seriously compromised by the environmental degradation which has occurred as the result of industrial development and a lack of infrastructure. 'Sun, sand, sea' tourism, and more recently nautical tourism, have been most affected by water pollution, but the quality image of all other forms of tourism is also impaired by poor environmental conditions. Amelioration of these conditions through the large environmental project proposed would have an important impact on tourism in the area. In particular, the image of Split would be enhanced and there would be some improvement in the quality of tourism in Kastela, where an upgrading of private and other accommodation might be expected to occur. Improved water quality would also increase the likelihood of the various marina projects going ahead, though care needs to be taken that such projects themselves do not adversely affect the environment.

Conclusions

The Split case study has revealed and illustrated some of the complexities of current changes in Yugoslav tourism consequent upon moves towards a more general restructuring of the national economy, trends in international markets and other external forces. The local study has also exemplified and validated many of the broader issues identified in the national Tourism Development Strategy, and it is worth emphasising notable features of these:

- the need to improve the organisation and operation of the tourism industry, particularly with regard to marketing and promotion;
- importance of foreign investment capital and the role of joint ventures;
- growing role of the private sector;
- possibilities and constraints in developing forms of tourism other than those based on the traditional three 'Ss', specifically urban-based historical tourism and nautical tourism;
- identification of tourism's needs in the improvement of transport infrastructure.

The Split example also highlights the need for a more comprehensive approach to tourism planning while at the same time indicating that bridging and uniting local, regional and national concerns and issues will be no easy matter. Challenging times certainly lie ahead as a very complex situation in Split and Yugoslavia continues to evolve. As suggested at the beginning of this chapter, similar issues will also emerge no doubt in other parts of eastern Europe following the events of 1989. In particular, questions of developing a more market-oriented tourism, the role of the private sector, and the nature and extent of foreign investment must be addressed by these new governments if they are to capitalise on the growing tourist interest in eastern Europe. While international tourism may provide a source of badly needed foreign exchange, it is doubtful whether tourism will be accorded any priority, given the gamut of other problems faced.

Postscript

The events and conflict which have occurred during 1991 as a result of political changes, particularly Croatia's moves towards independence, have significantly altered the situation in Split and throughout the rest of the country since the original fieldwork for this chapter was undertaken in 1989. These changes will have affected the situation in Split in two main ways. Firstly, demand, both from international and domestic tourists, will be considerably depressed. Secondly, the greater instability will have compromised attempts to open up the tourism industry to greater foreign investment. While the outcome of current events in Yugoslavia still remains very uncertain, similar developments elsewhere suggest that tourist memories can be fairly short and that demand will pick up quickly once stability returns. Private and foreign developers, however, will be much more wary of investing than previously, especially as investment in tourism plant usually brings returns in the medium and long term, rather than immediately. In any event, tourism will continue to play a major role in Croatia's economy whether Croatia remains within Yugoslavia or not. The issues facing tourism in Split remain largely unchanged but the challenges become greater.

Acknowledgements

This chapter draws on research that was carried out in 1989 under contract to and supported by the World Bank. Thanks are due to the many people in Split who made this study possible, particularly Mr Srdan Truta of URBS and Mr S. Mimica, Turisticki Savez Opcine Split. The assistance of Anton Gosar and Zlatko Pepeonik on an earlier visit to Yugoslavia is also acknowledged. All views expressed are solely the responsibility of the author.

Editorial note

The manuscript for this chapter was first submitted in April 1990, well before the political unrest in Yugoslavia. In our view the postscript correctly suggests that the political situation does not nullify either the findings of the investigation or the issues and implications arising from them; they will still be relevant once stability in Yugoslavia is restored, and still provide insights of relevance to current and future tourism development in other east European countries.

References

Allcock, J.B. (1986) Yugoslavia's tourist trade: pot of gold or pig in a poke? *Annals of Tourism Research,* 13(4), 565–588.
Barjaktarovic, D. (1988) *Tourism Development Strategy of the Socialist Federal Republic of Yugoslavia.* Federal Committee of Tourism, Belgrade.

239

Gosar, A. (1989a) Structural impact of international tourism in Yugoslavia. *GeoJournal*, 19(3), 277–283.

Gosar, A. (1989b) Second homes in the alpine region of Yugoslavia. *Mountain Research and Development*, 9(2), 165–174.

Griffin, M. (1988) *Yugoslavia*. International Tourism Reports, 4, 40–57.

Pepeonik, Z. (1984) Some characteristics of Hungarian tourist influx into Croatia in the postwar period. *Annales Universitis Scientiarium Budapestin ensis de Rolando Eötvos Nominatae, Sectio Geographica*, 18–19, 163–176.

Sallnow, J. (1985) Yugoslavia: tourism in a socialist federal state. *Tourism Management*, 6(2), 113–124.

Singleton, F. and Carter, B. (1982) *The Economy of Yugoslavia*. Croom Helm, London.

Vukonic, B. and Tkalac, D. (1984) Tourism and urban revitalization: a case study of Porec, Yugoslavia. *Annals of Tourism Research*, 11(4), 591–605.

Index

Air travel, 198,201

Computerised reservation systems,
47
Consumer/industry relationships,
28–34

Destinations
analysis of, 16–19
images of, 121–140
Egypt and Tunisia, 133
Languedoc, 136–138
Malta and Cyprus, 134
Mediterranean, 128
Turkey, 128–133
marketing of, 121,122,168–
177,178–180
components of tourism, 122–
125,167
opportunity sets, 23–24,26
Developing countries
Kenya
safari and beach holidays,
185-203
Mexico, 205–218
Yugoslavia, 234
see also Kenya; Mexico;
Yugoslavia

Farm holidays see Rural tourism
Foreign exchange
air transport and, 198–201
in Kenya, 185–203
leakages, 185–203
Yugoslavia, 234

Holiday choices, 165–181
analysing, 168–177
elements of choice, 165–167

evaluation of preferences, 37–
40,179–180
opportunity sets,
22,26,29,30,94
other considerations, 167–
168
place attributes, 168–177
range of, 167
special needs in, 178
tourist types, 170–180
see also Destinations; Package
holidays; Rural tourism;
Safari and beach holidays;
Skiing holidays; Sports
tourism
Holiday supply
choices, 165–181
filtering of, 57–59
ranges of, 167
role of IT in, 53,61
spatial differences, 55
tour operators' strategies, 91–
105
see also Holiday choices

Inclusive tours see Package
holidays
Industry analysis, 16–19
Information technology, 45–64
agency operation and, 60,61
back office systems, 47
benefits of, 49
competition, 48
computerised reservation
systems, 47
current trends, 48-53
future of in tourism, 62
impact on competition, 52

Information technology continued
impact on filtering of choices, 59
impact on tourism, 50–51,61–63
potential to influence sales, 54
role in holiday supply, 53,61
staff training in, 60,61
Thomson Open Line, 47,48,49
Viewdata, 46,49,50
videotex *see* Viewdata
Integration
company structures
France, 75
Germany, 75
Italy, 75
Spain, 73–75
UK, 71–73
concentration, 79–82
horizontal, 68–92
mergers, 69–70
vertical, 68,83–85
Investment, foreign
Spain, 76–77
IT *see* Information technology

Kenya, 185–203
air transport, 198–201
foreign exchange, 192–201
safari and beach holidays, 185–203

Marketing
analytical framework for tourism, 121–122
general, 121–122
image promotion and consumer behaviour, 140
market intervention, 123
organisation goals, 125
place images in, 126–138,168–177,179–180
Egypt and Tunisia, 133
Languedoc, 136–138
Malta and Cyprus, 134
Mediterranean, 128

Turkey, 128–133
place marketing, 122–126
components of tourism, 123–125,126
price mechanisms, 126
strategy, 138–140
tourism consumer, 123
tourist types, 170–180
tourism product, 124
Yugoslavia, 231–237
Mexico, tourism development, 205–220
effect on local communities
developmental, 210
mitigation of, 214–216
negative, 206
positive, 205
socio-cultural, 210
socio-economic, 211–212
exclusion of locals from, 216–217
FONATUR, 214–220
government participation in, 207–208
Las Bahias de Huatulco, 208–218
Models/modelling, 15–41
appraisal of, 19–20
core–periphery, 17
dynamic, 17
economic, 18
geographical, 16
industry, 24-28
management and marketing, 18
opportunity sets, 15
origin–destination, 17
psychological and sociological, 18
spatial, 17

National parks, 117

Opportunity sets
company, 33,95,96,97,98, 101,103,104
consumer, 22,26,30,94
contribution of to tourism

Opportunity sets continued
   analysis, 24–28
   destination area, 23–24
   general, 20–21
   operational models, 36–40
   theory, 34–36

Package holidays
   choices, 165–181
   destinations
      images of, 121–140
      marketing of, 121,122
   in developing countries
      Kenya, 185–203
      Mexico, 205–218
      Yugoslavia, 223–239
   potential of IT to influence
   sales of, 54
   relationship between operators
   and agents, 54
   rural holidays, 143–162
   significance of to UK
   industry, 53,54
   skiing holidays, 93–105
   sports holidays, 107–118
   tourist types, 170-180

Rural tourism, England and
   Portugal, 143–162
   accommodation, perceptions
   of, 148–156
   development of, 144–145
   economic diversification,
   145–148
   farm holidays,
   146,147,154,158
   locations, perception of
      England, 156–159
      Portugal, 159–160
   tourist types, 170–180
   Turismo Habitação,
   146,147,148,155,156

Safari and beach holidays
   Kenya, 185–203
      demand for, 189–192
      foreign currency earnings
      from, 192–195

Skiing holidays, 93–105
   comparison of UK and Dutch
   programmes, 102–105
   from UK, 95–99
   from Netherlands, 99–102
   via package holidays, 93–105
   see also Sports tourism
Sports tourism, 107–118
   changing styles of, 107,111
   facilities for, 108–111
   spas, 110–111
   sports cruises, 111–112
   sports
   festivals/championships,
   115–117
   sports halls of fame, 113–
   115
   sports holidays, 111–113
   sports museums, 113–115
   see also Skiing holidays

Tour operators
   comparison of UK and Dutch
   skiing programmes, 102–105
   contractual arrangements,
   83–85
   destination images and
      Turkey, 128–133
   impact of IT on, 61–62
   role in providing holidays,
   26,28,33
   strategies of, 91–105
Tourism industry
   air travel and, 198–201
   analysis of, 16–19
   company structures, 71–75
   concentration in, 79–83
   contractual arrangements,
   83–85
   cross-country comparisons,
   75–76
   developing countries and,
   185–203,205–218,223–239
   foreign exchange and, 185–
   203
   information technology in,
   45–64
   foreign investment in, 76–79

Tourism industry continued
  integration in, 67–87
  modelling, 15–41
  opportunity sets, 15
  and package holidays, 53,54
  relationships with consumers, 28–34
  research into, 2–5
  vertical ownership, 83–85
Tourist types, 170–180
Travel agencies
  agency operation and IT, 45–64
  Certificate of Travel Agency Competence (COTAC), 60,61
  contractual arrangement with tour operators, 83–85
  relationship with operators, 54
  staff training in IT for, 60,61

Videotex *see* Viewdata
Viewdata, 46,49,50

Yugoslavia, 223–239
  Tourism Development Strategy, 224–225
    constraint and challenges to tourism, 233–239
    regional differences, 230–233
    in Split, 225–230